Revolutionizing
Motherhood

Revolutionizing
Motherhood
The Mothers
of the
Plaza de Mayo

MARGUERITE GUZMAN BOUVARD

SR BOOKS

Lanham • Boulder • New York • Toronto • Oxford

Published by SR Books
An imprint of Rowman & Littlefield Publishers, Inc.
A wholly owned subsidary of The Rowman & Littlefield Publishing Group, Inc.
4501 Forbes Boulevard, Suite 200
Lanham, MD 20706

PO Box 317
Oxford
OX2 9RU, UK

The poems herein appear in *With the Mothers of the Plaza de Mayo* (Bedford, NH:
Igneus Press), © 1993 by Marguerite Guzmán Bouvard. The author gratefully ac-
knowledges the photojournalists of the Mothers of the Plaza de Mayo for permission to reprint the photographs in this book.

Library of Congress Cataloging-in-Publication Data

Bouvard, Marguerite Guzmán, 1937–
    Revolutionizing motherhood : the mothers of the Plaza de Mayo / Marguerite
Guzmán Bouvard.
        p. cm. — (Latin American silhouettes)
    Includes bibliographical references and index.
    ISBN 0-8420-2486-7 (alk. paper). — ISBN 0-8420-2487-5 (pbk. : alk. paper)
    1. Madres de Plaza de Mayo (Association). 2. Disappeared persons—
Argentina. 3. Human rights—Argentina. 4. Political persecution—Argentina.
I. Title. II. Series.
HV6322.3.A7B68   1994
323.4'9'0982—dc20   93-41428
                                                                          CIP

For Pierre, Laurence Anne, Michele, and Neil,
who have always been the center.

For the children of my heart: Karen Shipula,
José Arroyo, and Vanhkham Singnam Lavorn.

For the children who were *disappeared*
but who remain alive in spirit.

C O N T E N T S

ACKNOWLEDGMENTS

I extend grateful acknowledgment to my family for their understanding and support: my husband Jacques for his countless hours of help with formatting and printing; my son Pierre, who gave me frequent-flyer tickets for Buenos Aires; and my daughter Laurence, who checked my syntax and meticulously copyedited with the eye of a linguistics expert. I especially thank Mona Harrington for her painstaking reading, excellent suggestions, and unfailing moral support; Martha Collins for her careful reading and helpful suggestions; Molly Lyndon Shanley for her reading and support; Ludmilla Mimó for her translation of my correspondence; Héctor and Primi Mohina for the loan of videos and the hours of watching their videos of the Mothers at their home in Buenos Aires; the Mothers' photojournalists for sharing their work; Carmen d'Elia for sharing her special insights and experience; and Kevin Noblet and Oscar Serrat of the Associated Press. The assistance of Christopher Keith Hall of Amnesty International is also greatly appreciated.

I gratefully acknowledge the support and encouragement provided by the Wellesley College Center for Research on Women from 1989 to 1992, the Women's Studies program at Brandeis University, the Virginia Center for the Creative Arts, and, for the time and space to write the final draft, the Leighton Artists Colony, Banff Centre for the Arts.

FEAR

When you put on your white pañuelos
at the airport so I could recognize you, the crowd
edged away in fear. I embraced you,
but I carried my own fear; of colonels
and torturers, the bored voice of the embassy official.
Later, I was afraid of the waiter who brought tea
to my room each morning and looked
at my scattered notes from under the beetle-brows
of the security police. I remembered the advice
of friends, *If you see the same person*
in front of your hotel, take note.
The first time I went to the plaza for your weekly march,
I was afraid of the unmarked cars of the police,
the eyes of their video cameras through the car windows.
But you fanned out through the indifferent streets
as if you owned them, settling on the stone benches
of the plaza like a cloud of butterflies.
When you marched, I followed as if I were following
holy footsteps. The rain that pummeled the square
filled my shoes, and the old masks fell away.

The Mothers
of the
Plaza de Mayo

The Argentine Mothers of the Plaza de Mayo appeared on the political scene in the aftermath of the military coup of 1976, which ushered in one of the most flagrant and brutal military dictatorships in recent times. Fueled by anger at the *disappearance* of their children and by an extraordinary courage, a group of middle-aged women belied the perception in a traditional, patriarchal society that the aged and women in general are powerless. Against the military values of hierarchy, obedience, and the unchecked use of physical force, the Mothers practiced pacifism, cooperation, and mutual love. They developed a political organization and style which contradicted that of a culture whose politics historically had been based upon ideological fragmentation and military intervention.

Most of the Mothers were housewives, and those who had worked were employed in areas reserved for women, such as primary-school education, social work, and retail sales. Few had received an education beyond high school (a number of them had completed only primary school), and only two had previous political experience. Yet they were the only group that dared to confront a repressive military government. In defiance of a regime that operated in secrecy, they began to demonstrate in Buenos Aires before the presidential palace in the Plaza de

Mayo, the square where Argentina first declared its independence from Spain and where many groups have come to claim their rights throughout Argentine history. The Plaza de Mayo is the seat of power in the country, flanked not only by the presidential palace but also by the cathedral and the most important banks. People regularly cross the square to conduct business at the banks and in government offices. During the time of terror, however, the omnipresent security police made it dangerous for a group to gather there.

The Mothers first met in 1977, a small group of women who dared to brave the security police. Their numbers soon swelled to the hundreds and included a network of Mothers in the interior provinces and support groups staffed by exiles and nationals throughout Western Europe. At a time when any opposition was banned and even friends and family members of people suspected to be opponents of the regime were being *disappeared*, the Mothers not only continued to demonstrate in the Plaza de Mayo but also, in 1979, openly constituted themselves as an organization promoting democratic values.

By the time a constitutional government replaced the military junta in December 1983 the Mothers had claimed the Plaza de Mayo as their sacred space. Here they would honor their *disappeared* children by continuing their political programs and working on behalf of a new generation of young people. They transformed the Plaza de Mayo so that it not only reflected power and dissent but also celebrated their unique battle for human rights and their radicalized, collective version of maternity. Their Thursday afternoon marches around the Plaza and their annual twenty-four-hour celebration of Human Rights Day have attracted hundreds of well-wishers from abroad, including international figures such as Italian president Sandro Pertini, Nazi hunter Beate Klarsfeld, the rock composer Sting, and the Spanish poet Rafael Alberti. Through their international reputation the Mothers have claimed the Plaza de Mayo as their world stage, confirming the universal significance of their search for justice.

I first visited the Mothers in August 1989 to work on an oral history project on women human-rights activists around the world. As a professor I had watched my students turn inward and away in response to an increasingly bewildering international situation. By providing role models I wanted to help them believe once again in the effectiveness of individual and collective efforts toward change so that they could find a way out of their sense of hopelessness. I focused on women who were human-rights workers because their long-practiced roles and their unique contributions have not been accorded the attention they deserve. In this century, women have been active fighters in the movements for independence in Africa, Asia, and Central and Latin America. During World War II, for example, women acted as leaders and members in the various resistance movements. Today, in Sri Lanka, women who had previously never left their homes save for running errands are in the forefront of the peace movement to end the slaughter between the Tamils and the Sinhalese. I began to gather testimonies from such women from various countries and planned to devote a chapter of this projected publication to the Mothers of the Plaza de Mayo. Through Liv Ullmann, whom I had met at an Amnesty International celebration and who had played the lead role in a film about the Mothers, *La Amiga*, I was able to contact them.[1]

Because I was afraid of sharing the Mothers' grief and the avalanche of emotions that would assail me upon my arrival, I postponed my trip a number of times. Anyone with children or closely involved with young people has had dark fantasies about the harm that can come to them. I knew that if my own children had grown up in Argentina during the time of the military junta, they might have ended up in one of the detention centers created during that period. My students who volunteered in shelters for the homeless or who taught Sunday school might have been *disappeared*, as well as the young people who regularly come to my door canvassing for some environmental or political cause. All those who expressed a social conscience in Argentina were candidates for grisly tortures by the military. Some of the Mothers had been concerned about the political activities in which their children had been engaged, but the worst they had feared was that their children might be imprisoned. None of them could have imagined the horrors to come. When I finally did leave for Argentina I had some trepidations about political systems where the military holds the balance of power. Also, I had read about the Mothers and their extraordinary bravery, but they were getting on in years, and I wondered how this would affect what they hoped to accomplish as an organization.

As I walked through the gates into the arrival area of the Buenos Aires airport, I saw two elderly women. They immediately put on their white shawls so that I could identify them, and as they lifted their shawls and began to tie them under their chins the crowd anxiously edged away. This was my first encounter with the fear that pervades Argentina. Many North Americans live with fear in their daily lives, but we do not live with the raw political fear that shadows so many people in countries like Argentina. There, fear is like the grit that swirls from the pavement: it settles everywhere and is what keeps the population quiescent.

At first sight the two Mothers who had come to meet me seemed frail. But the smaller one, Juana de Pargament, was brisk and energetic. She could not have been five feet tall, yet she grabbed my suitcase and placed it on the bus talking all the while with great animation about the meeting that would take place at the Mothers' office and about Argentine politics. I could hardly keep up with the pace of her thoughts. Susanna de Gudano, on the other hand, spoke very little. Her beautiful pale face was etched with lines of sadness but radiated dignity and inner strength.

After a long, bumpy ride we arrived at the Mothers' House in time for their weekly lunch meeting, where I found the commission members of the Mothers' organization arrayed around a table. They welcomed me into their office—which seemed more like the residence of a large and active family—then continued their business, including me in the discussions.

This was the beginning of one of the most profound experiences of my life. I shared the Mothers' days and plunged into their hectic pace. I had to get used to the police cars with video cameras trailing the women as they marched around the Plaza, to the threatening telephone calls they routinely received, and to the hotel waiter who brought up my tea in the morning but who looked more like a plainclothesman and seemed overly interested in the notes scattered on the table. I had to revise all of my conceptions about the meaning of motherhood and the meaning of power. Here was a group of elderly women who lived and breathed a dangerous politics yet who also displayed a grandmotherly concern for visitors such as myself. In the midst of writing a press release Susanna de Gudano would take up her shopping bag and leave in order to be able to cook a special meal for me because I was on a restricted diet.

To meet the Mothers of the Plaza de Mayo is to witness and understand the inner transformation that they herald as the prior condition of a new political way. Their personalities and circumstances differ greatly, but I sensed that each one of them had risen to the heights of her possibilities. Their persons made as profound an impact on me as their unusual organization and their political style.

Although I met a number of the Mothers from the chapter in La Plata and from outlying chapters, I spent most of my time with the members of the Mothers' commission in Buenos Aires, women such as Juana de Pargament, who shepherded me through the organization. Juana is now seventy-eight years old, although vanity prompts her to say she is seventy-seven, and her agility and vitality are incredible. She is up early to clean her large house, which she refuses to sell for a more convenient home because the deed is in her *disappeared* son's name and in order to do so she would have to admit his death. When I visited her there she opened up his medical office on the first floor; everything was still in place, his array of medical books, his desk, his instruments. The sense of presence, and the pain of absence, was overwhelming. After her housework she goes to her daughter's to help out. Her daughter has a demanding job as head of a biochemical lab at a hospital, and at home she juggles parenting and caring for a disabled husband. Juana typically reaches the Mothers' House at 10:00 A.M. and from that moment on she is involved in managing correspondence and greeting streams of visiting journalists and guests. It is not unusual for her to close the office late at night.

Juana used to accompany the president, Hebe de Bonafini, on her travels throughout the world. She recalls how during her absences her house was vandalized by the security police and the walls splashed with the accusation, "Mother of a Terrorist." Her toughness comes out of her many encounters with the security police and the difficult and dangerous early years of the organization. I have seen her stride up to a plainclothesman harassing one of the Mothers' young helpers and demand that he "take his hands off that kid." The other side of Juana's nature is her sensitivity to everyone's needs, typical of the Mothers' attitude toward people who come to visit and to those who come to the

Mothers for help. To retain one's humanity in the face of what the Mothers and their children endured and in the throes of a system that continues to threaten them physically and psychologically is a form of defiance.

Elsa Fanti de Mansotti, one of the younger Mothers, was in her forties when her only son was *disappeared*. He and his wife were dragged away by the security forces while staying at his mother-in-law's house with their little girl and their nine-day-old baby so that his wife could recover from the delivery. Added to the anguish of the *disappearance* of the young couple have been the years of conflict between the two families over custody of the grandchildren. Each family felt that the children would be better off with them. Because the maternal grandmother had been recently widowed and needed retraining in order to find work, Elsa and her husband initially took care of the children, but as soon as the grandmother found a job the disputes over custody commenced. The maternal grandmother ultimately won. Elsa and her husband see the children on holidays and during school vacations, traveling considerable distances to fetch them and bring them back.

Elsa is outspoken about Argentina's economic difficulties and the pressing need for social reform. She also has an unwavering kindness and asked me about my own children with such keen interest that I could not help but feel how easy my own life was in comparison to hers. She shares with the Mothers a depth of generosity that draws them to many people and enables them both to handle their own difficulties and to embrace the world. Their wrath is trained only on the abductors of their children and the politicians who pander to those responsible for the *disappearances*. The Mothers are not saints, however. They are real human beings who can quarrel and who also know how to enjoy themselves. Their ability to manage the personal and the political stems from their own growth coupled with their desire for maximum political effectiveness. That their sights are set on goals beyond the self is a matter of wisdom as well as heroism. They have seen how self-interest can cause people to remain silent, as it did during the worst excesses of the terror under the junta.

Not all of the Mothers are outspoken. There are Mothers like Gloria Fernandez de Nolasco, who is in charge of the Mothers' archives and who was one of the founding members of the organization.

Although she participates wholeheartedly in their many activities she prefers to remain in the background, a woman who bears the immense solitude of widowhood and the loss of her only son with a quiet dignity. She is strikingly beautiful, her eyes revealing the sorrow that finds no expression in words.

Ada María Feigenmuller, or "Cota," as she is affectionately called, is one of three Mothers who turned eighty in 1993, and she sometimes falls asleep during long meetings.[2] She has delicate features, a gentle smile, and she barely reaches my shoulder, but, when at a demonstration, she can raise her fist and shout with the others. While I was marching with the Mothers in the Plaza in November 1990, a bloody melee broke out among baton-wielding police, members of the General Confederation of Labor, and followers of a colonel jailed for an attempted coup. In the midst of the commotion suddenly Cota was running, leading me away at top speed.

The children of Aurora Alonzo, a tall, willowy woman in her midseventies, do not like to talk about their lost brother and are uncomfortable with the reformist activities that doomed him. She, however, is deliberate about her political views. She may not raise her voice during demonstrations, but her face reveals her strength and doggedness.

There are Mothers who are both quiet and self-effacing, such as María Gutman, who, despite her health problems, takes care of the filing in the Mothers' office. She is a listener, and her presence fills the room, where she sits at the typewriter. María, who was widowed, kept a small store where she sold handbags and leather goods when her nineteen-year-old son Alberto was *disappeared*. He was attending the university as a mathematics student, a young man who had so many friends that María remembers always having a full house. "His only crime was to have a good heart," she told me ruefully.

Susanna de Gudano is also one who speaks little, although she is an energetic participant in the Mothers' political activities. Her weapon is her irony. The morning after one of the Mothers' huge demonstrations she searched the newspapers in vain for some coverage of the event. When a visitor queried her about the public response to the demonstration, Susanna replied, "Of course, there was a telegram from the president congratulating us." Her *disappeared* son conducted research at the army's institute for nuclear study. When the security forces came to take him away they left behind his wife and three-month-old baby. Susanna's granddaughter is now thirteen and looks like her grandmother, but neither she nor her mother approve of Susanna's politics. Because the Mothers defy not only the Argentine political culture but also a society that still upholds the image of woman as homebound and submissive, such disapproval is not unusual.

Josefa Donato de Pauvi is a frail-looking, distinguished woman of sixty-nine years, but beneath her social veneer is a courageous and independent mind. When she joined the Mothers' organization she was severely depressed over her son's *disappearance* and had lost much weight. She told me that working with the Mothers gave her a strength she had not believed she possessed and remarked with pride that the Mothers' endurance had increased as they expanded their political activities.

"I think there is something superior that gives us strength," Josefa told me. "I still believe in God. It is not very easy. I can't go into a church because I don't like the priests who govern the church. I can't go and confess with a priest because we feel they have been accomplices of the military, but inside me I feel there is a supreme being. Otherwise I would not be the way I am today. Many years ago when I was feeling very bad, I had a dream in which I saw my son and he told me, 'Mother, don't be so sad. I am well.' His face was so soft and that dream stayed with me."

María del Carmen de Berrocal is a former primary-school teacher who exudes a quiet dignity and strength. Her grandchildren are frequent visitors at the Mothers' office and always look for their father's picture on the poster that dominates the meeting room. When we talked about her son, María del Carmen told me that "everything was important about him, his studies, his work, his political ideas. Every part of his life was important, his marriage, the birth of his children, his work. He had so much, his work, his dream, his ideas, all cut off." His mother supported his socialist ideas, but, though she was concerned about him, the worst she feared was a jail sentence. She told me, "He *disappeared* physically, but he is with me in all I do, all I think, all I plan. He is with me not only at the Mothers' House in my work, but also in my home."

Hebe de Bonafini, president of the Mothers of the Plaza de Mayo (*photo by Daniel Cohen*)

Evel Aztarbe de Petrini in the Plaza de Mayo

Susanna de Gudano

Aurora Alonzo

Hebe de Bonafini in the Mothers' House
with a poster of the *disappeared* children in
the background

Evel Aztarbe de Petrini and María del
Rosario de Cerruti in the Mothers' House

Hebe María Pavero de Mascia

María Berigellieti de Miani

Aline Moreno del Hodel

Ada María Feigenmuller

Front, wearing dark glasses, the author, with a group of Mothers

The most fiery and outspoken of the Mothers is Mercedes Mereno, who grew up in Spain and experienced the worst excesses of the Spanish civil war. Her father was an important official in the anarchist trade-union federation, and she remembers going to meetings with him as a child and exulting in his political activity. Because her parents were anarchists they cut themselves off from the Catholic church, a stance which ultimately created terrible problems for Mercedes. At the age of twelve she was seized by Franco's soldiers, who shaved her head and accused her of being overly intelligent and giving Communist speeches to members of the anarchist labor union, the CNT (National Confederation of Workers). She was forcibly baptized, the man who had arrested her father acting as her godfather during the ceremony. Because of these events and the subsequent execution of her husband, Mercedes's mother emigrated to Argentina with her two daughters. But, despite the scars of her years under fascism and the *disappearance* of her only child Alicia in 1977, Mercedes has retained the buoyancy and joy of her experience in the labor movement. A free spirit, she is a voracious reader of anarchist literature. At the meetings of the Mothers' commission her voice always sails above the others, and during routine activities she sings with an ease and abandon that belie her circumstances.

What brings these strong individuals together are their determination and their political convictions: there are thousands of mothers of *disappeared* young adults but, now, only a few hundred Mothers of the Plaza de Mayo. Although each Mother does not consider her own suffering as more important than that of the other Mothers, each welcomes opportunities to talk about her child because to do so gives her child a social presence and helps to combat the terrible intent of *disappearances*—to annihilate the memory as well as the person. Officially, the Mothers consider themselves as mothers of all the *disappeared* children and believe the fates of their children and of all Argentine children are inextricably linked.

The Mothers are more than just political comrades. They behave like an extended family, sharing each other's joys and difficulties since most of the problems they confront are particular to their tragic circumstances. Many of them are bringing up grandchildren, facing the problems of adolescent children with the added psychological burden of their situation and their oftentimes greatly reduced circumstances. Such tragedies tend to tear families apart, and many Mothers endure estrangement from family members who do not approve of their political activity or who are afraid of being associated with them. When I was marching with the Mothers in La Plata a young man bounded in line to walk beside his grandmother. Elvira's face lit up with a rare joy. "It's the first time he has come to the Plaza," she told me. "He lives with the other grandparents."

The Mothers' lives are filled with triumphs as well as difficulties. They share a special pride in having survived as an organization against such odds, of having defied the police and the military when no other group was able to do so. A friend who spent the war years in Auschwitz for her involvement in the Resistance against the Nazis once remarked to me that because of her terrible experience, she is better able to savor simple pleasures and to understand how precious life is. The Mothers know how to enjoy themselves. Seated around the table at their monthly meetings, they discuss the political situation, but their discussion is intermingled with genuine pleasure in each other's company. What is memorable about them is their great range of being. They carry an agony few of us can imagine, yet they are able to experience profound joy and, in doing so, have explored the full range of human feeling. They are more alive than most people I have met in my life.

Some people in Argentina who admire the Mothers have elevated them to a mythical status. But they do not want to be put on a pedestal because they have an important message for Argentines and for people around the world—that we can take hold of our destinies and that we all have the capacity to address our problems if we make up our minds to do so. María del Rosario de Cerruti, the editor of the Mothers' newspaper, told me this story about a poor neighborhood eighty kilometers from Buenos Aires that had formed a committee to improve living conditions and had invited the Mothers to give a talk. When the Mothers arrived and began to speak, the audience grumbled and complained, "What do the Mothers and their programs have to do with our problems?" The committee, embarrassed, explained that the Mothers were people who knew how to fight for their interests. "Yes," some people in the crowd yelled, "but we need food and housing and we can't always be demonstrating in the streets." Two months later a storm demolished the roofs of the poorest houses. Someone in the neighborhood said, "We have to do what the Mothers do." They marched to the city hall every day until they managed to get eight thousand corrugated sheets for those roofs. Most of all, they confirmed the Mothers' example.

At the end of that first visit with the Mothers I was so moved by what I observed that I decided to postpone my oral history project and trace their story. Discovering and assessing the Mothers' political achievements in a world where both political thought and action have been defined by men proved a continual challenge, one that required new theoretical perspectives. I also found that the reality the Mothers created could not be neatly subsumed within the various schools of contemporary feminist theory. They brought to their work an authentic style, clear, unmediated, and true to their own experience. As women who defined themselves both as mothers and as revolutionaries, they saw no contradiction between these roles. Their organization revealed the possibilities and the importance of political motherhood, a role that has been forged by members of resistance movements around the world and which is being realized within the United States by community activists.

What struck me as I observed the Mothers' unique political style was that they were redefining power as the claiming of the different spaces that influence our political lives. I therefore focused on the manner in which the Mothers thrust themselves into the arenas of political power, such as the shaping of political dialogue and therefore of political consciousness. By their continual repetition of the truth and by defining their own political vocabulary in a way that united the public and private spheres, they forged a space in political awareness. They echoed the work of the Brazilian social theorist, Paulo Freire, who wrote that power begins with the formulation of our perceptions of reality. The space that the Mothers claimed for ethics illuminated the lies in the junta's propaganda just as the junta's efforts to silence them revealed the Mothers' profound influence.

Gathering in the open spaces of the Plaza and pouring through the streets in large demonstrations are also a form of power since both acts represent a suspension of governmental authority. Refused entrance to established political institutions, the Mothers thrust themselves into the arenas of the sidewalks, the parks, and the public squares throughout Argentina, thus defying a secretive political system. Denied access to the means of communication, the Mothers published their own newspaper and traveled throughout the country on speaking tours. By establishing a network of international support groups and by contacting foreign leaders, they created an international presence, thus influencing their own government. The capturing of these alternative spaces reflects some of the strategies used by nationalist groups fighting colonial governments and by some of the black organizations in South Africa, notably the United Democratic Front, which has used its ethical stance and international reputation as levers against the government.

The Mothers combined in their work an intensity of feeling, an ethical position, and shrewd political assessments, thus challenging prevailing political thought that stresses reason as superior to and more reliable than emotion. Unleashing their fury in a society that regards anger as an inappropriate emotion for women proved a significant source of political power.

Refusing to be co-opted by existing political groups, the Mothers created their own organization based upon equality, ties of affection, and the promotion of radical goals. They challenged and transformed traditional interpretations of maternity by redefining it in a collective and political manner: they described themselves as mothers of all the *disappeared* and of a new generation of Argentine youths, acting as their political mentors. They referred to the young people who gathered around them in support groups as their own children, meaning that, like their *disappeared* children, these young people had become linked to them through their passion for political reform and their concern for the disadvantaged. Referring to these youths, the Mothers described themselves as "permanently pregnant," heralding a new generation of political leaders.

The Mothers of the Plaza de Mayo not only asserted the claims of motherhood against the state during the time of the military junta but later also sought to transform the political system to reflect their definition of maternal values as concern for the well-being of all children, a concern expressed through health care, education, full employment, grass-roots participation in governance, and the international pursuit of peace. They provide us with an alternative model of political action based upon familial and community responsibility rather than upon individual goals. As the Mothers confront the government, engage in international diplomacy, and serve as mentors for grass-roots efforts toward political change, they explode the myths that the private sphere is isolated from and irrelevant to the political system and that middle-aged and elderly women are powerless. In these claims and in their defiance of the governmental policies of presidents Raúl Alfonsín and Carlos Saúl Menem, they came to refer to themselves as revolutionary Mothers.

The grounds for the Mothers' extreme position came from a radical interpretation of Christianity on the one hand, even though a number of the Mothers are Jewish, and the adoption of an anarchist position that true change could only come from the spontaneous linking of grass-roots efforts. Characteristically, anarchism focuses on the process of change, providing no blueprint for the future aside from the goals of justice and equality. As anarchists the Mothers were intent upon transforming the political process to allow a voice for all social groups. They insisted, however, that they were only paving the way for a new reality, refusing to provide a design for the political system and therefore opening themselves to the criticism that they were unsophisticated political thinkers.

After the return of constitutional government in 1983, the organization's radical political stance resulted in a drop in membership. A number of Mothers left because they believed that justice would be best served by supporting the new government and working with the political parties, most particularly the Radical party, which specifically appealed to women's votes. The Mothers' political style and their transformation of maternity created a split in their organization in 1986 when a group of about a dozen Mothers formed the Línea Fundadora, or the Founding Line (some of these Mothers had been in the original group that began demonstrating in the Plaza). The Founding Line intended to carry on a less radical style of politics and to work within the political system. Class distinctions and education, as well as organizational models and attitudes toward the political process, distinguish the Mothers of the Founding Line from the Mothers of the Plaza de Mayo. The former are closer to the socioeconomic and educational backgrounds of many feminists, among whom the split has aroused much controversy. Prominent scholars in both the United States and Argentina have supported the Línea Fundadora, criticizing the Mothers of the Plaza de Mayo for their political style. The women in both groups, however, have displayed exemplary courage and tenacity in the pursuit of their goals, proving that efforts in search of justice and human rights are well served by a plurality of approaches.

NOTES

1. *La Amiga* was written and directed by Jeanine Meerapfel and produced by Journal Film Klaus Volkenborn, in coproduction with Jorge Estrada Mora Producciones Buenos Aires, and Alma Film GmbH in 1988. The film is about an ordinary woman who becomes a Mother of the Plaza de Mayo after her son is *disappeared*.

2. The other two are Mimí Alvarez de Rojas and Teresa Oberti de Suárez.

JOSEFA'S DREAM

My son and his wife were lawyers.
When they took him away, she told me not to worry.
She would draw up a writ of *habeas corpus*.
He would be returned in a few days. The days
stretched into weeks. I couldn't leave the house
in case he might come back. The weeks
multiplied and he didn't appear.
The days were bearable, but nights I lay there
wondering if he was hungry, if he was cold.
The possibilities created their own
darkness. After months passed,
his wife left the country. Years
slipped by. The textbook he had written
was finally published. His wife returned
from exile. But he didn't appear,
he who devoured new books and passed them
on to me. He was so busy helping others
he forgot about his own safety.
He would be over forty now with children,
with clients lined up outside his office,
and people who couldn't pay but knew
where they could get advice.
A few months ago, I had a strange dream.
The grass was sparkling like a field of mica,
and my son stood before me dressed
in white. He was smiling as he spoke to me,
Mother, I am happy now, why are you weeping?

CHAPTER 1

The Dirty War

I think you are suggesting that we investigate the Security Forces—that is absolutely out of the question. This is a war and we are the winners. You can be certain that in the last war if the armies of the Reich had won, the war crimes trials would have taken place in Virginia, not in Nuremberg.

General Viola, responding to a journalist about the need for an investigation into the problems of the *disappeared*. *El Clarín*, March 18, 1981

The tyrant's old approved beliefs about right and wrong which he had as a child will be overpowered by thoughts, once held in subjection, but now emancipated to second that master passion. Now that this passion has set up an absolute dominion, he has become all his waking life the man he used to be from time to time in his dreams, ready to shed blood or do any dreadful deed.

Plato, "Despotism and the Despotic Man," in *The Republic*

On March 24, 1976, three commanding officers of the armed forces—General Jorge Rafael Videla of the army, Admiral Emilio Eduardo Massera of the navy, and Brigadier Ramón Agosti of the air force—staged a successful coup and adopted the Statute for the Process of National Reorganization, later referred to as the Proceso, that gave it power to govern. They suspended the Congress, installed their own appointees in the Supreme Court and provincial high courts, and dismissed most members of the judiciary. The few who were reconfirmed had to swear to uphold the articles and objectives of the process by which the military junta ruled. The junta displaced, with little public protest, the tattered remains of the civilian government headed by Isabel Perón.

Since 1930 the military had repeatedly mounted coups against elected civilian governments. General Juan Carlos Onganía, however, who overthrew the government of President Arturo Umberto Illía in 1966, both provided a precedent for the junta's repressive measures and fostered the conditions which led to the intense turmoil in the early 1970s culminating in the coup of 1976. Once in power, General Onganía had banned political parties and all political activities, rejecting the role of any interest group in policy making. He responded to labor strikes with military force and the imprisonment of union leaders, while his interior minister ordered state intervention in the previously autonomous universities, abolishing their internal government and student federations. Onganía viewed political plurality or even passive dissent as subversion against the state and put forth the doctrine of ideological borders, according to which the army's role of protecting the nation's borders was extended to protecting the public from "exotic ideologies." He thus bequeathed to the junta that took power in 1976 the military's role in preserving the moral and ideological health of the nation as well as the concept of the enemy as internal.

The suppression of popular political expression led not only to a series of riots and civil disturbances during the last year of his rule but also to the appearance of leftist armed guerrilla activity in 1970. While paramilitary groups on the right had long been a feature of Argentine history, leftist guerrilla organizations previously had been confined to rural areas and had exerted little influence.

Three left-wing Peronist groups formed and then united under the Montoneros, named after the guerrillas who had fought the Spanish from horseback. Led by Mario Firmenich, the group included students and new professionals from affluent middle-class families who were disgruntled with the traditional left and its impotence in the elections and among the unions. It identified with the urban-based populism of Peronism and proclaimed popular revolution as its immediate goal.[1] The People's Revolutionary Army (ERP) was the armed wing of a small Trotskyite party formed in 1970, the Revolutionary Workers' party. It mistrusted Peronism as overly bourgeois and reformist and aimed to mobilize a new political constituency among non-Peronist workers and shantytown dwellers, labeling itself *Guevarist* after Che Guevara.

These groups drew tactical inspiration from the shift of guerrilla activity away from the rural uprisings to urban terrorism, especially kidnappings and random violence. In Buenos Aires radical leftists took a handful of prominent conservative leaders and foreign businessmen hostage and exploded car bombs to demonstrate the government's inability to maintain safety in the city. Reactionary vigilantes responded with violence and the murders of known and suspected leftists. They abducted students and union militants, either torturing or *disappearing* them. An extreme right-wing group called *Mano* (Hand) dramatically escalated the violence and abductions, so that by 1971 one such *disappearance* occurred every eighteen days.[2] Those who sought to maintain a semblance of due process—people such as civil-rights lawyers, judges, journalists, and trade-union members—were caught in the cross fire and threatened by terrorists on the right and the left. Below the surface of everyday activity was a confusing subterrain of violence; leftist guerrillas held clandestine news conferences, and right-wing death squads headed by police assassinated both leftists and those associated with them.[3]

As a result of a series of violent demonstrations against military rule, power was passed from General Onganía to General Roberto M. Levingston in 1970 and then to General Alejandro Lanusse in 1971. Lanusse promised elections to restore civilian government but nevertheless maintained military rule for another two years. Finally, in response to increasing popular pressures and expanding guerrilla operations, he lifted the ban on political parties and scheduled elections. In the presidential election of October 1973, the Peronists were victorious and Juan Domingo Perón returned from exile to begin his third elected term as president.

Perón's first year in office was favored with an unexpected world commodity boom and a rise in exports. His political support, however, was composed of heterogeneous forces: on the right was the business community, in the center was the highly bureaucratized General Confederation of Labor (CGT), and on the left was a large group of middle-class youths, intellectuals, and the Montoneros. Over time, the various social forces polarized to form an extreme right and an ultra left. Republican institutions were ignored as political action occurred within universities, in factories, on the streets where students and workers held large demonstrations, and in the urban shantytowns and rural areas where residents organized mutual-aid groups.

The Montoneros established fronts in universities and shantytowns and assassinated union leaders, while the ERP prepared for renewed guerrilla warfare. In January 1974 it mounted an assault against the army garrison in the city of Azul.[4] Right-wing violence was also on the rise, and an array of death squads was formed from armed sections of the large labor unions; parapolice organizations within the federal and provincial police; and the AAA (Alianza Anticomunista Argentina), founded by Perón's secretary of social welfare, López Rega, with the participation of the federal police.[5] Both sides funded their activities by kidnapping, blackmail, and robbery, and it was not uncommon for businesses to pay both right- and left-wing groups that threatened them.

On July 1, 1974, the elderly President Perón died of heart failure and the fragile political settlement he had forged foundered. In the midst of rising political violence and economic inflation his widow Isabel assumed the presidency. Guerrilla warfare resumed against the army and police and, to a lesser degree, against union leaders and politicians. The ERP began a drive for control of Tucumán, and the Montoneros stormed an army garrison in Formosa. In 1974 the AAA murdered seventy intellectuals and lawyers; by 1975 it was assassinating fifty per week.[6]

Yielding to the armed forces and the police in November 1974, Isabel Perón's government decreed a state of siege, thereby giving the army free rein to deal with the guerrillas. The following year the army mounted a ruthless campaign against guerrillas in Tucumán and staged reprisals against those suspected of harboring them. Five thousand troops were marshaled to crush 120 guerrillas, an indication of the repression forthcoming under the junta.[7] Aided by the state security police, the three branches of the armed forces were now engaged in outright war, each forming espionage networks and clandestine operational units, and some establishing secret detention centers. These forces soon overpowered their adversaries with indiscriminate violence, broadening the definition of subversion to include any dissent by political parties, the press, universities, legal professions, and unions.

Many members of these groups simply were *disappeared*; later, their corpses floated downriver or were found on refuse dumps in unrecognizable states.

Soaring oil prices created by the Arab-Israeli conflict added to the political turmoil and European bans on imported Argentine meat helped create spiraling inflation, thus increasing pressure on the government. Waiting until the last elements of government support caved in, the army prepared to make its move.

By the time the junta came to power, the guerrillas were in decline. Their sympathizers had been weeded out of the unions, the universities, and the media, and their newspapers had been suppressed. Throughout these violent years, the guerrilla groups had failed to obtain a broad popular base. The Montoneros were unsuccessful in penetrating the unions, and the ERP had been eradicated in Tucumán in 1975. Between 1970 and 1975 victims of the guerrillas numbered two or three hundred at the most. The junta would *disappear* many thousands in reprisal.[8]

The military that brought General Jorge Rafael Videla to power in 1976 saw itself as the natural ruling caste of Argentina, the guardian of the nation's values. It regarded leftist terrorists as a lethal threat to the Argentine way of life and made their destruction one of its main goals despite the fact that such leftists had been decimated by the time of the coup. Through its speeches and pronouncements, the junta couched its aims in eschatological terms, drawing upon the "Just War" theory of medieval Christianity and claiming that it was preserving the God-given natural order of harmony, unity, and obedience by eliminating subversion, which it equated with pure evil.[9] It portrayed its efforts as a religious crusade—a Holy War that subordinated any concerns of due process or human rights. Thus began what the junta called the Dirty War, directed not only against the weakened guerrillas and leftist terrorists but also against anyone suspected of being a subversive.

In the military's reorganization, antisubversive operations were made the direct responsibility of each regional army commander.[10] Task forces were created, their job to capture and interrogate all members of suspect organizations, their sympathizers, associates, and anyone else who might oppose the government. As the junta aimed to protect what it called Western Civilization, its definition of the enemy was ominously and deliberately loose.

The stage was set for one of the worst periods of terror and violation of human rights in modern history. The junta, however, intended
to carry out its aims without compromising its image abroad, and thus
it invented its deadly policy of *disappearances*. Under a semblance of
normality, thousands of people were dragged from their homes, their
places of work, from the streets by plainclothesmen in fleets of unmarked cars. Their families and friends were hurled into a limbo of
terror and nightmare while the country continued to conduct its business as if nothing had happened.

The Mothers remember that in the middle of the night, or in the
hours just before dawn, Ford Falcons without license plates would
slide through the streets like sharks. A fleet of them would park
outside an apartment or a home while large groups of armed security
forces dressed in plain clothes stormed inside, tying up families,
breaking furniture and dishes, pillaging, and, ultimately, dragging
away a son or daughter.

One such example recalled by a Mother is typical of the brutality
of these abductions.[11] The winter of 1977 was ruthlessly cold, and
Evel Aztarbe de Petrini remembers that when the doorbell rang she
was preparing a flu remedy for her older son Sergio, who was suffering from a sinus infection. Her husband was working that night, so she
was alone with her two sons. When she answered the door she found
herself face to face with ten heavily armed men. They were looking for
a thief in the neighborhood, they said. When they saw Evel's two sons,
they asked if anyone else was in the house. Evel replied, "No."

The men dragged the boys out onto the patio, threw them on the
ground, and began kicking them in the genitals. They held them at
gunpoint while they searched the house, pillaging, taking ties, belts,
even an iron. When they found some cords belonging to her son that
were used for attaching patches to blue jeans, they claimed the cords
were for making bombs, which Evel roundly denied. Then one of them
asked which one of her sons was Sergio—they were going to take him
away.

Sergio wanted to know why they were taking him. "Why do you
have to take him?" Evel cried. "Take me instead, if you are going to
take anyone." But they put a revolver to her son's head and hit her
when she tried to protect him. They left her younger son on the floor
and, as he tried to get up, they kicked him, saying, " Stay and take care

of your old woman." Evel ran after the men, tripping on a bicycle. When she reached them they had already put Sergio in a truck and were pulling away. It was the last time she saw her son.

The security forces dragged away young parents in front of their infants or small children. Elvira Díaz de Triana's daughter and son-in-law had a two-and-a-half-year-old son and a new baby girl.[12] On October 26, 1976, four days before the young woman's twenty-second birthday, the couple was taken away at dawn. Their abductors took the children to a neighboring apartment, telling the residents that if no one came for the children within a week, they should take them to the nearest police station.

Later that day while Elvira and her husband were having lunch, the doorbell rang. Her husband went to open the door and returned ashen-faced, holding the little boy. The child had been able to recite his name and address to the neighbors, who then traced his grandfather, a well-known doctor. Elvira's husband left the child with her while he went to fetch the baby, but they never found their daughter or son-in-law.

Noemie de Alvarez Rojas recalls her son's *disappearance* that same month.[13] Her son was a physicist at the National Commission of Atomic Energy, and his wife Hilda Graciela Leikis de Alvarez Rojas, also a physicist, was an employee of Bairesco S.A. In the early morning hours a group of heavily armed men broke into their apartment and physically assaulted the couple in front of their three terrified children, who were twelve, nine, and two years old. They trashed the apartment and took a number of valuables, including the car, before dragging the couple away and leaving the children in the apartment with the maid.

Noemie and her husband were living in Mendoza, a province more than a thousand kilometers from Buenos Aires. Their lives were changed overnight. Noemie moved to Buenos Aires to take care of the children and to begin the search for her son and his wife. Although her son's scientific colleagues around the world sent hundreds of letters and petitions to the government, neither Noemie nor her son's friends ever received a single reply.

The security forces dragged away pregnant women. They kidnapped entire families and then tortured them in front of each other. People were taken from wheelchairs and hospital beds. One young

Noemie de Alvarez and Elvira Díaz de Triana

María del Carmen de Berrocal

Gloria Fernandez de Nolasco

Juana de Pargament

woman was abducted while recovering from a serious operation on her spine and was encased in plaster from the waist to the knee.[14] Hundreds of adolescents disappeared, and even the elderly and the very young were taken away. After their parents were *disappeared*, children were left with neighbors or left alone in their homes. The less fortunate were placed in detention centers for the children of the *disappeared*, in the custody of the Women's Brigade of the provincial police. Those who had physical disabilities were murdered or left to perish.

Sometimes the abductions happened in broad daylight, or on the streets, the security forces flaunting their refusal to be bound by law or to be subject to any restraints. There were mass abductions in the provinces. In June 1976 blackout nights in the province of Jujuy provided cover as hundreds of students, workers, and professionals were rounded up in army trucks, police cars, and trucks belonging to a large enterprise in the towns of Calilegua and Libertador General San Martín. After the fall of the junta, it was discovered that the army, the chief of police, trade-union leaders, and the head of Ledesma, a large enterprise employing much of the population there, had all been involved. The bishop of Jujuy and chaplain to the armed forces, Monsignor José Miguel Medina, responded to relatives' anguished pleas for help by claiming that there were many Communists among the population. He refused to receive them.[15] Conscripts from all three branches of the armed forces were also *disappeared*—some of them had seen too much. As a ruse, they were sent on errands that placed them outside the barracks. They were then picked up, and, afterward, the service listed them as deserters.

What made these raids so terrifying was the fact that they were carried out with anonymity. The security forces did not identify themselves or wear their uniforms. Assuming that a mistake had been made, the frightened relatives believed that as soon as they notified the relevant authorities and explained that their loved ones had done nothing wrong, they would be returned. Instead, the parents, husbands, or wives of the *disappeared* faced a long and disorienting ordeal as they made the rounds of police stations, hospitals, and military garrisons only to be told that there were no records of their loved ones and that they would have to direct their efforts elsewhere.

In his analysis of the Dirty War, Frank Graziano has pointed out that the systematic discrepancy between the force required and the force deployed in carrying out the abductions suggested a need for disclosure beneath the junta's public denials.[16] Among those who witnessed the abductions were those who closed their windows or turned up their radios to mask the screaming, pretending that they had seen nothing and trying to distance themselves from such a terrible reality. In the staged display of the abductions, however, everyone was required to be aware and present, to realize that whether one was abducted or not was merely a matter of chance. By actually witnessing or hearing about the abductions through whispered rumors, the public was forced to acknowledge the power of the junta and its own help-lessness and fear.

Occasionally, someone who had been abducted was returned. This was the case with Graciela Geuna, who was released after her imprisonment and ultimately shared her experiences when she escaped abroad.[17] One afternoon in June 1976, Graciela and her husband Jorge, both students in the School of Law and Social Sciences at the National University in Córdoba, were leaving their home to go out. Jorge went ahead, and as Graciela locked the door of their apartment she heard him shout that he was being abducted. Seconds later, twenty heavily armed men in civilian clothes grabbed her and began beating her and her husband with rifle butts. Graciela was gagged and pushed into the trunk of a car, her hands tied behind her back. As the car gathered speed she realized that they had left the city and were traveling along the highway.

Her destination was La Perla, one of the most notorious concentra-tion camps, housing between fifteen hundred and two thousand pris-oners during the time of the junta. When Graciela arrived she was stripped and handcuffed to a bed where she was tortured with electric prods. For days she was systematically and brutally tortured. In the intervals, she could hear screams and beatings in the cells around her. Without leaving a trace, Graciela had entered the netherworld of clandestine detention centers that were scattered throughout Argentina.

When the abducted arrived in the detention centers they were immediately subjected to torture that continued for days. They were methodically, sadistically, and sexually abused, not to extract information—for few had any information to give—but to break their spirits as well as their bodies. Afterward, they were kept hooded, hungry, chained, and living in their own filth. As former prisoners who were released later testified, the practice of hooding was intended to disorient prisoners and increase their sense of vulnerability and isolation because they could be assaulted at any time without being able to defend themselves.[18] Given that omnipresent possibility, the psychological torture of the hood was perhaps worse than the physical torture. As a further indignity, prisoners were assigned numbers, which stripped them of their identity and helped to maintain the secrecy of the operation. In order to prevent any news from leaking out not even the guards or prison wardens were allowed to know the prisoners' names. Inmates were frequently transferred from one camp to another, not only as a form of psychological pressure but also to prevent them from learning too much about particular detention centers.

As in the Nazi concentration camps, doctors were present during the tortures whose role was to keep the victim alive as long as possible.[19] Some hospitals were transformed into detention centers where victims were given heavy doses of psychoactive drugs. In all of the centers ubiquitous army chaplains ministered to the commanders and the guards and would later answer the pleas of distraught relatives with the insistence that they knew nothing.

Jews were subjected to the worst horrors; swastikas were painted on their prison walls and recordings of Hitler's speeches blared throughout the night. The special ferocity meted out to them attested to the close relations between the Argentine and German armies in the 1930s and 1940s and the emigration into the country after World War II of thousands of Nazi officers, including the Third Reich's most notorious criminals. It was also a reflection of the anti-Semitism that historically has plagued the Argentine right.[20] Religion and ideology were strangely mingled in the minds of the repressors. "I am a crusader, an envoy of God," a captain shouted to the prisoners he was torturing. "You are devils. Our mission is to purify Argentina."[21] Prison walls were frequently covered with slogans: LONG LIVE HITLER, WE ARE GOD, LONG LIVE GENERAL VIDELA. Some guards gave Nazi salutes and forced prisoners to do the same.

These details became known only in snatches, slowly over time, because a wall of secrecy surrounded the location of the 340 detention centers. Some were located in police stations or on military premises, such as the Naval Mechanics School and the Campo de Mayo military barracks in Buenos Aires, and La Perla in Córdoba. A distraught parent vainly searching for her daughter could be passing by the very location where she was kept without even realizing it. One of the Mothers, Hebe de Bonafini, discovered through a released prisoner that her *disappeared* son Jorge had been held in a police station not far from her own home.[22] Some detainees were hidden in the basements of factories, radio stations, or in residential neighborhoods. People in the neighborhoods sometimes knew what was happening because of the large concentration of trucks, helicopters, ambulances, and heavily armed plainclothesmen, but they were too terrified to say anything. In addition, the governments of Chile and Uruguay collaborated with the Argentine Dirty War; a number of detention centers were located in these countries and operated on behalf of the junta.[23]

Secrecy was a hallmark of the junta's Dirty War. The leaders did not want to repeat General Augusto Pinochet's mistake in Chile. He had staged a military coup ousting the left-wing regime of Salvador Allende and his United Popular Front government in 1973, initiating a widespread and blatant repression that earned him international condemnation. In Argentina the abductions were carried out beneath a veneer of normalcy so that there would be no outcry, so that the terrible reality would remain submerged and elusive even to the families of the abducted. An important part of the terror was psychological: the most terrible deeds were committed without records and without a trail of information. Government officials at all levels, members of the judiciary, the police, and the armed forces were instructed to claim that they had no information about the person in question. The families of the *disappeared* felt as if they were searching within a darkened room, a room without windows or doors where both sound and memory were banished.

Secrecy was not only necessary to protect the image of the nation abroad but also to mask actions that were illegal and unconstitutional at home, since the Dirty War violated the legal tradition in Argentina—the right to due process and the primacy of the right to life. The press was discouraged from publishing information about the *disappearances*, and a large number of editors and journalists were *disappeared*, including a number of foreign journalists. Many others fled into exile, and those who remained were effectively silenced. Jacobo Timerman, editor of *La Opinión*, one of the only newspapers that published lists of the *disappeared*, was abducted, taken to a detention center, and ultimately forced into exile. Robert Cox, the editor of the *Buenos Aires Herald*, which also reported the abductions, was hounded out of the country. Radio and television newscasters were usually silenced, although Ariel Delgado, a brave radio commentator and program director, continued to speak of the *disappearances* until he was forced to flee to Uruguay. He kept broadcasting from that country until his life was again threatened by the Argentine security forces, then fled to Italy and Nicaragua for the remaining years of the junta's reign.[24] In 1989 the Mothers of the Plaza de Mayo published a list of *disappeared* journalists; it included 93 persons.

There is no agreement on the actual number of the *disappeared*. The National Commission on the Disappeared (CONADEP), formed at President Raúl Alfonsín's ascension to power in 1983, ultimately published the number of *disappearances* as 9,000, which included a breakdown of the *disappeared* by sex, age, and occupation. The commission arrived at this figure and accompanying information on the basis of testimony that it had received. The director of the local branch of the commission in Mar del Plata, however, claimed in an interview with *La Voz* that "it is not an exaggeration to speak of 30,000 disappeared persons." Based on their own surveys conducted throughout the country and reports received from families of the *disappeared*, the Mothers of the Plaza de Mayo have always insisted that at least 30,000 were *disappeared*. They claim that many relatives of the *disappeared* were too frightened to come forward and cite as examples the city of La Plata, which suffered 2,000 *disappearances*, only 800 of which were officially reported, and a factory where 250 workers were *disappeared*, of which only 80 were reported. Ramón Camps, the chief of police of the province of Buenos Aires during the junta's rule, said that more than 45,000 were *disappeared* in the country.[25] These numbers do not include the countless cases where entire families were *disappeared*, leaving no one to come forward with a claim. The number

30,000 is therefore symbolic and may represent a much larger number of cases.

Looting was part of the abduction, and even the most modest homes were systematically robbed. Security forces carted off not only china, silver, and linen but also such humble household objects as ironing boards. At times the kidnapped were tortured until they signed away the deeds to their homes and cars. After the treasurer of the province of Tucumán was abducted by security police who sacked his home, the commander of the Fifth Infantry Brigade, General Antonio Domingo Bussi, ordered his bank accounts frozen.[26] In fact, a number of kidnappings were carried out for the sole purpose of extorting money.

An even more sinister aim of such abductions was to further intimidate the relatives of the *disappeared*. Most of the *disappeared* were abducted in their homes, although some were taken in the street or at work, as in the case of Alberto Horacio de Berrocal.[27] His mother, María del Carmen de Berrocal, reports that on January 21, 1977, her son was leaving the cafeteria at his office after eating lunch. As he walked down the stairs, a group of men entered the building and bundled him outside and into a waiting car. His wife called María del Carmen that evening when Alberto Horacio did not come home or pick up their two children at the day-care center, and the two of them went to his office the following morning. Alberto Horacio's employer was afraid and insisted that he neither saw anything nor knew anything about what had happened. They learned the truth from an uncommonly brave man in the neighborhood.

Usually, the abduction was staged at the end of the week, at night, so that time would elapse before relatives could take any action. The timing and violence against the victim and his family were intended to terrorize and thus silence the relatives. But the army also made certain that neighbors and entire communities were intimidated. Sometimes the electricity was cut off for a sector where a raid was being planned. Local police were overruled or were accomplices in the raids. On occasion, whole districts were sealed off while helicopters hovered overhead. People were terrified of talking about what they had seen. They feared that they, too, would become targets.

In conjunction with its policy of spreading terror throughout the country, the junta initiated a propaganda campaign abroad to create an attractive image of Argentina. In 1978 it employed the services of Burson-Marstellar, a large, international public-relations firm based in the United States, to produce appealing supplements on Argentina for newspapers around the world.[28] The firm also created a proposal for launching a major public-relations effort in eight important countries —the United States, Britain, Japan, Canada, Colombia, Mexico, Holland, and Belgium—and identified a large number of influential foreign journalists who could be invited to Argentina to be given red-carpet tours.

The junta responded to inquiries about what was happening in Argentina with self-righteous and heated denials. In 1979 the Organization of American States' Inter-American Commission on Human Rights came to Argentina to investigate allegations of *disappearances*. The month before that visit, Buenos Aires police raided the offices of three national human-rights organizations and seized files on the *disappearances* that had been prepared for the commission's visit.[29] The raids had been ordered by a judge on the claim that the documents were needed for an investigation into perjury in the *habeas corpus* petitions signed by the families of the *disappeared*.

The Mothers of the Plaza de Mayo testified before the commission about the problems they had encountered in trying to convince the public that *disappearances* were not a fabrication. "When we told the passersby in the Plaza de Mayo why we were there, they would ask us, 'Disappeared? But you know where they are.' No, that is what we want to know. 'But they are not in prison, they have not been tried?' No. And every Thursday, every day, we tried to explain this ineffable reality, which our compatriots were unable to understand unless they had been touched by it either directly or indirectly."[30]

The commission's report concluded that special autonomous command units had been created in the armed forces, and that these units were involved in the *disappearance* and possible extermination of thousands of people. It placed the responsibility for this activity on the highest level of the military.

Angrily rejecting this conclusion and producing a lengthy document that denounced it, the Argentine government gave its own explanation for the whereabouts of the missing persons: some *disappearances* resulted from the operations of "terrorist groups," some of the names of missing persons had been invented, and others were names of terrorists who had gone underground without telling their relatives or who had gone abroad to spread their campaign of subversion. Finally, they claimed that many of those reported missing were killed in armed clashes. The Mothers, too, were given these answers during their repeated attempts to seek information. When the parents of the young woman with the spinal injury who was dragged away from her hospital bed filed a writ of *habeas corpus,* they were summoned before a naval officer who told them that their daughter had been detained for her "subversive activities" and was killed in an armed confrontation.[31]

After the Mothers turned their efforts toward the Human Rights Commission of the United Nations, the Argentine foreign minister to that body, Gabriel Martínez, began a long campaign to undermine the head of the commission and keep him from delving too deeply into what was happening under the junta. Intent upon its systematic policy of exterminating distinct groups in society, the junta avoided responsibility or any kind of accountability. In December 1977 in an interview with *Gente* magazine, General Videla claimed, "I categorically deny that there exist in Argentina any concentration camps or prisoners being held in military establishments beyond the time absolutely necessary for the investigation of a person captured in an operation before they are transferred to a penal establishment." A year later General Roberto Viola insisted, "There are no political prisoners in Argentina except for a few persons who may have been detained under government emergency legislation and who are really being detained because of their political activity. There are no prisoners being held merely for being political or because they do not share the ideas held by the government."[32] Throughout the years between 1976 and 1983, when the junta was in power, it roundly denied any abuse of human rights.

Within Argentina, the junta was equally concerned in keeping a veil of secrecy over the *disappearances*. It tried to accomplish this by silencing the media as well as by terrorizing the relatives and those released from detention centers. Graciela Geuna was one of a select number of people fortunate enough to emerge alive from these concentration camps but whose freedom was severely restricted. Two years after her abduction she remained under constant army supervision and was not allowed to leave the country.[33] The commander of La

Perla threatened that if she told anyone what had happened to her or talked about the camp, the lives of her relatives would be endangered. She was instructed by a second lieutenant in the camp to tell her husband's parents that she did not know what had happened to him. A year later during an upheaval within the Third Army Corps, which was responsible for released prisoners, she managed to get a passport in her maiden name and leave the country. Despite attempts to blackmail her, she testified to Amnesty International about the organization of La Perla and the members of the armed forces who had participated in the torture there.

The silencing of individuals and the control of communications were intended both to mask the ugly reality of terror and oppression and to create a sense of fear and helplessness throughout the population, isolating people from each other and disjointing reality. The semblance of normality that surrounded these events made the *disappearances* even more unbearable to relatives and friends of the *disappeared*. In the early years of the *disappearances* only those who had been personally touched had any awareness of what was happening. Argentina had a dual reality: Everyday life proceeded as usual, with soccer matches celebrated in great fanfare and national holidays observed while thousands of people were being plucked from their lives without a trace.

The ultimate victim of the policy of *disappearance* was the family, whose stability, structure, and privacy were deeply affected. The children and siblings of the *disappeared* suffered severe traumas and were plagued with psychological problems. The adults were either too frightened to act or began a time-consuming effort to find their loved one at local police departments, army garrisons, prisons, and hospitals. The CONADEP has documented that the assault on the family went even further: relatives were often used as hostages for a member who was being sought. Sometimes, if the police were unable to find the person for whom they were searching, they would rob, torture, and inflict *disappearances* on his or her family.[34] At other times, torture was shared or witnessed by a suspect's relatives.

When a family suffered the *disappearance* of one of its members, it was propelled into a netherworld where there were no rules, no institutions to which one could direct one's concern, and no death to mourn. The family lived in a surreal limbo; deprived of all information and recourse and stripped of social support and comprehension, relatives found themselves in complete isolation. Often this tragic event created divisions within the nuclear and extended family, destroying the ultimate bastion of the individual against the power of the state. In her studies of totalitarianism Hannah Arendt has noted that while the isolation of individuals in the public spheres is intended to cripple political opposition, the destruction of social bonds at their most fundamental level is intended to engender loneliness, to sever ties to a community and therefore leave the individual utterly at the mercy of the state.[35]

Historically, the justification for state-sponsored terror on a mass scale and for the practice of genocide has been the naming of the other: the Jews in Nazi Germany, the Armenians in Turkey, the Kurds in Iraq, and the subversive in Argentina. After the fall of the junta, Ramón Camps, former chief of police of the province of Buenos Aires, claimed, "We didn't disappear persons but subversives."[36] Such an officially designated outsider is thus reduced to a less-than-human status, justifying the violation of his or her every right. In all of these examples, targeted groups were treated as scapegoats for the countries' problems, and the governments announced that once their countries were rid of these groups, they would again be pure and whole. From this point of view those who tortured and exterminated presumed subversives were heroes. In Argentina, after the junta's fall, the military hierarchy continued to defend itself in this light.

Members of the junta argued that local subversion was part of a world phenomenon centrally directed by Communist countries. They saw Argentina as a theater of operations in the confrontation between the atheist USSR and the United States and thus an important player in the global confrontation of ideologies. The junta believed itself to be Western, Christian—the preserver of natural order, the Argentine soul and nation, and the political Right. In the other camp was the enemy, the associates of Leftism, Marxism, atheism, anarchy, disorder, and sin. In terms of this simplified opposition and the medieval Christian depiction of the saved as seated at the right hand of God and the damned on the left, the enemy became metaphysical. The junta was a crusader defending the soul of the West, and the military's role was exalted as paternal and powerful.[37]

Members of the military were trained by the French terrorist Organization of the Secret Army (OAS), and then by the United States in counterinsurgency techniques. They saw their legitimacy as coming from their mythologized goals rather than from political institutions, the constitution, or the consent of the population, and they regarded themselves as self-appointed saviors. The oft-repeated "God is with us" became both the national and external justification for their activities, and the Catholic hierarchy's private support and public statements lent them added legitimacy. According to General Jorge Rafael Videla, a terrorist is not just someone with a gun or a bomb; it is anyone who spreads ideas that are contrary to Western or Christian civilization.[38] The enemy therefore included not only subversives but also those with seditious mentalities. This category was broadly interpreted and included people such as the pianist Miguel Angel Estrella, who was sent to a detention center in Uruguay where he was tortured for nine months until paralyzed. Ultimately released and forced into exile in Paris, he claimed, "The military told me that I wasn't a guerrilla, but that I had a rotten head because I played for the workers and the peasants."[39] In the junta's estimation, a subversive was anyone who expressed concern for the poor or—even worse—who tried to unite and empower them.

Jacobo Timerman has stated that the junta had clearer ideas of what it rejected than of what it wanted to establish in the country. Caught in its monolithic and simplified view of reality, the junta saw subversives everywhere. In the eyes of a paranoid anyone concerned with human rights, anyone teaching in the social sciences or the humanities or in the helping professions, and especially anyone who treated the poor was a subversive. Therefore, psychiatrists and doctors were dragged away from their offices, psychiatrists often singled out, Timerman claims, because the intelligence services believed they had special connections with guerrillas and that their mission was to keep up the spirits of guerrillas. Sociologists and other professors were taken from the universities or secondary schools where they worked, and in La Plata, whole classes of medical students were *disappeared*. Nuclear physicists were *disappeared* from their laboratories, leaving the National Commission of Atomic Energy decimated by the *disappearance* of many of its engineers and physicists. Journalists, radio announcers, editors of magazines, and even the publisher of *Padres*, a magazine for parents, were abducted. Lawyers constituted a special target because the junta wished to undermine the independence of the legal system and because, under the Argentine constitution, everyone is entitled to a defense lawyer. Over a hundred lawyers were *disappeared*, not including those who were murdered or detained in prisons without being tried or charged. The lucky ones escaped into exile.[40]

There were many who were *disappeared* because they were witnesses to incidents associated with the terror. The mother of a young woman abducted when she was pregnant received an anonymous card informing her that her daughter had given birth in a hospital. After she visited the hospital, two nurses, the paternal grandmother and aunt, and the young woman's father were all *disappeared*.[41]

Although the *disappearances* occurred throughout the country, the vast majority took place in the Buenos Aires area during the first two years of the junta's rule. The highest percentage of those *disappeared* were blue-collar workers because the leaders of the junta were determined to crush the labor movement and reverse economic nationalism, thereby destroying the popular base of Peronism.[42] Early in its rule the junta outlawed strikes and collective bargaining and closed shops and trade-union meetings. The General Confederation of Labor was proscribed, and labor leaders were banned from political activity; military officers assumed their place. Scores of workers were *disappeared*, often with the complicity of union leaders, revealing a deadly connection between Finance Minister Martínez de Hoz's free-market economic policy and the decimation of the rank and file of the unions. Martínez de Hoz lowered trade barriers and encouraged investment from abroad, a policy that would only succeed with a docile and inexpensive labor force.[43] Blue- and white-collar workers accounted for 48 percent of the *disappeared* reported to the National Commission on the Disappeared. According to the CONADEP, 72 percent of the *disappeared* were male and 28 percent female.[44] Among the women were many who were pregnant and whose children were taken away and given up for adoption, often to military officers who were unable to have their own children. In a number of hospitals there were lists of the wives of military officers who wished to adopt.

The government spurred public spending for housing, highways, and a huge increase in military wages. This was a period of easy money for the privileged, some of whom traveled to Europe and the United States for shopping sprees. The junta borrowed over a billion dollars in one year, but earnings from Argentina's traditional exports of grain and beef failed to cover the cost of imports. Ultimately this policy would undermine the economy with its crushing international debts and unemployment.

Other groups that posed a threat to the leaders were students, professionals, teachers, actors and performers, and nuns and priests associated with Liberation Theology. Many of the former were members of the Peronist party or the Socialist party, groups wishing to work toward social reform. But there were also many *disappeared* who were nonpolitical and whose only subversive activity was teaching Sunday school. Sometimes the people who were *disappeared*, such as the fifty-year-old housewife mentioned in the Mothers' bulletin, had always lived quietly.[45] Others were abducted simply for their active concern about the welfare of fellow citizens. With that measuring stick, an important segment of the population in Western countries such as France or the United States could be characterized as leftist subversive. One of the most notorious and tragic instances of *disappearance* occurred during the first year of the junta's rule, an incident that came to be known as the Night of the Pencils, in reference to the Night of the Long Knives under the Third Reich. Sixteen high-school students who had protested the rise in fares for their schoolbus confessed their participation to their parish priest, Christian Von Wernich, who then violated the secrecy of the confessional by giving them away to the military authorities.[46] He was instrumental in their arrests and also present in the detention center where all but three of the adolescents were tortured to death.

The junta's net was a wide one. Politicians, senators, and diplomats, such as Elena Holmberg, the government's press attaché in Paris, were *disappeared*. A number of children of prominent military families and local government officials were *disappeared*. In Corrientes the minister of public works, the bishop of Goya, the daughter of a minister, priests, and several directors of agricultural unions were *disappeared*.[47] Compared to these other so-called subversives, the actual number of leftist guerrillas such as the Montoneros and members of the ERP *disappeared* was quite small.

Foreign nationals also wound up in the detention centers, and, despite repeated overtures from their governments, few were ever seen again. The situation of Latin American refugees within Argentina was particularly precarious. A number of them had fled the tide of military rule to settle in Argentina only to succumb to the fate they believed they were fleeing. Even before the junta came to power the paramilitary AAA had begun to prey on them because they had sought refuge on account of their political views, and after the coup the junta issued a decree stating that any foreigners whose presence affected national security would be liable to expulsion. Two months later, two prominent Uruguayan exiles, both former senators, were abducted and later found shot to death in the trunk of a car. In July of that year twenty-three more Uruguayans were kidnapped in Buenos Aires in an operation that revealed complicity between the security forces of the two governments. When an Uruguayan journalist came to Argentina with his daughter-in-law to investigate the whereabouts of his son, he, too, was *disappeared*. After his eventual release he spoke out from his homeland about all the Uruguayan prisoners he had seen in the detention center. The *disappeared* included 123 Uruguayans, 6 Swiss, 36 French, 164 Spaniards, 304 Italians, 48 West Germans, 10 Brazilians, 6 Peruvians, 37 Chileans, 55 Paraguayans, 400 Israelis, and 3 United States citizens, all of whom were presumably exterminated in the detention centers.[48] At the trial of the generals in 1986 it was revealed that almost six hundred foreigners had *disappeared* and that fifty governments had made diplomatic inquiries regarding almost three thousand *disappeared*.

Some commentators have compared the Argentine state-sponsored terror with the Nazi policy of Night and Fog, whereby members of the Resistance were abducted and terror sown throughout Nazi-occupied Europe. According to that policy offenses against the occupation forces that could be clearly proved would be subject to local military courts. In the majority of cases, however, where guilt could not be established, prisoners were secretly transferred to Germany and then simply vanished without a trace. No information was provided on either their whereabouts or their fate. Punishing the suspicious as well as the guilty created an eerie absence that was intended to paralyze the Resistance.

As in the Nazi-occupied territories, the Argentine phenomenon of *disappearance* constituted a form of state-sponsored torture that unleashed terror not only on the *disappeared* but also on society as a whole. It was a crime with no legal recourse. After the fall of the junta, when the military courts were trying those responsible for the Dirty War, many of these people could not be sentenced for murder because there were no bodies as evidence and no laws that covered this practice. *Disappearance* means just that: no proof remains of the whereabouts or the death of a person, who has lost his or her legal and social identity.

The one official channel available to the distraught family was a writ of *habeas corpus*, which in Argentina could be submitted to the courts by human-rights organizations, or by relatives of the *disappeared* or lawyers representing them. Theoretically, after receiving such a petition, the courts are obligated to request information about the missing person from the Ministry of the Interior, the federal police, armed forces, command units, and, if necessary, the local police. The effectiveness of this procedure depends upon the existence of a strong and independent judiciary willing to demand a justification of detention from the executive power. But the majority of judges were appointed by the junta, and the remainder were effectively cowed. In fact, the government threatened many defense lawyers who filed these petitions so that it became dangerous to provide legal services to the *disappeared*. When a wife asked a judge to investigate her husband's death in prison, the judge threatened her with imprisonment if she persisted in her request, and the autopsy was never ordered.[49] Given the elastic definition of "enemy of the state," the military came to identify defense lawyers with their defendants, and these lawyers were swallowed up in detention centers. Not surprisingly, many refused to aid the families who came to them for help.

Most appeals were either halted for supposed lack of jurisdiction or denied for lack of information. The families of the *disappeared* were routinely informed by the courts that there was no information about their loved one and that therefore the petition was being dismissed. Other responses to such requests were, "It doesn't belong to this jurisdiction," "Come back in two weeks," or, "This appeal will only worsen the situation without accomplishing anything." From the over five thousand submissions for *habeas corpus* in the Buenos Aires area in the first three years of the junta's rule, not one resulted in a serious investigation.[50] By blocking these efforts the junta intended to instill in the population as a whole a feeling of utter defenselessness before its absolute power and impunity.

If the detention centers were kept secret, so were the murders of many of the detained. Many prisoners were tortured to death, their bodies cremated to avoid detection.[51] Sometimes so many bodies were cremated at once that the smell and smoke had to be deliberately masked by pyres of burning tires. There were mass executions by firing squads, with prisoners forced to dig pits for their own bodies beforehand, the graves then concealed. Helicopters would also dump bodies into the ocean, and some of the corpses washed up on the beaches as gruesome testimony of the terror. Generally, the victims who had not been killed were given an injection of drugs before being thrown out of the helicopters, but this was not always the case. Bodies were covered with cement and thrown into rivers, and corpses wrapped in plastic bags were buried in old cemeteries under existing graves. After the fall of the junta a number of exhumations of mass graves revealed corpses with their hands cut off to erase their identity. This destruction of the bodies was an important part of the policy of *disappearance*. Wiping out the identity of corpses increased the ambiguity hanging over the fate of the thousands of *disappeared* and gave relatives hope that their loved ones might still be alive. Thus, family members were effectively terrorized, convinced that they must do nothing to annoy the government and that their own actions might decide the fate of their loved ones. Of course, the policy of secretly disposing of bodies also stalled investigations into the facts and the assigning of responsibility for these deeds.

Some of the *disappeared* were freed and returned to their families, their release intended to serve as windows—as public reminders of the clandestine violence and torture occurring in the detention centers. Like the overacted abductions, strategic revelations were not inconsistent with the denial of violence. This deliberately mixed message was intended to cloud and confuse the public, spreading fear and an overwhelming sense of the regime's power.[52] Not all of the released were as defiant as Graciela Geuna. Some were so terrorized that they could not talk about their experiences or even mention the names of the other prisoners in the detention center. But a group did eventually form the Association of Ex-Detained, Ex-Disappeared, which accompanied the Mothers on their weekly marches after the fall of the junta and the return of constitutional government.

Many of those who had remained untouched by the *disappearances* sought refuge from their fear in the belief that if one remained quiet and concentrated one's attention on one's personal life, nothing would happen. The government's official denial of what was taking place strengthened the tendency for denial, and public statements regarding subversion gave rise to frequent refrains among witnesses that "He must have done something"—desperate attempts to create meaning out of senseless brutality. People who lived near detention centers took longer routes rather than pass in front of them; the less one knew, the better. A dense silence descended upon the country, the same silence of self-preservation, apathy, and hopelessness that prevailed in Germany while the Nazis were taking away Jews, Communists, Gypsies, and other enemies of the people. Anyone who sought to speak out was considered extremely dangerous by the population at large. Thus, the citizens became accomplices to the impunity of the government. As the Mothers of the Plaza de Mayo commented after the junta's fall, "The fear and silence imposed by those in power produced a paralysis which led many sectors of the population into a tragic passivity. The intention was to make all the Argentineans disappear as persons and as citizens. That is to say, they meant to disappear our national identity."[53]

NOTES

1. David Rock, *Argentina 1516–1987: From Spanish Colonization to Alfonsín* (Berkeley: University of California Press, 1987), 353.

2. Ibid., 354–55.

3. Andrew Graham-Yooll, *A State of Fear: Memoirs of Argentina's Nightmare* (New York: Hippocrene Books, 1986), 13–24, 113–26.

4. Rock, *Argentina 1516–1987*, 363.

5. Leonardo Senkman, "The Right and Civilian Regimes, 1955–1976," in *The Argentine Right: Its History and Intellectual Origins, 1910 to the Present*, ed.

Sandra McGee Deutsch and Ronald H. Dolkart (Wilmington, DE: Scholarly Resources, 1993), 135.

6. Rock, *Argentina 1516–1987*, 363.

7. Ibid., 367.

8. Ibid.

9. Frank Graziano, *Divine Violence: Spectacle, Psychosexuality, and Radical Christianity in the Argentine "Dirty War"* (Boulder, CO: Westview Press, 1992), 107–46.

10. *"Disappearances," A Workbook* (New York: Amnesty International USA, 1982), 9.

11. Evel Aztarbe de Petrini, interview by Marguerite Bouvard, November 1990.

12. Elvira Díaz de Triana, interview by Marguerite Bouvard, November 1990.

13. Noemie de Alvarez Rojas, interview by Marguerite Bouvard, November 1990.

14. *"Disappearances," A Workbook*, 94.

15. Madres de Plaza de Mayo, *Monthly Newspaper* (Buenos Aires), June 1985.

16. Graziano, *Divine Violence*, 65–73.

17. *Testimony of Graciela Geuna on La Perla Camp (Córdoba)* (London: Amnesty International, 1980).

18. *Nunca Más: The Report of the Argentine National Commission on the Disappeared* (New York: Farrar, Straus and Giroux, 1986), 52.

19. Ibid., 54.

20. Senkman, "The Right and Civilian Regimes," 129, 135–40.

21. *Nunca Más*, 67.

22. Matilde Sánchez, ed., *Historias de vida Hebe de Bonafini* (Buenos Aires: Fraterna del Nuevo Extremo, 1985), 125.

23. Iain Guest, *Behind the Disappearances: Argentina's Dirty War against Human Rights and the United Nations* (Philadelphia: University of Pennsylvania Press, 1990).

24. Ariel Delgado, interview by Marguerite Bouvard, November 1990.

25. Madres, *Newspaper*, May 1988.

26. Madres de Plaza de Mayo, *Boletín Informativo*, no. 16 (Buenos Aires), April 1984. See also *Nunca Más,* 271–74.

27. María del Carmen de Berrocal, interview by Marguerite Bouvard, August 1989.

28. Guest, *Behind the Disappearances*, 69.

29. *"Disappearances," A Workbook*, 117.

30. Ibid.

31. Ibid., 12–14, 98, 156.

32. *Nunca Más*, 340.

33. *Testimony of Graciela Geuna on La Perla Camp*.

34. *Nunca Más*, 322–28.

35. Hannah Arendt, *The Origins of Totalitarianism* (New York: Meridian Books, 1958), 475.

36. Madres, *Newspaper*, May 1988.

37. Graziano, *Divine Violence*, 107–17.

38. *Nunca Más*, 248–52, 442.

39. Madres, *Boletín*, no. 19 (July 1984).

40. Jacobo Timerman, *Prisoner Without a Name, Cell Without a Number* (New York: Alfred A. Knopf, 1981), 94, 97–98.

41. Madres, *Boletín*, no. 15 (March 1984).

42. Alfredo Martin, *Les mères "folles" de la Place de Mai* (Paris: Renaudot et Cie., 1988), 21–26.

43. Guest, *Behind the Disappearances*, 28–30.

44. Alfredo Martin, *Les mères "folles,"* 55–57. See also *Nunca Más*.

45. Madres, *Boletín*, no. 15 (no date).

46. Ibid., no. 16 (no date). See also Eduardo Luis Duhalde, *El estado terrorista argentino* (Buenos Aires: Ed. Caballito, 1983), 155–56, 183–84; *Nunca Más*, 318–31; and María Seone and Héctor Ruís Nuñez, *La noche de los lápices* (Buenos Aires: Editorial Contrapunto, 1986).

47. Madres, *Boletín*, no. 15 (no date).

48. Guest, *Behind the Disappearances*, 110, 349.

49. Ibid., 158.

50. Ibid.

51. *Nunca Más*, 230.

52. Graziano, *Divine Violence,* 80.

53. Madres, *Boletín*, no. 12, December 1983.

IN ARGENTINA

for Juanita

In another country, you would be telling stories
to your grandchildren. You would be sweeping
your house with gusto,
not with defiance. You want to sell

the too large house, but you would have to admit
your son's death, the deed
is in his name. Instead, you scrub the room
that was his medical office.

In another country, your house would not be
trashed by the police
whenever you travel, or spray-painted
mother of a terrorist.

At 75, you move with the ease
of a dancer. You prefer standing
when you talk, to make a point.
Your arms trace a wide arc:

There is no space large enough
to contain your wrath. Like my great-aunt
in Normandy who presides over flocks,
you are smiling and apple-cheeked.

But you lead demonstrations.
You shake your finger at a plainclothesman,
hissing, *Take your hands off
that kid*. In another country,

you would be a diminutive grandmother
making preserves. In Argentina,
you tower above the caudillos,
the heroes, and the statues in the squares.

CHAPTER 2

The Politics of Violence and Terror

How could the horrors, the monstrous cruelties of the Dirty War, occur in modern Argentina? This is the same question that arose from the revelations of the concentration camps after World War II. How was such barbarism possible in the country of Goethe and Schiller? Political analysts of Nazi Germany focused on that country's long authoritarian past. Despite Germany's economic and political achievements it had experienced only a brief period of democracy, and that brave yet fragile experiment, the Weimar Republic, was scorned by much of the population. Germany had remained impervious to the liberal democratic revolutions that swept Western Europe throughout the nineteenth century and instead clung to the values of hierarchy, elitism, and the preference for order against the often unpredictable workings of a democratic system.

After World War II, Germany experienced a period of foreign occupation that helped create a new political culture in the Western sector of that country. Argentina was not so fortunate. After the Dirty War waged by the junta and the restoration of constitutional government, Argentina would remain trapped in the results of its turbulent history. The contradictions, the tendency toward extremism, and the threat of violence that perpetually simmered below the surface soon emerged. Argentina's impressive industrial capacity, its resources, and its highly educated population remained captive in a culture historically riven by political violence.

Like Germany, Argentina has wrestled with an assertive nationalism and recurrent crises of national identity. It sought to incorporate waves of immigrants that came from Italy, Spain, and Portugal in the nineteenth century, swelling the ranks of the working class in its great cities and helping to usher in a period of rapid industrial expansion. Today, Argentina remains a nation of immigrants who hail from France, England, Germany, Eastern and Southern Europe, the Middle East, and Korea, as well as from other Latin American countries, and Argentines often point to this as a source of difficulty in creating a national identity.

Another obstacle in the path of achieving unity within the political system was created by an unresolved conflict in Argentina's heritage. On the one hand Argentina was influenced by the imperial Spanish presence and the Iberian political heritage of the *caudillo*, or military dictator, with its authoritarian underpinnings and its reliance on the Catholic church. However, it was also heir to the liberal European model of constitutional democracy.[1] After independence was wrested from Spain in 1816, a forty-three-year period of unrest passed before a liberal constitution was adopted, and even that event did not bring stability to the country. Over time there has been an intermingling of both heritages, but the country generally has swung from rule by a charismatic and authoritarian leader to episodes of constitutional democracy, ultimately unable to settle on either model. Democratic and authoritarian propensities coexist, with acceptance of constitutional forms and processes such as elections on the one hand, and of authoritarian executives and enhanced roles for corporate interests such as the church and the military on the other.

Argentine history is troubled not only by differing political models but also by competing national myths. Since the beginning of the Argentine republic two currents of thought have dominated the country's political self-image: the liberal but not necessarily democratic position of the educated upper classes that looked to Europe and the United States; and that of the nationalists, who have harbored contradictory tendencies from populism and nativism to aristocratic paternalism.[2] This divisiveness subsumed economics and pitted the interior provinces of the country and the poor against the oligarchy. From this vantage point the caudillos were genuine popular leaders, their violence justified given the domineering policies of the capital and its elitist governments. Argentine nationalism has been fascinated by strong leaders, and Argentine history is rife with colorful and charismatic leaders such as José de San Martín, Juan Manuel de Rosas, Domingo Faustino Sarmiento, Hipólito Yrigoyen, Carlos Gardel, and Juan and Evita Perón, people who continue to evoke powerful emotions even today.

Of these leaders, Juan Domingo Perón had a particularly powerful influence on Argentine political culture throughout his intermittent rule, which began in 1943 with his rise to power through the ranks of the military and ended with his death in 1974. His influence continues to cast a shadow over Argentine politics. In developing his policies, Perón drew upon nationalist phobias against communism and working-class revolution, and on corporatist doctrine that reflected a Christian view of social justice. Corporatism stresses harmony between socioeconomic interests over class conflict and emphasizes the responsibility of the state in integrating the various sectors. By promoting this doctrine and ultimately revising the constitution, Perón managed to centralize power in the presidency at the expense of other institutions and the provinces.

Perón's tenure was notable both for achieving social justice for the working class, women, and other neglected sectors of the population and for the authoritarian methods he bequeathed to future governments. At the beginning of his first term he enacted striking measures of social reform, increasing wage earners' incomes against those of other sectors and promoting the construction of low-cost workers' housing, hospitals, schools, and clinics.[3] Before Perón, labor had had negligible political influence. Under his tutelage the General Confederation of Labor (CGT) became one of the most powerful organizations in the country.

Although Perón was ousted by a military coup and driven into exile in 1955, he continued to exert influence in Argentina through his public pronouncements and his many lieutenants who remained behind. The interplay between his supporters and enemies dominated politics even after his death. While opinion on Peronism continues to be divided and the interpretation of that movement controversial, it nevertheless has had a strong impact on the political system and is one of the factors undermining a respect for pluralism in that embattled country. By founding the Peronist party and movement, sometimes referred to as the Justicialista movement, Perón left an indelible mark on the nation, and his doctrine of social justice continues to inspire reform-minded Argentines. Currently, the Peronist party is split between a right and a left wing, the left wing supporting social reform but not necessarily democratic methods, and the right wing representing business interests. These two interpretations of Peronism are at war, the left wing accusing the Peronists in Carlos Saúl Menem's government of betrayal. Like Perón, Menem used the left to achieve power, only to turn to the right once in office.

By the end of his presidency, embattled by economic problems and rising opposition, Perón sought to silence his foes by purging the universities and subordinating the workers to the state through control of the unions. He broadened police powers by creating new police bodies with special sections to infiltrate labor unions and political parties. He impeached Supreme Court justices who disagreed with him and removed judges of lower tribunals. Under his leadership the Congress passed laws curbing political dissent and denied his opponents access to radio broadcasting and newspapers, precedents eagerly followed by the Peronist President Menem. Perón was not squeamish about using violence and urged his supporters at mass rallies to take power in the streets and confront his opponents with violent means. Today, Peronism still controls the unions. As a result of legislation passed under Perón, the unions are organized into industry-wide blocs under a hierarchical bureaucracy supported by compulsory membership dues, a structure lending itself to control from above.[4] By providing significant social and economic benefits to the unions, Perón gave them a stake in governmental intervention.

In industrial democracies, incorporating the working class into the political system has meant its inclusion in the political process as well as its representation in political parties and a variety of interest groups. In Argentina, however, the working class rose into a political culture that emphasizes strong interests at the expense of political institutions. The unions are able to express their considerable power by taking to the streets, which is important in Argentina. Through their collection of dues and their management of social programs for workers, they control a significant amount of money. Union leaders have not been above collaborating with the military, and during the Dirty War leaders of the CGT were instrumental in the large-scale *disappearances* of workers. The Mothers of the Plaza de Mayo believe that the leadership of the CGT is as antidemocratic as other significant interests in society, and that is why they have focused their efforts upon the grass roots of the labor movement. They have learned the lesson that few of their countrymen have been able to grasp—that powerful special interests undermine democracy.

The Catholic church traditionally has played an important political role in Argentina. Although the church is not monolithic, its right wing is the dominant element among church members and in the hierarchy. The Catholic right grew significantly during the 1920s and 1930s, when it forged an alliance with the army in order to attack the growing "evils of religious tolerance, democracy, North American materialism, Judaism, and communism."[5] During that decade, the political stand of the church embraced the European ideologies of fascism and nazism. A number of Catholics supported the Axis powers during World War II and continue to uphold a combination of cultural conservatism and political authoritarianism.

In the late 1960s the Vatican II conference produced a document entitled "The Church in the Modern World," which would divide the Argentine church. Stressing the importance of human liberation in this life as well as the next, the decree pointed to both atheistic socialism and liberal capitalism as sources of social turmoil and described underdeveloped countries as victims of capitalism.[6] This was the beginning of the Third World Priest movement and Liberation Theology, which attracted many young people in Argentina who wished to improve the lot of the poor. The Catholic left came to include both moderate factions and extremists associated with the Montoneros, the left-wing guerrilla group within the Peronist party.[7] The Argentine church became divided between those who supported the military government and a relatively small number who sought its overthrow.

Historically, the church has promoted authoritarian values such as obedience and deference to hierarchy.[8] Standing apart from the church in other Latin American and Central American countries because prominent members have played leading roles in the corridors of power, the Argentine church supported military and Peronist governments since these allowed it dominance in education, and it is through education that it has prevented the development of democratic attitudes and of individual initiative and responsibility.[9] In keeping with its past record of supporting military coups, the Catholic hierarchy welcomed the coup headed by General Raphael Videla that overthrew Isabel Perón in 1976. In turn, Videla appointed prominent Catholics to his combined Ministry of Religion and Foreign Relations.

In Argentina, nationalism and religion traditionally have been linked, the Catholic church often acting as the connection between conservative military officers and elitist intellectuals of the far right. Many nationalist cabinet ministers not only taught at military institutions but also held posts at Catholic universities. They have been active in important ministries such as the Ministry of the Interior, with its control of the police and its authority over local governments. The Ministries of Education and Culture, and of Religion and Foreign Relations, also lent themselves to the propagation of the faith.[10]

Throughout Argentine history rightist Catholic intellectuals provided the ideology for military governments and extremist paramilitary bands. Jordán Bruno Genta, for example, was the principal theorist for a paramilitary group of civilians and retired military personnel, the National Counterrevolutionary League, founded in 1964. Although Genta's doctrine of counterrevolutionary war went unnoticed in the mid-1960s, it became the basis of the junta's national security doctrine, stressing that communism had infiltrated all levels of the state, society, and culture. To combat this evil Genta suggested that the country gear for internal war, that Roman Catholicism be publicly and officially professed in Argentina, that public schools abolish secular teaching, and that international capitalism and worker movements be declared incompatible with Argentine nationalism, their activities proscribed.[11]

The time of the junta is truly a dark period in the Catholic church's history. Members of the church hierarchy were closely associated with the leaders of the government, and even the papal nuncio, Monsignor Pio Laghi, was not immune from charges of collaboration. The clergy held solemn High Masses for the various members of the junta, and their public communications, while sometimes deploring the kidnappings, lent support to that regime by noting that the guerrillas had brought the country to a state of disorder. They were accomplices to the *disappearances* in a number of ways, such as by suppressing information about the *disappeared*, which they were privy to because of their close connection to the government; and by their sinister assistance during the tortures in the detention centers. The National Commission on the Disappeared (CONADEP) and the testimonies of former prisoners about the detention camps have corroborated the role of the clergy in these torture centers.[12] "The Lost Honor of the Argentine Bishops: Their Collaboration in Abduction and Torture," published by the International Association Against Torture, in Geneva, Switzerland, is a chilling document that details the behavior of members of the clergy during the Dirty War.[13]

Hebe de Bonafini, the current president of the Mothers' organization, recalls that when her son Jorge was *disappeared* on February 8, 1977, she went to seek help from Monsignor Antonio Plaza, the bishop of La Plata. Bishop Plaza brought her into his office, where he introduced her to a retired policeman. Although he had promised Hebe she would get information about her son, it soon became clear to her that the bishop and his policeman friend were more interested in grilling her and trying to get information about her son's friends than in helping her.[14] She left hurriedly and without ceremony. In another instance, when Evel Aztarbe de Petrini's son Sergio was abducted, she immediately rushed to the parish of San Martín, where her son taught Sunday school, and asked to see the bishop.[15] He refused, and thus began her painful introduction to a hierarchy that would turn away from the Mothers while supporting the military.

Three bishops and a number of priests were repelled by the government's behavior and railed against it, and on occasion the hierarchy did come forward to speak out on behalf of the *disappeared*. But their words were always too little and too late as far as the Mothers were concerned, and in the early years of the search for their children their organization repeatedly felt it had to remind the church of its pastoral duties. Monsignor Novak of Neuquin, Father Rubén Capitanio, and many of the lower clergy were devoted and brave supporters of the Mothers. It was as dangerous for the clergy to speak out as it was for the general population, however. Two bishops and twenty priests, nuns, and seminarians were *disappeared* because of their opposition to the brutality of the regime, but the church barely raised a voice in protest.[16]

In the absence of a strong democratic tradition to adjust varying interests, powerful groups such as labor, the Catholic church, and the military have sought extraparliamentary means to realize their goals. This proclivity arises also from the failure of political institutions to reflect the needs of major socioeconomic groups. The two houses of the Congress are weak in comparison to the executive branch and unable to incorporate the programs of the wealthy, the middle class, the working class, reformers, the church, and the military. Historically, these sectors have viewed their positions as mutually exclusive, and in a system that gives dominance to the executive branch, Argentine presidents have governed in the spirit of winner-take-all, ignoring large segments of the population. As a result disgruntled sectors have turned to political violence; in the absence of legitimacy, the use of force to acquire power and of coercion to remain in power have become accepted practices.

Violence affects all segments of society. It affects the upper class, which pays both right- and left-wing terrorists for protection from the omnipresent threat of kidnapping, and it envelops those who seek reform but have little faith in the political process. To complicate matters the welter of terrorist groups is often wedded to officialdom; during the Dirty War, junta leader Admiral Emilio Massera hired leftist Montoneros guerrillas who were in detention centers to work on his behalf because he admired their skills.[17] After the junta fell, members of the ERP found employment with the military.[18] Violence is also rooted in the workings of the political system, in police and security forces who continue to use unchecked physical force against peaceful demonstrators and suspects they routinely round up.

The political spectrum in Argentina ranges from the far right to the extreme left, with each tendency fragmented into a myriad of groups and subgroups, some of which include paramilitary elements. Because of the conservative influence of the church, a traditional fear of the workers' revolutionary potential, and the fact that the far right has captured nationalist sentiment, the left has been regarded with suspicion. A number of leftist movements exist, from the socialists to small fringe groups, but these have been unable to transcend their differences and work together. In their desire for justice and social reform, the Mothers of the Plaza de Mayo have identified themselves as clearly on the left and have unsuccessfully urged the left toward unity. That their program, which aims for the achievements of many West European democracies in health care and education, is considered dangerously radical in Argentina is telling.

The right is also fragmented, with the far right exerting an influence out of proportion to its actual power through its connections to the military and because of the absence of a moderate right. Paul Lewis has identified two types of rightist tendencies that have influenced Argentina's military governments in recent years: the Nacionalista, which is authoritarian, corporatist, and looks to the country's Hispanic heritage; and the right-liberal, which believes in authoritarian capitalism. Right-liberals are divided by their attitudes toward military rule, with the ultras favoring military rule and the moderates favoring a modified version of democracy. They differ from the Nacionalistas, who favor autarchy, in their desire to link Argentina to the world economy and in their pursuit of technological and commercial progress. Both rightist tendencies have been attracted to military regimes because they do not have a sufficient base to acquire power through the political process and under such governments they are free to carry out their policies without interference.[19] The Peronist right periodically has cooperated with the Nacionalistas in its desire to stave off reformist and revolutionary activity from the union grass roots. The right has played an important role in politics because it has captured the image of Argentine nationalism, placing nationalist issues in the forefront of its agenda and capitalizing on the factionalization of Argentine politics.

Civilian intellectuals such as Genta and technocrats on the far right have provided military governments with legitimating ideologies and technical expertise. A number of avenues bring these people in contact with the military, and some intellectuals have achieved cabinet positions through membership in nationalist clubs like the Ateneo de la República; Catholic lay organizations; exclusive social organizations such as the Jockey Club; the Argentine Rural Society; the Chamber of Commerce; and the Industrial Union.[20] Movement of personnel between military and civilian life is continual as retired military officers acquire positions in industry, and as civilians enter military govern-ments through contacts forged during professorships in the various military schools.

In Argentina political divisions are further reinforced by socio-economic differences; few institutions offer people of differing views the opportunity to come together. Argentines debate their political outlooks passionately, with little bent for compromise. Friendships that can bridge political tendencies are rare, and few can uphold a politically neutral position when the various political groups maintain that those who do not agree with them are automatically against them.[21]

For many Argentines politics is a romantic or a deadly pursuit. In its historical revisionism and its emphasis upon country and culture the far right has portrayed itself as heroic. In its tireless concern for the poor and neglected, the left also regards itself and its mission as extraordinary. Both poles of the political spectrum have a tendency to elevate their goals at the further expense of compromise.

Strands of political culture have resisted military solutions, and there have been intervals of constitutional government, however short-lived. Intellectuals and the moderate left and center parties constitute the main opposition to the armed forces. The differences among parties opposed to military rule are so strong that they cannot work together in coalitions. Each group regards its interests as exclusive, and these parties are no measure for the two dominant parties, Raúl Alfonsín's Radical Civic Union and President Carlos Saúl Menem's Peronist party, which have alternately held power because of their numerical strength and also because of their response to the demands of some of the most powerful interest groups—including the military.

Young people in Argentina are politically conscious at an early age, and it is not unusual for high-school students to become political activists, inspired by a keen desire for social reform and justice. Because there are so many programs and ideologies for achieving social change, however, and because children are not taught to work together, the faults that separate the political views of the adult popu-lation begin to appear when Argentines are in their adolescence. One becomes a Peronista, a Socialist, a Communist, or a member of the Youth Group of the Radical Party, and that allegiance is passionate and exclusive. This is why the Mothers of the Plaza de Mayo insist that any young person wishing to join their support group must not be tied to a political party or ideology. They frequently address students in high schools and universities, where forging a common ground among these various groups is one of their persistent aims.

In seeming contradiction, the schools where so many ideologies flourish among students function in an authoritarian manner. There are no civics courses and few extracurricular outlets in which young people can assume responsibility and self-governance in matters that concern them. The Ministry of Education maintains tight control over school districts and curricular requirements. Superintendents and principals rein in teachers who in turn exercise strict control over their students, including their political activities.[22] In 1987, for example, the principal of the Lomos de Zamoro school informed police that two of his students were organizing a candlelight procession to commemorate the Night of the Pencils. The two were arrested in the doorway of their school as the demonstration was about to begin.[23]

Universities in Argentina are likewise subject to authoritarian control. Peronist and military suppression of student politics and purges of professors who do not maintain the correct attitudes have accounted for the emigration of many intellectuals in the past quarter century. During the military dictatorship of 1976–1983, teachers and university professors were *disappeared* in great numbers. Many educators and intellectuals fled to exile in Spain, France, England, Italy, and Germany, swelling a diaspora of artists and intellectuals who have emigrated to countries around the world over the years. Tragically, some of these exiles could have imparted a more democratic set of values to the next generation.

One of the overriding problems that has plagued Argentina throughout its history has been the presence of a strong, economically powerful military that has displayed a contempt for democracy. When Argentina gained its independence from Spain, the military enjoyed more popularity than the revolutionary politicians and became the only institution with any legitimacy.[24] The close relationship between politics and the military has been maintained throughout the nineteenth and twentieth centuries, the army repeatedly intervening at times of political crisis in an attempt to establish its own order and impose its own solutions to political and economic problems. Its geographic concentration around Argentina's three largest cities, Buenos Aires,

Rosario, and Córdoba, and its easy reach of government offices have facilitated its repeated intrusions. The Campo de Mayo garrison, for instance, is a short two blocks away from the presidential palace. These concentrations of force represent an ominous threat to the stability and survival of political institutions.

A large army that has absorbed as much as 12 percent of the budget and that does not have a mission represents a great threat to a political system. Though its budget was cut by Presidents Raúl Alfonsín and Carlos Saúl Menem and the average number of conscripts in training fell dramatically, the command structure remained intact.[25] Today the army puts forth a large number of demands, not the least of which is vindicating its role in the Dirty War and obscuring anything that might hold it accountable for its behavior. Since constitutional government was restored in 1983, four attempted military coups, the latest in December 1990, have been thwarted, each inspired by a desire to restore the military's image as well as increase its share of the budget and modernize its services.

Throughout Argentine history, however, the blame for the army's periodic foray into politics must also be extended to civilians who either have welcomed its ascension to power or who have failed to support the constitution. Appeals to the military by various political groups have not been uncommon, and since the 1960s upper- and upper-middle-class Argentines have regarded the army as a bastion against Communist subversion. In times of chaos such as the years under the rule of Isabel Perón, citizens have looked to the army as a means of reestablishing order. Fear of terrorist activity led the upper and upper-middle classes to support the coup of March 1976. Civilians are not without weapons such as general strikes against military domination, but their willingness to use them rests on how deeply they value the civilian alternative. In 1982 it was military incompetence during the Falklands War rather than social protest that brought down the junta.

Given Argentine political culture and history, eliminating the influence of the army in the affairs of the country is no easy task. The problem is not merely compounded by numbers, geographic concentration, or the portion of the budget the armed forces absorb. The military is embedded in the Argentine political system through a powerful and far-reaching military-industrial complex. As one of the biggest landowners in Argentina, the military controls a significant portion of capital. Each branch of the armed forces owns or has control over vast state enterprises. The air force, for example, controls aircraft production, national airlines, air insurance, and travel agencies. The navy controls the merchant fleet, shipyards, and weapons research and production. The army controls a huge industrial conglomerate, the General Directorate of Military Factories, which was created in 1941 and has undergone continual expansion since then; it now comprises 5 percent of the gross national product. Members of the armed forces also sit on the boards of state enterprises such as the National Telephone Company and hold large shares in mixed state-private enterprises in such areas as steel and petrochemicals.[26] Any political leader who would reduce the military influence in the country must also account for its pervasive presence in all sectors of the economy. President Menem's campaign of privatizing state-owned industry ultimately may be a way of lessening military influence in the economy.

Argentine soldiers had not waged a battle against foreign enemies for a hundred years when they entered the ill-fated Falklands War of 1982. To justify their size and budget, the armed forces dramatized the internal threats they perceived from ideological foes. They continually claimed that guerrillas armed by the Soviet Union and trained by Cuba posed the major security risk to Argentina, refusing to see that their own oppressive actions helped create the very small leftist guerrilla movement that was all but wiped out during the Dirty War. Despite the tarnishing of the army's image as a result of its role in the Dirty War and its debacle in the Falklands War, the military continues to be an important behind-the-scenes player in the contest for political power. That its continuing power is recognized by the important interest groups and members of the political elite reveals the weakness of civilian institutions.

It was into this culture of violence that the Mothers of the Plaza de Mayo appeared in 1977, raising a voice that had never been heard in Argentine politics. A group of middle-aged women, most of whom had never participated in or even thought about politics, forged a set of democratic and humane values out of their own searing experiences in the search for their *disappeared* children. They would hold up these values as an alternative to a system that unleashed terror against its own citizens during the Dirty War and that, even after the return of constitutional government, would continue to yield to the military and deny basic human rights to those who dissented.

The Mothers progressively claimed space within a closed and male-dominated society. These women came out of the shadows, out of a cultural, historical, and social invisibility and into the center of the political arena to challenge a repressive government. Fired by their own vision of the truth about their children's *disappearances*, they forged a space in political vocabulary and hence in political consciousness, unmasking the truth of successive regimes and raising troubling ethical questions. They became self-proclaimed custodians of a history of terror and injustice against leaders who first tried to obliterate the identity of the *disappeared* and later sought to draw a veil over the crimes of the military junta. Contemporary Argentina, like Germany in the aftermath of the Third Reich, is muffled in an eerie silence. There are even attempts to rewrite history by characterizing the Dirty War as a fight against subversion. The Mothers continually shatter this silence, carving out a sanctuary for memory and for their lost children in the public awareness. Through their choice of yearly slogans they both educate and empower their followers. The angry responses of the government prove that the Mothers have retained the initiative in the political dialogue. Like Cassandra they continue to challenge and provoke those who would rather turn inward and away.

Because they were not admitted to the chambers of governmental power they claimed the geography of dissent, the Plaza de Mayo, where Argentina proclaimed its independence from Spain in 1816 and where groups of citizens have gathered since then to demand their political goals. Because the newspapers denied them coverage they distributed their own newspapers, pamphlets, and posters throughout the country and around the world. In defiance of a regime that caused people to retreat into their homes and private lives, they took the open spaces of the streets and parks, shouting the truth in a country rendered mute by fear.

As they pursued the search for their children, the Mothers also presented the Argentine people with alternative values and modes of being. Their efforts to infuse politics with ethics and with respect for universal human rights are reminiscent of the work of Gandhi and Martin Luther King, Jr. Ultimately the Mothers' constituency over-

Hebe de Bonafini, president of the Mothers of the Plaza de Mayo, addressing a crowd in the Plaza de Mayo, 1989 (*photo by Don Rypka*)

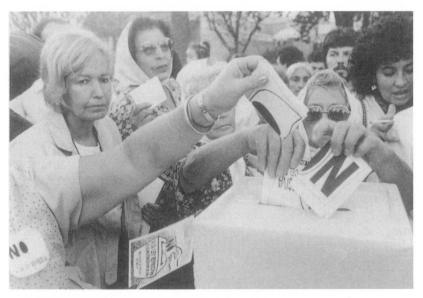

The Mothers stage a mock vote in 1989 against a law increasing the power of the military in internal security (*photo by Inicio de la Campaña*)

flowed the boundaries of the nation-state to demand the protection of maternal bonds against the state and the rights of young adults everywhere to freedom and dignity.

Their story is one of becoming, of an unfolding of the spirit and a creation of political awareness. Their initial effort as a group was to seek a response from the government about the fate of their children. They did not question the government or the Catholic church but regarded themselves as good citizens and church members. Their quest, though, led them to the discovery of a pattern of oppression as they unmasked the intentions of a government that sought to eliminate all opposition under a facade of normalcy and with a studied public-relations campaign. Working in the open with nonviolent methods, the Mothers eventually challenged the entire military regime. Repeated instances of terror and police brutality, including the assassination of four of their members, could not stop them, instead revealing the limits of both force and fear.

The Mothers' movement is about presence, the proclamation of alternative modes of thought and innovative political action within a system that has traditionally refused to tolerate opposition. Their presence is power and occurs in political and ethical consciousness, in the streets, in the homage of international leaders such as former Italian president Sandro Pertini and in their many international support groups. It resonates in the heart where that politically dangerous feeling—hope—sends out sparks. As such, the Mothers' organization is built upon the collaboration rather than the conflict between private and public space, contradicting a vision of power as wholly public.

The Mothers not only transformed political action, but they also revolutionized the very concept of maternity as passive and in the service of the state into a public and socialized claim against the state. Their vision of maternity ultimately served as a springboard for demanding a political system that would reflect maternal values and assure human rights, universal participation, and social welfare: they proclaimed themselves revolutionary Mothers. The organization they forged out of their anger and pain serves as a model, founded on equality and mutual respect, proving that it is possible to honor democratic values in repressive settings. Although the Mothers are growing older and will eventually vanish from the scene, their example will continue to evoke the possibilities of the human spirit.

NOTES

1. Susan and Peter Calvert, *Argentina: Political Culture and Instability* (Pittsburgh: University of Pittsburgh Press, 1989), 11–36.

2. Nicolas Shumway, *The Invention of Argentina* (Berkeley: University of California Press, 1991), 214–22.

3. Rock, *Argentina 1516–1987*, 263.

4. Ibid., 284, 302–3.

5. Calvert, *Argentina: Political Culture,* 29.

6. Daniel Poneman, *Argentina: Democracy on Trial* (New York: Paragon House, 1987), 111.

7. Calvert, *Argentina: Political Culture*, 33.

8. Emilio Mignone, *Iglesia y dictadura* (Buenos Aires: Ediciones del Pensamiento Nacional, 1986).

9. Poneman, *Argentina: Democracy on Trial*, 113.

10. Paul Lewis, "The Right and Military Rule, 1955–1983," in *The Argentine Right: Its History and Intellectual Origins, 1910 to the Present*, ed. Sandra McGee Deutsch and Ronald H. Dolkart (Wilmington, DE: Scholarly Resources, 1993), 177.

11. Senkman, "The Right and Civilian Regimes," 126–32.

12. *Nunca Más*, 248–52.

13. *L'Honneur perdu des évêques argentines: La collaboration des évêques catholiques dans la pratique des disparitions forcées et de la torture* (Geneva, Switzerland: Cahiers de l'Association Internationale contre la Torture, 1990).

14. Hebe de Bonafini, interview by Marguerite Bouvard, August 1989.

15. de Petrini, interview.

16. *Nunca Más*, 321.

17. Guest, *Behind the Disappearances*, 72–75.

18. Conversation between former member of the Argentine Communist party and Marguerite Bouvard, November 1990 (name withheld for safety).

19. Lewis, "The Right and Military Rule," 147.

20. Ibid., 149.

21. While I was in Argentina, the people I spoke with queried me regarding my politics as a way of gauging their reactions to me. I spent a great deal of effort trying to persuade one of the Mothers' supporters that even though I did not have a high regard for Fidel Castro, we could nevertheless remain friendly.

22. Poneman, *Argentina: Democracy on Trial*, 114–16.

23. Madres, *Monthly Newspaper*, June 1987.

24. Calvert, *Argentina: Political Culture*, 78–79.

25. "Argentina, Shaken and a Little Stirred," *The Economist* (December 6, 1990): 52.

26. Poneman, *Argentina: Democracy on Trial*, 100–107.

A WHITE SHAWL

You chose white
because you refuse to mourn.
Your scarves illuminate

the stained streets, the steps of the subway,
the bus depots with their tired passengers.
You wear white to confound the enemy,

to be distinguished in a crowd, your white wings
scudding ahead of the racing ocean.
Your pañuelos carry the wisdom

of the household, of two hands becoming twelve,
the multiplication of loaves and fishes.
Tied together, they make a cordon

to protect your young helpers from the police.
They surround a paddy wagon with a Mother inside.
On the tenth anniversary of the pañuelo

thousands fluttered in streamers
among the torches in the square
as if snow geese were arriving from the Arctic.

Wherever the politicians and their henchmen gather,
you stand before them, your white scarves
a mirror before their averted faces.

You chose white, the milky sky
before dawn. You chose as your uniforms,
a simple diaper, a baby-shawl.

CHAPTER 3

The Mothers Come Together

Our lives were divided into before and after.
Mothers of the Plaza de Mayo

The *disappearance* of their children represented a watershed for the women who came together to form the Mothers of the Plaza de Mayo. When they began their frantic search for their children, they were primarily homemakers, content with their absorption in family and household and expressing little interest in the world beyond. They had been socialized into these roles by a traditional Argentine society that regards the male as the dominant figure, the sole participant in public life and the undisputed head of the home. Not many of them had completed secondary-school education because in the generation of the 1930s and 1940s, only males went to school.

At first these Mothers did not realize that they were embarking on a journey which would transform them into political activists—that the act of searching for their children and their subsequent union in this search would lead them to an independent analysis of the system that had made such a tragedy possible. On the basis of that analysis they would wage a courageous resistance to the regime and develop an entirely new mode of political expression. From their resistance to state-sponsored terrorism they moved to a demand for a complete transformation of Argentine political life, including respect for human rights. Ultimately they would demand the return of a democracy that guaranteed pluralism and eliminated the role of the military and intelligence services. During the seven-year reign of the junta, they traveled light years. Instead of worrying about what they were going to cook for dinner, they were confronting armed policemen who turned water cannons and dogs on them. They revolutionized their way of life, their perceptions, and created new models of opposition for Latin America and beyond. They would use hitherto untapped sources of power, confounding the military with their cohesiveness and their continual public unmasking of the truth about what was happening behind the carefully constructed political facade.

Searching for their children at police stations, hospitals, and army barracks was a brutal introduction to the world outside the home, including its political system. The bewilderment they felt at their children's *disappearance* was compounded by the psychological torture of their loved ones' uncertain fates as well as by the physical stress of standing in line at ministries or prisons for hours without food, water, or sanitary facilities—only to be told at the end of a long day, "Come back tomorrow." The Mothers' personal lives, the comfort and structure of their routines were turned upside down as if from a death.

The *disappearance* of a son or daughter was a shocking personal tragedy that ultimately undermined the foundations of their social, political, and psychological worlds. The first institution to buckle under the violence of the terror was the family. In Argentine society, home and family form the pivot of a woman's life. Those Mothers who worked outside the home had jobs in sectors traditionally reserved for women, such as primary-school education, clerical work, and social services. The Mothers did not rebel against this. They were content in socially ascribed work and as parents and household managers, expecting to enjoy the growth of their children, their marriages, and the coming of grandchildren. When their sons and daughters were dragged away without a trace, relationships within the nuclear and extended family were also shattered. Suddenly the Mothers were away from their homes during the day, searching for their children while younger siblings of the *disappeared* were left behind. Fathers faced their wives' uncertain safety and a drastic change in responsibilities and routines.

The *disappearances* were calculated to make both parents feel powerless as the inviolability of the home was destroyed. If the house could be entered in the middle of the night while the family slept, there were no longer any real doors—security forces might come back for another child. The trashed rooms, the stolen china, the rifled books and papers were reminders that there was no more safety, which is just the reaction that a repressive system wishes to engender to keep individuals isolated, lonely, and constantly vulnerable.[1]

Many of the Mothers describe the first weeks and months after the *disappearances* of their children as times of hopelessness. Often they lay curled up on their beds, stricken with anguish and unable to grasp their situations. Initially, the families responded with shock and a sense of helplessness. They assumed that a mistake had been made and that their children would be returned as soon as it was rectified. Many of them were immobilized not only because of their grief but also because of fear of reprisals and fears for their other children. One Mother recalls that "there were mornings when I woke up and told myself, he must be someplace, he must be alive. But the next day, I imagined the contrary. I thus lived tortured, driven mad, thinking of him the entire day, seeing him in each young man I passed on the streets, jumping every time I heard the telephone or the doorbell, believing I had heard his voice."[2]

Somehow they were able to get through the days, but the nights took the greatest toll on the Mothers. They lay awake wondering if their children were hungry or cold, if they were being mistreated. Josefa Donato de Pauvi, whose son, a lawyer, was abducted in the early morning hours two weeks after the military coup, remembers being so depressed she could barely leave her bed or her house.[3] She had learned from some friends in the lower echelons of the military that her son was in the Campo de Mayo detention center, and, until she joined the Mothers months later, she lay awake nights unable to move beyond her pain.

The Mothers were the first to leave their homes and interrupt their daily routines in order to search for their children; the fathers had to go to work. As Argentine women in a traditional society, they were wary and did not speak to the others around them. Although each Mother was obsessed with the task of securing the return of her child, she believed this could be accomplished within a brief period of time. Initially, each believed that she alone had suffered this terrible tragedy. The incessant activity helped the women deal with their anguish and ultimately move beyond both fear and pain. Then, as they pursued their dreary rounds of prisons, police stations, and military barracks in search of their children, they began to notice other women waiting in line or sitting on the benches of waiting rooms. As the weeks and months passed they recognized the same worried faces on the trains and buses into the city. They began to talk to each other, comparing notes. At first they did not exchange names and addresses, merely talking about the best way to write a *habeas corpus*.

Ironically, the Ministry of the Interior helped bring the Mothers together. At the ministry a small office had been set aside for the Mothers so that their cases could be investigated. In fact, the office was a way of getting more information. While the friendly police-woman in the ministry was offering her sympathy and promises of help, she was also taking down the names and addresses of the Mothers and of their children's associates.[4] Some of the Mothers slowly realized the danger of the situation and moved on to different government departments in search of information. But in the corridors outside that office they began to compare their stories and decided to start meeting in each other's homes.

One Mother, Azucena de Villaflor de De Vincente, stood out because of her energy, her initiative, and her unforgettably radiant smile. Although her parents had been trade-union leaders and Peronist politicians, she had grown up with an aunt and uncle and had begun to work in a factory at the age of fifteen. When she married she stopped working and henceforth devoted her life to her children. Shortly after the coup that brought the junta to power, her son Néstor, a student and a member of the Peronist party, and her daughter-in-law Raquel were *disappeared*. Until then Azucena rarely had left the house alone except to shop or visit a friend. Ultimately, she became the one who urged the mothers to have courage and to forge ahead in their struggle. An inspiration and a tower of strength, she was always ready with new ideas, unfailingly generous with her comfort and support. The Mothers met at her home on weekends to write letters, plan their activities, and exchange ideas, often spending whole days there.[5] Azucena found out the addresses of Amnesty International and the Organization of American States' Inter-American Commission on Human Rights. She decided where the Mothers should direct their letters during a particular week and insisted that they scour all the daily papers for information on important visitors to the country whom they might interview and petition.

The Mothers also gathered in churches to conduct their business because they felt safer there. While they were meeting in the Church of Stella Maris, Azucena first thought of going to the government offices in the Plaza de Mayo—they could draw up a petition asking for an audience with the government and try to find out what had happened to their children.[6] It proved to be a momentous move.

On April 30, 1977, fourteen Mothers assembled in the Plaza de Mayo. Among them were Azucena de Villaflor de De Vincente, Juana de Pargament, María del Rosario de Cerruti, and María Adela Antokoletz.[7] Filled with trepidation, they arrived separately, with just bus fare and their identity cards in case they had to flee. In the surge of emotion and determination that followed their decision, they had settled on a day when they were all free, a Saturday. No one had thought of the fact that since stores and businesses were closed for the weekend the Plaza would be empty. They decided to meet again the following Friday when there would be an audience for their demonstration.

In the interval the Mothers gathered the addresses of the women they had seen in the ministries and courts and tried to recruit as many mothers as possible, going to each home to explain their mission. Not all the women were interested, many responding with fear and alarm. Nevertheless, in a bold and spontaneous decision a group of Mothers started meeting in the Plaza on Fridays. The Mothers had decided to work openly against a regime that enforced secrecy and total compliance, and their Friday meetings represented the beginning of a long and courageous struggle to claim space for truth and dissent in the very setting of governmental power.

On the third week of their meetings they delivered a collective letter to the president. Azucena de De Vincente and Mária del Rosario de Cerruti entered the Casa Rosada, but no one would see them. They kept coming back every week until two months later an under secretary in the ministry told them that the president would meet with them that day. They returned at 7:00 that evening while a large crowd of Mothers waited for them outside in the Plaza. The meeting turned out to be most unsatisfactory—the president told the Mothers that their children had left the country. "How could they be detained if I know nothing about it? What do the writs of *Habeas corpus* say? They say that they are not detained. Well, then, they are not detained. Many of these young people were mixed up in subversion and have left the country. The young women who leave the country are prostituting themselves in Mexico and your sons must have gone with some girl." Azucena de De Vincente and María del Rosario de Cerruti were furious. They replied, "You are not going to remove us from the Plaza anymore until you tell us what has happened to our children. Even without legs, we will continue to march here until you tell us what they have done with our children. You don't sign death warrants for those that you kill, you won't take responsibility for what you do, you are more cowardly than anyone."[8] They left that meeting even more determined to persist in their search and to keep coming to the Plaza until they found out what had happened to their children.

Initially, only a few Mothers had the courage to meet by the pyramid in the center of the square. But by the time they had their interview with the president their numbers had swelled to sixty. The authorities first believed they were just a group of poor old women. When they kept coming, the government sent a policeman who barked at them that the country was in a state of siege and that sitting there was tantamount to holding a meeting and would mark them as an illegal organization. "Keep moving, keep moving," he ordered.[9] And so they began to walk by twos, arm in arm. The Plaza is huge and they could have dispersed among the crowds, but they began to approach the pyramid and to circle, walking counterclockwise to demonstrate their defiance. Much later they described their walks as marches, not as walking, because they felt that they were marching toward a goal and not just circling aimlessly. As the Fridays succeeded one another and the numbers of Mothers marching around the Plaza increased, the police began to take notice. Vanloads of policemen would arrive, take names, and force the Mothers to leave. But the women kept coming back. Eventually, they decided to convene on Thursdays because then there were more likely to be passersby. One of the Mothers also believed that Friday was a day of bad luck.

Hebe de Bonafini, the current president of the Mothers' organization, remembers how she first decided to come to the Plaza with the other Mothers.[10] She had been talking to a woman whom she had seen in the various places where she went for information about her son.

The woman suggested they take the bus together since they had seen each other on the same route before. As they rode past the city the woman told Hebe that her pregnant daughter was *disappeared* five months previously, and that because there were so many women in this situation a group of them had begun to work together, arranging for interviews with people who might help them and drawing up documents. They would be meeting at the Plaza de Mayo on Thursday to sign a petition and seek an interview with a priest, and the woman wanted Hebe to join them.

Hebe's first reaction was one of alarm. She agreed to go but then wondered whether she was doing something foolish, something that might provoke a scandal among her family and acquaintances. She also worried that it might endanger her other children. In short, she was terribly afraid. When she got home, she and her husband had a long discussion, and ultimately she decided to go as a way of helping her *disappeared* son. She arrived a little early on Thursday, filled with anxiety and wondering what she could accomplish, whether she had done the right thing. As she saw the Mothers slowly begin to gather, she drifted over to them. They were talking rapidly in low tones.

Although the Mothers then believed that they were only looking for their children and that they would find some support, this was but the first step in what would become a long act of defiance against the terrorist state established by the junta. The women went to a variety of human rights' organizations—the League of Human Rights, the Permanent Assembly on Human Rights, and the Center for Legal and Social Studies—but they felt that they were a distinct group and that the other organizations did not understand them, that it would be better to work on their own.[11]

Often as the Mothers gathered they would be met by policemen who threatened them with weapons and dogs. Because soldiers sometimes arrived and sprayed them with tear gas, the Mothers learned to carry moist handkerchiefs with them as protection.[12] One Mother remembers the police approaching with water cannons in an attempt to stop the women from entering the Plaza. She had traveled an hour and a half to get there and had no intention of turning back, so she kept walking toward the Plaza and the police. When she felt the click of a gun cocking at her back, she just kept going.[13]

Plainclothesmen became permanent fixtures at the Plaza and are still there today, parked in light blue cars or out on the sidewalk filming the gatherings and demonstrations. During these marches the Mothers learned the tactics of solidarity and the strength of unity. If a policeman demanded the identity papers of one of the Mothers, all of them rushed in with their papers. "If you take one, you have to take all of us." Often they were hauled off in police vans and kept at the police station for twenty-four hours. When there were too many to fit in a van, the police would empty buses and take away as many as seventy Mothers. At the police station they would be grilled about their gatherings, but the Mothers refused to give any information. When one policeman arrived with his typewriter to take her statement, taunting her with the question "Why are you a Communist?" María del Rosario de Cerruti recalls answering, "I am coming to the Plaza to look for my son." "Your son is a Communist," the policeman charged. "My son is not a Communist. He is a young person who thinks and acts politically. I don't care what party he belongs to because I am not defending a political party. I am looking for my son who has the right to think."[14] After a statement was completed, a person could appeal the arrest before a judge for a nominal charge. Each time, the Mothers filed an appeal and, to the astonishment of the police, left an extra sum of money to cover when they next would be brought in. Time after time the police were caught off guard by these women who refused to respond to bullying.

At the time the only safe place to meet was in the few churches that tolerated their presence. One day when the police had barricaded the Plaza to keep the Mothers out, they met in the cathedral to sign their letters and conduct their affairs. After the police stormed the cathedral and dragged them to the station, Cardinal Pedro Eugenio Aramburu gave orders to deny the Mothers access to the church. Even parish priests were afraid of compromising themselves by allowing the Mothers to gather in their pews. Though many churches let the Mothers know that they were not welcome, the women managed to find a different place to meet each Thursday, thus eluding the police. They looked for churches with squares in front of them and benches where they could sit together as if they were just gossiping. Then they would file into the church, say their prayers and rosaries, and pass letters and petitions among themselves for signatures. Juana de

Pargament remembers one church where someone turned the lights on as they filed into the pews—they had found a friend.[15] Infiltration, however, was a constant concern, and they had to be on the lookout for Mothers no one recognized.

By that time the Mothers' group had begun to establish a division of labor. Some of the women dealt with the myriad of forms they needed to fill out, some went to the courts, others went to the various ministries or to the army corps.[16] Without realizing it, the Mothers were gaining not only the strength of their numbers but also the inner strength that comes from mutual support and companionship. Under the urging of Azucena de De Vincente, they kept up a continual flow of letters and petitions. They also began to receive letters of thanks from the interior, from families who also had been affected by the *disappearances*. This network of communications and goodwill gave them heart. Their intelligence and imaginations were continually challenged, and, to their amazement, they found themselves more than equal to the tasks to which they had set themselves. Azucena was always there, bringing food, keeping up everyone's spirits, and urging them on. She seemed tireless, a whirlwind of energy.

The Mothers also developed their own spy system and communications network. By questioning former detainees they found out the names of those who took away their children and who tortured them, where they lived, and the names of their wives and children.[17] They found out how their children were tortured, for how many days they were hooded or raked with electric prods. In some cases the security police sent a few of the Mothers pictures of their tortured children, intending to terrorize them and render them inactive. At first the Mothers memorized names and events; then they began to write them down. As soon as a young person was released from a detention center the Mothers came in a flock, pelting that person with questions. Sometimes these people were so terrified that they denied ever having been imprisoned. Often they were kept under constant surveillance by the police, but ultimately those former detainees who were willing to talk became the links in the Mothers' underground information network.

Each bit of news was more terrible than the last. When they thought that they had heard the worst, the Mothers discovered a fresh horror. But each new horror transformed them, and because of that there was no turning back. These women, who had spent their lives in the sheltered arena of the home and the neighborhood, began to understand what they were up against. This new intelligence and understanding helped them to survive their ordeals and also brought them to new heights of courage.

Now that they had developed their own unofficial organization, the Mothers began to think about how to identify themselves as a group when they were out in the streets. The issue came to the fore in September 1977, when the Catholic community of Buenos Aires was planning a procession to Luján. Azucena de De Vincente thought it would be a good idea to join the procession because people talk to each other to pass the time during the long walk, and this might represent an opportunity for the Mothers to explain their cause. Because the parade would cover the fifty kilometers from Buenos Aires to Luján, there was much discussion about how the Mothers would be able to meet—not every Mother was able to walk that distance. Unlike the priests and nuns leading the column, many people, including some of the Mothers, preferred to take buses and trains, stopping periodically to join those who were walking. Then, one of the Mothers suggested that they wear something distinctive so that they could recognize each other from a distance. "A shawl on our heads or a mantilla," one woman proposed. But not everyone had a mantilla. Then one Mother chimed in, "How about a gauze shawl, a diaper? It will make us feel closer to our children."[18]

The Mothers all donned white shawls as they joined the procession at various points along the way. They gathered by twos and threes, then more and more of them converged until they were like a broad white stream in the crowd. People began to notice them, and when the police started to follow them, the Mothers mingled with the Marist priests. As the police moved in they began to pray, reciting the Our Father and Hail Mary until they reached the Cathedral of Luján. When the crowd reached the basilica, the Mothers stood there reciting the rosary. People approached them and asked them who they were, the Mothers responding that they were praying for their *disappeared* children.[19] A number of persons told them that they too had lost children. While others went inside the church to pray for world peace and to celebrate a country that was supposed to be moving forward, the Mothers sat in the pews with their rosaries and their white shawls in terrible witness to the dark underside of reality that the junta was trying to mask. Afterward crowds of young people came over to talk and to find out who they were. The Mothers remained in the cathedral all night in order to be present for the five o'clock Mass, hoping that the *disappeared* would be mentioned. The bishop ignored them.

A week later everyone in Luján was still talking about the women with the shawls. The Mothers decided then that the shawls would be their identifying sign but that they would make them out of batiste because gauze was too flimsy and would not last; they were beginning to understand that their struggle would be a long one. In adopting the baby shawls as their insignia the Mothers embarked on the use of powerful symbols that would not only identify them but that would also represent a reality in stark contrast to the brutality of the military regime. The shawls symbolized peace, life, and maternal ties, and they represented the claim of family bonds and ethical values in the public arena.

In October the Mothers decided to hold a general meeting to discuss their next step. By that time they numbered about 150, and therefore finding a place to meet presented a difficult problem. Mária del Rosario de Cerruti remembers that they chose a large park thirty kilometers from the center of Buenos Aires, pretending that it was a retirement party for some of their friends.[20] As they settled on the ground they formed four groups, deciding who would be responsible for each group and how they would communicate over the telephone. It was their first attempt to create an organizational structure. They developed telephone chains and a vocabulary of code words which ultimately proved amateurish but which nevertheless gave them a sense that they were making progress. Once under surveillance—a car with two people inside idled near the edges of the park—the Mothers quickly gathered up their picnics and left.

As the Mothers circled the Plaza each Thursday other women sometimes joined them, grandmothers, sisters, or relatives of the *disappeared* and some brave well-wishers. People also came to their meetings to get information about relatives who were *disappeared*, many of them staying on to help collect money or signatures and to write letters and petitions. Among those who flocked to them was a young man with blond hair and a cherubic face named Gustavo Niño.[21] He had started joining them in the Plaza in August, telling the Mothers that his brother was *disappeared* and that he was looking for information about him. Because of his youth and his diligent efforts to help the Mothers, he appealed to their maternal feelings. He not only marched with them in the Plaza but also accompanied them on their missions to various army command posts and to their meetings in the churches. The Mothers became protective of him and repeatedly told him, "Gustavo, please be careful."[22]

Even though the number of Mothers circling the Plaza had increased to hundreds, the newspapers made no note of them or of the *disappeared*. The *Buenos Aires Herald* mentioned them, but it was an English newspaper, its readership restricted. Occasionally they received notice in *La Prensa*, but mostly in negative terms. Therefore the Mothers decided to try to place paid advertisements in the newspapers listing the names of the *disappeared*. Azucena de De Vincente suggested they contact *La Nación* and *La Prensa*. "They can ignore one of us, but two hundred?"[23] Even scraping together the bus fare for transportation into the city was a hardship, so they would have to raise money. Managing to gather funds from among themselves and their husbands, they took out their first paid advertisement on October 5, 1977. It was their first foray into this world, and they were ill-equipped. When they presented a handwritten article they were told that the newspaper could accept only typewritten material. They found someone willing to let them use a typewriter and hastily typed their advertisement. The headline read WE DO NOT ASK FOR ANYTHING MORE THAN THE TRUTH, the text referring to President Videla's remarks during his recent visit to the United States, when he said that no one who told the truth would suffer reprisals.[24] The names of the *disappeared* were listed along with their pictures, and the article was signed by each Mother with a demand for a clear statement about the fate of her child. Thus the existence of the Mothers and their mission was revealed to the country at a time when neither radio, television, nor newspapers were reporting the *disappearances*.

Inadvertently, however, the Mothers were also courting a new danger. The newspapers insisted not only that their advertisements be typewritten and the names of the children listed alphabetically, but they also stipulated that the Mothers give their names and addresses documented with a certificate of domicile, requiring that the women go to the police station to secure the certificates.[25] At the time they did not realize the danger of leaving such trails of information.

In December the Mothers decided to place another advertisement in the newspapers for Human Rights Day. Once again they were faced with the necessity of raising money, but by this time they had a number of helpers besides young Gustavo Niño, including the French nun Sister Alicia Doman. Hebe de Bonafini remembers spending Saturday afternoons at Azucena de De Vincente's house, working for the Mothers and preparing for their advertisement that December. Azucena's husband Pedro was suspicious of Gustavo Niño and warned his wife to be careful and keep her distance from him, but Azucena insisted that with such an angelic face he could never hurt a fly.

On December 8 a group of Mothers and their helpers met at the Church of the Holy Cross to gather funds for their advertisement. A few of them noticed that the church was surrounded by strangers, but they forgot their suspicions as they busied themselves with the task of collecting funds during Mass. Spotting Gustavo Niño, one of them asked why he was there—it was dangerous. Replying that he wanted to be with them on this important day, Gustavo seemed particularly disappointed that Azucena de De Vincente was not at the church. After the collection he said he wanted to go out for a breath of air and left. A few of the Mothers followed, in a hurry to leave. Others had stopped to talk for a few minutes when a group of men raised their rifles and shouted, "Drug operation!" Attacking two of the Mothers and pinning two others against the wall, the men beat the women as they struggled and screamed, threatening, "Shut up, you old crazy women, if you don't want to come with us!" They took away two of the founding members of the Mothers, Mary Ponce and Esther Balestrina de Creaga, as well as Sister Alicia Doman.

The following day, tears and confusion marked the Mothers' meeting. They were devastated when they realized that a spy was in their midst. Though some of them wanted to abandon their advertisement project, Azucena de De Vincente insisted that they go ahead regardless of what happened. "We have to get our friends out, too, as well as our children. After all, they were taken away for gathering money for this advertisement."[26] Taken by surprise at the power of the enemy, a number of Mothers wondered how they would be able to continue.

On December 10, the day the advertisement appeared, Azucena de De Vincente was abducted in front of her house as she went out to buy a copy of the newspaper. Sister Léonie Duquet, a French nun who had worked closely with Sister Alicia Doman, was also arrested, as well as a young artist who had helped the Mothers. They have not been seen since, although the Mothers had news that the two sisters were in detention centers and had been badly tortured, and that Azucena de De Vincente had been seen in the notorious ESMA, the Naval Mechanics School that served as a detention center.

The abduction of Azucena was a terrible blow to the Mothers. Though they had been harassed continually by police and security agents in the Plaza and had been followed to their homes, they had cherished an illusion that as middle-aged mothers they would never be arrested. Now, their leader had been brutally seized from among them along with two nuns from a country with close ties to Argentina. People had been afraid to associate with the Mothers before; now it meant risking one's life. Membership in the Mothers' organization fell as the group experienced the worst period of repression it was to endure. Many now realized the risks for themselves and their families. Some Mothers who had lost one child suffered the *disappearance* of yet another one, and one Mother lost all three of her children. They wondered if they had the strength to go on now that they saw just what they were up against. But many of them continued because they remembered what Azucena had once told them: "If you let down your guard, they will triumph."[27] A fall and subsequent rise in membership followed every blow the next year. When a group of Mothers was hauled away to the police station while they were at the Plaza, the membership would fall. Then people regained confidence and returned.

The junta issued a statement on December 16 blaming the *disappearances* of the people connected with the Mothers on "nihilistic subversion."[28] Responding with a boldness and courage that would become their hallmark, the Mothers called a press conference in the Plaza de Mayo to deny the statement and to blame the kidnappings on the government. Thus began the war of words, the battle between the Mothers and the government to retain ascendency over the political dialogue, the Mothers not only demanding the truth about the *disappeared* but also publicly proclaiming the validity of their experience and their perceptions. The only journalists who had the bravery to appear were a group of foreign reporters, and because of their presence the Mothers were not threatened even though they were heavily outnumbered by police and plainclothesmen.

That Christmas the Mothers endured a day of sorrow in homes that were shadowed by absence while the country celebrated and banners wishing the population peace and good tidings were draped over the headquarters of various army barracks. Nevertheless, at the end of their first year, the Mothers experienced a profound inner transformation in response to the tragedy of their loss. Those Mothers who banded together were redefining their sense of self, analyzing their own situation as part of a broader pattern of repression, and discovering their own inviolable dignity and worth. Just finding a way to meet as a group took great courage and ingenuity. At this time the Mothers still perceived their main course of action as sending petitions to the president and his wife, asking their parish priests for help, and contacting the authorities. They continued to believe that because their children were innocent they would be returned. It was possible to find redress within the political system and succor from the institutional church, and the Mothers were not rebels but good citizens and churchgoers.

As a tactic to isolate and weaken them the government deliberately ridiculed the women as an example to any group who might wish to oppose the regime. The carefully designed campaign labeled the Mothers as *Las Locas* (crazy women), effectively discouraging people from associating with them. Even some of the mothers of *disappeared* children closed their doors against the Mothers, and those who were active in the organization began to notice the withdrawal of friends and family. Visits from cherished cousins and uncles became more and more sparse. When they met old friends on the street they received hasty and distant greetings. At first the Mothers were hurt and offended as their former friends became strangers and telephone calls ceased, but as they ventured away from their homes it no longer mattered.

They found themselves with two lives, one in the organization, which meant standing in line or meeting with other Mothers, and one in the home. Still responsible for a husband and other children, they suffered divided hearts, one half yearning for the *disappeared* child, the other worrying about those who remained. Their peaceful household routines were replaced by a nightmare of trips into the city, their lives made hectic as they tried to juggle their duties at home and their search abroad. The Mothers were experiencing all the conflicts of women who straddle the worlds of work and home. Husbands faced similar challenges; they still had to go to work and earn a living, but they also had to take care of the house and children in their wives' absence. These hardships strengthened some marriages but destroyed others.

For women who did not read the newspapers and whose only view of the outside had been the carefully controlled images presented on television, the new circumstances were traumatic. They were afraid and confused by the changes in their lives and often felt guilty about having less time for their other children. Like Hebe de Bonafini, who still had a young daughter at home, they worried about neglecting these children and their households. In short, they suffered the chaos of feelings that assail women with little public experience who try to pursue broad goals with their own resources. And they faced the omnipresent threat of governmental violence.

Many Mothers were alone in their grief, isolated socially and politically in a country that went about its business as if nothing alarming were happening. But the act of reaching out to one another was the first of a continual series of choices that transformed them from victims into self-confident political activists. For it is choice that makes the difference between surrendering to tragedy and using tragedy as a stepping-stone to growth and new meaning. Reaching out to one another to form a group in search of their children may not seem like a heroic feat in an open society. But in the context of a terrorist state and within a society that has traditionally kept women in marginal roles, it was a tremendous step, one that began a process leading them to construct new frames of reference.

The vase of the Mothers' lives had been smashed by the *disappearances* of their children, and they were reclaiming the shards to form a new and more resistant shape out of the broken pieces of the universe that had once housed them—the church, the inviolable home, the husband as protector, and their own safety as middle-aged women in a society that revered women even while it marginalized them. Whether they gathered on stone benches in front of a church or circled the Plaza, the Mothers were experiencing a growing solidarity and a new path in their maternal roles. They were still the protectors of their children, but in this distorted universe that meant entering the labyrinth of the political system instead of cooking or ironing their clothes.

At this stage the Mothers were still waiting to be admitted to the powers that be, but their life in the public arena had begun.

Nineteen seventy-eight was the year of the World Cup soccer match in Argentina. Despite the continuing *disappearances* the country was in a frenzy of preparation and celebration, and national attention was focused on the match. The public euphoria heightened the Mothers' grief and isolation.[29] The soccer match covered up all the terrible things that were happening. Who would believe them when they tried to publicize the growing number of *disappearances*?

The inner circle of the Mothers' organization knew that the country would soon be filled with tourists and the media, and that they needed to gain access to them. They were worried about how they would communicate because they had no experience and could speak no foreign language. The solution came spontaneously, as all the other aspects of the extraordinary development of their organization. "It's easy," one of the Mothers said. "When a journalist asks for a question, you simply say, 'We want our children. They must tell us where they are.' "[30] In addition, the Mothers decided to send hundreds of cards to foreign political leaders and television networks.

That same year the International Conference on Cancer Research and its visiting doctors were received in Buenos Aires with great fanfare. The Mothers made a point of speaking with the doctors, and a few days later two came to march with them in the Plaza, wearing badges from the conference as protection. Suddenly, the Plaza swarmed with police and the Mothers headed for the street at its corner, with the doctors walking ahead of them. Breaking their silence, one of the Mothers began to shout in defiance, THEY TOOK THEM AWAY ALIVE, WE WANT THEM RETURNED ALIVE. The other Mothers followed suit, repeating the cry over and over, though minutes later they scattered into the Avenida de Mayo as their march was dispersed.[31] So began their foray into a political dialogue in which they would both seize the initiative and unmask the ugly reality behind the government's protests of normalcy. Through the constant public chanting of their slogans they created a presence for themselves in the political arena, engaging in a dialogue that would simultaneously express their anguish as Mothers, expose the duplicity and dishonesty of the government, and create an ethical space in a country that seemed to have lost its conscience and its soul.

Although the words they chose were simple, they addressed a most perplexing reality—the fate of the *disappeared* and those responsible for the abductions. Leaders of the junta referred to the *disappeared* as "terrorists, delinquents, or killed during armed conflicts."[32] But the Mothers refused to accept this version of their children and insisted that they had not died, were not on trips, but had been made to *disappear* because they were political dissidents. By their presence in the streets and on the Plaza and by their voices that challenged the government's version of political events, the Mothers entered the political arena as an opposition group. From the beginning they were criticized for their stridency and hysteria, castigated because they defied the cultural norms of femininity and because they assumed a more extreme and autonomous position in a society where dissent was portrayed as socially pathological and revolutionary. Their raised voices proclaimed their presence in a society where absence was enforced through *disappearance* on the one hand and fearful silence on the other, thus exposing and challenging the very premises of the system itself.

Throughout May the Mothers played cat-and-mouse with the police. In order to keep them out of the Plaza the police waited for them there. The Mothers would march on the opposite side of the Plaza and, as the police approached, would hurry to the other side, their objective to reach the center and the pyramid where they could be better seen.[33] It was a time of terrible fear, and many Mothers recall that they always went out with extra underwear in their purses in case they were arrested and sent to prison. On June 1, the day of the inauguration of the World Cup, while Argentine channels showed footage of doves being launched in the air, foreign journalists and television crews were in the Plaza filming and interviewing the Mothers. Television cameramen from the Netherlands videotaped the Mothers as they marched around the pyramid, and police had to keep their hands off.

María del Rosario de Cerruti remembers a woman named Sally, a journalist from the United States who came to the Plaza with her tape recorder.[34] While she was taking notes two men from the security forces grabbed her tape recorder and passport. As she shouted, the Mothers mobbed the men, pushing them to the ground and piling things on top of them to keep them down. The Mothers managed to retrieve the recorder and the passport, and three of them took Sally to the American embassy in a taxi.

The junta's efforts to conceal the *disappearances* were also foiled by a growing number of political exiles who fled to France and other European countries. The Mothers were in constant contact with these exiles, enhancing their communications network and thus their political effectiveness. They developed a system of metaphors to send news to their supporters abroad. Poems about birds and whether their flights were interrupted became a way of describing their marches in the Plaza. In the spring of 1978 they received a disturbing letter from a Mother in France who had worked with them before going into exile. She wrote that a young man with blond hair and an angelic face was working with a group of exiles, the Argentine Center of Information and Solidarity.[35] They suspected that he was an infiltrator and was collaborating with the intelligence service of the navy. He called himself Alberto Escudero. From the enclosed photo the Mothers recognized Gustavo Niño.

Niño, whose real name was Alfredo Astiz, was working with the Pilot Center in the Argentine embassy, an organization established by the government in June 1977 to counteract adverse publicity coming from exiles. It was headed by the diplomat Elena Holmberg and staffed by ESMA officers. Astiz operated under many aliases, including the Angel, the Crow, and the Blond, as part of a policy to hide the identity of those who tortured and abducted the *disappeared*. In January of the previous year he had carried out a brutal abduction of a Swedish national that would propel him into international controversy and notoriety. Dagmar Hagelin, a seventeen-year-old woman with a joint Swedish-Argentine nationality, was going to visit her friend María Antonia Berger in the early morning. Astiz's squad was hiding in the bushes, apparently waiting for her friend María. When María's father opened the door Dagmar heard one of the naval officers shout, "Stay where you are!" She turned and ran, but Astiz overtook her and then shot her in the head. A policeman commandeered a car idling in the vicinity, and they drove up to where Dagmar lay bleeding on the sidewalk, jamming her into the trunk. Two women who survived the ESMA testified that they had seen Dagmar the day after she was shot, chained to a bed and bleeding.[36] A week later one of the women saw

Dagmar's abandoned shirt and sandals and deduced that she had died. After the kidnapping Dagmar's father went to visit the foreign minister with the Swedish ambassador. A few weeks later the Swedish cabinet met and sent an outraged telegram to the Argentine foreign minister protesting the act. Because of this incident Swedish-Argentine relations deteriorated, rupturing completely in 1980 as Sweden became one of the Mothers' strongest supporters.

From the early days of the military coup Argentina's human-rights record attracted the world's attention, and ultimately this publicity strengthened the Mothers' efforts. Throughout 1976 and 1977, Argentina's ambassadors in the United States and Western Europe were continually summoned by their host governments for interviews about the reports of tortures, political murders, and *disappearances*. The junta received unwelcome attention not only from its allies but also from groups such as Amnesty International and the International Commission of Jurists, organizations that were active in alerting international opinion to human-rights abuses and that appeared regularly before meetings of the United Nations Commission on Human Rights.

In November 1977, Amnesty International sent a three-person team to Buenos Aires to investigate the *disappearances*. The team included U.S. Congressman Father Robert Drinan, Lord Eric Avebury from Britain, and Patricia Feeney, who headed the Argentina desk at Amnesty International headquarters in London. Under pressure from the junta the Argentine press conducted a smear campaign against the group, calling them Marxists who did not understand the threat of terrorism. Demonstrations against the group seethed in front of their hotel, even though such gatherings were not permitted under the junta. Nevertheless, the junta could not prevent reverberations from the visit or the subsequent report released by Amnesty International. Father Drinan became one of the most forceful advocates of suspending U.S. military aid to Argentina, and Lord Avebury began a series of successful efforts to secure the entry of Argentine refugees into Britain.[37] Amnesty International's report was the first of a series on the *disappearances* and was filled with names, dates, and places. Ultimately, these reports were facilitated by Argentine refugees who poured into Europe, stopping first at the London headquarters to bring information.

The junta made special efforts to counter the increasingly negative image of the country abroad, paying particular attention to the United Nations. As a member of that organization the government was bound by its human-rights provisions and had voted for the Universal Declaration of Human Rights in 1948 and for the Convention of Vienna that protected diplomats and foreigners. In addition, it had ratified the conventions of the International Labor Organization, which included the right to form free trade unions. Six months after the coup the ILO published a list of detained and *disappeared* trade unionists in Argentina. Prince Sadruddin Aga Khan, the United Nations High Commissioner for Refugees, broached the issue of the two Uruguayan refugees, the former senators who had been found murdered in Argentina.[38] The junta instructed its ambassador to the United Nations to present positive images of the country and portray the deaths as the work of terrorist subversives.

Gabriel Martínez was selected by the junta as its apologist at the United Nations. As ambassador to that body his mission was to prevent any public debate that would lead to criticism of the junta by name and to ensure that Argentina remain off the confidential list of Gross Violators of Human Rights.[39] In order to accomplish this he manipulated the rules of the United Nations, destroyed the careers of diplomats such as Theo Van Boven, head of the Human Rights Commission, and attacked Non-Governmental Organizations (NGO) accredited to the United Nations, such as Amnesty International and the International Commission of Jurists. He was incessantly active, making important allies, buttonholing people, and singling out those especially interested in human-rights activity as special targets. Ironically, Argentina's strongest allies in this campaign were the Soviet Union and the Eastern bloc nations, a curious twist for a country that was on an anti-Communist crusade at home.

The policy of *disappearances* also ran afoul of changing U.S. foreign policy. After the disclosure of CIA involvement in the coup that overthrew Salvador Allende in Chile and ushered in a repressive military rule in one of the most democratic nations in Latin America, Congress began writing measures that banned foreign aid to repressive regimes. It proposed amendments to the Foreign Assistance Act, calling on the president to deny security aid to governments that engaged in consistent patterns of gross violations of internationally recognized human rights. Led by Representative Donald Fraser, the House subcommittee on International Organizations held hearings on human rights.[40] Its hearing on Argentina in September 1976, which included lawyers from Argentine human-rights groups as witnesses, helped focus national attention on the *disappearances*. When Father Drinan returned from his Amnesty International mission he added his voice to the outcry, and a number of human-rights groups, including Amnesty International, sent letters to newly elected President Jimmy Carter asking that he take firm action to stop the *disappearances*.

Under Carter the State Department was directed to issue human-rights reports on all governments receiving U.S. security aid. A new human-rights bureau and a human-rights legal adviser were created within the department, and Patricia Derian, wife of writer and publisher Hodding Carter, was appointed under secretary of state for human rights. She became an outspoken advocate of human rights in Latin America and in 1977 made three visits to Argentina that would fill her with outrage and generate hostility to the junta.[41] She left for her first visit already appalled by the reports coming from Argentina. Upon her arrival the press attacked her as a snooper, the representative of a country that acted as the hemisphere's policeman. She had some unsatisfactory meetings with members of the junta and with Minister of the Interior Albano Harguindeguy, but the government could not prevent her from meeting with the various human-rights groups. She formed a deep attachment to the Mothers, and her friendship as well as Amnesty International's focus on Argentina's human-rights record helped the Mothers direct their efforts abroad.

By now the Mothers had begun to attract attention in West European political circles as well as in the United States and were carving out a space for themselves in the international setting. Lisbeth Den Uyl, the wife of the prime minister of the Netherlands, created the Support Group for the Mothers of the Plaza de Mayo in Argentina (SAAM), the first such champions for the Mothers, which brought together women from all walks of life: professionals, writers, executives, politicians, and housewives.[42] SAAM organized demonstrations, sponsored exhibits, and raised funds to help finance the Mothers' activities. Its members also were able to pressure their own governments, giving the Mothers yet another weapon against the junta. SAAM was soon followed by other support groups throughout Western Europe as the Mothers pressed their cases abroad.

At the end of 1978 the Mothers decided it was time to bring their cause to the United States and Western Europe, a daunting project. Not only did they have to raise funds, but they also had to organize the trip, arrange for contacts, establish connections with politicians, and solve the worrisome problem of languages; none of the Mothers spoke a foreign language, but they were nevertheless undeterred. Hebe de Bonafini, María del Rosario de Cerruti, and Elida Galetti sent out dozens of letters to announce their arrival in the United States, not knowing what they would find or even what to expect.

An Argentine contact met the trio of Mothers at a Washington airport. "Show me your identification papers," the Mothers demanded, as if they were still in Argentina. While in the U.S. capital they managed to address the Organization of American States and to get appointments with senators, congressmen, and State Department officials with the simple statement, "We are the Mothers of the *disappeared* from Buenos Aires, Argentina, and we are coming to discuss human rights."[43] From Washington the Mothers flew to New York City to meet with journalists and human-rights groups. They went to the United Nations in the first of many visits where their white shawls distinguished them and raised the ire of Gabriel Martínez. The General Assembly had passed a resolution that year expressing concern over the *disappearances* of persons as the result of excesses on the part of security forces. Because of Martínez's efforts, however, it had not named Argentina.

The Mothers met Theo Van Boven the following February when the Human Rights Commission convened in Geneva. He was profoundly moved by their stories and would become a staunch supporter. Because of Van Boven's activist policy toward Argentina, Gabriel Martínez had his telephone tapped and waged a relentless war against him with a campaign of charges, complaints, and memos directed to Van Boven's superiors.[44] He was temporarily foiled by the intervention of Patricia Derian, who asked the U.S. ambassador to the United Nations, Donald McHenry, to make it clear to Van Boven's American supervisors that he had the full support of the U.S. government. President Carter regarded the United Nations as one of the cornerstones of his human-rights policy and supported that organization's goal of drafting and implementing credible international standards. In his first major speech at the United Nations he had made it clear that the torture and mistreatment of persons anywhere in the world was everyone's concern, and that members had the responsibility to speak out against such practices.

In New York City the Mothers also visited a Christian organization called Tibor House, where they told an astonished priest that they intended to visit the pope. (Hebe de Bonafini remembered how a released prisoner had told her that her son Jorge had confided to him, "My mother will go to the pope to get me out."[45]) He attempted to dissuade them but finally made phone calls on their behalf, and as a result they were soon on their way to Rome. This combination of spontaneity and daring was becoming one of the characteristics of their political style. In Rome, the Mothers stayed in an empty apartment an Argentine contact had found them, sleeping under their coats and cooking their own meals. They forged some useful contacts, and Susanna Agnelli, a member of parliament who had lived in Argentina for many years, arranged for an interview with President Sandro Pertini. The meeting proved to be the beginning of a long friendship, and when the junta fell, President Pertini would announce that he had had three secret meetings with the Mothers. María del Rosario de Cerruti recalls how the Mothers arrived at the presidential palace carrying their shopping bags.[46] They were greeted by a butler with white gloves who took their coats and groceries and ushered them into a room where the president rose to embrace them. He served them coffee in exquisite china and told them how his own mother had been in prison for her political beliefs when he was an adolescent. After the interview a car pulled up beside the Mothers, a person inside calling out, "*Signoras.*" They were terrified, thinking it was the police. Instead, it was a government minister offering them a ride.

The Mothers were unable to get an audience with the pope, but an Uruguayan bishop managed to place them in front of a receiving line so they could speak with His Holiness as he passed by. Hebe de Bonafini thrust pictures of their children into his hands, crying out, "Please help the *disappeared!*" He allowed the pictures to slip through his hands onto the floor and kept walking. Hebe cried out once again, "Do something for the *disappeared!*" "There are *disappeared* in many countries," he replied. Hebe kept insisting, "Help us the way you help the Poles!" All they received was a blessing as he exited the room.[47] This was the first of a number of encounters in which the Mothers vainly sought the pope's help in applying pressure on the Argentine government and interceding on behalf of their children.

The trip to Rome initiated a frenetic round of visits abroad that brought the Mothers to any country willing to receive them and listen to their message, nations from Sweden to North Korea, from Canada to Australia. With their white shawls and their dignity they began circling the globe, self-appointed ambassadors on behalf of the victims of state-sponsored terrorism. They never prepared their speeches because by now they were adept at telling the simple and terrible truth about the *disappearances* and about their own efforts. Travel abroad had one important consequence for the Mothers. It meant that even though they would continue to be harassed and to receive death threats, their lives were no longer in immediate danger. The junta was too concerned with its image to risk the adverse publicity an assassination would provoke.

By now the Mothers not only challenged the government at home but also sought to confound its diplomatic efforts abroad. Like the resistance movements of nascent nations throughout Africa and Asia in the early 1960s, they learned the power of the international media in drawing attention to political oppression and the abuse of human rights. They were claiming space in opinion sectors throughout the world for their plight and for their humanitarian values. From their intrusion into a political arena that proscribed any form of opposition, they had moved on to join the arena of international diplomacy.

NOTES

1. Alan F. Westin, *Privacy and Freedom* (New York: Atheneum, 1967), 23–51.

2. Madres, *Boletín*, no. 1 (no date).

3. Josefa Donato de Pauvi, interview by Marguerite Bouvard, August 1989.

4. Juana de Pargament, interview by Marguerite Bouvard, August 1989.

5. Matilde Sánchez, *Historias de vida Hebe de Bonafini* (Buenos Aires: Fraterna del Nuevo Extremo, 1985), 130.

6. Madres de Plaza de Mayo, *Historia de las Madres de Plaza de Mayo* (Buenos Aires, 1988), 2.

7. Ibid., 2–3.

8. María del Rosario de Cerruti, interview by Marguerite Bouvard, August 1989.

9. Madres, *Historia*, 8.

10. Sánchez, *Historias de vida*, 109–11.

11. de Pargament, interview.

12. Madres, *Historia*, 12.

13. de Alvarez Rojas, interview.

14. de Cerruti, interview.

15. de Pargament, interview.

16. Ibid.

17. Sánchez, *Historias de vida*, 127–29.

18. Ibid, 141.

19. de Pargament, interview.

20. de Cerruti, interview.

21. de Pargament, interview.

22. Sánchez, *Historias de vida*, 140–47.

23. Ibid.

24. John Simpson and Jana Bennett, *The Disappeared and the Mothers of the Plaza* (New York: St. Martin's Press, 1985), 159.

25. Sánchez, *Historias de vida*, 180.

26. Ibid., 149.

27. Ibid., 161.

28. Ibid., 149.

29. One Mother recalls that her son was *disappeared* two days before the World Cup and that while everyone was watching television in a state of great excitement, she was in her room crying, feeling as if she were going mad.

30. Ibid., 158.

31. Ibid., 160.

32. Diana R. Kordon et al., *Psychological Effects of Political Repression* (Buenos Aires: Sudamericana/Planeta, 1988), 33–39.

33. de Cerruti, interview.

34. Ibid.

35. Sánchez, *Historias de vida*, 160.

36. Guest, *Behind the Disappearances*, 46–48, 70–73.

37. Ibid., 80–86.

38. Ibid., 110–17.

39. Ibid., 109.

40. Ibid., 151–53.

41. Ibid., 150–63.

42. Madres, *Boletín*, no. 17 (May 1984).

43. de Cerruti, interview.

44. Guest, *Behind the Disappearances*, 126–29.

45. Sánchez, *Historias de vida*, 171.
46. de Cerruti, interview.
47. de Pargament, interview.

THE MOTHERS SAY NO

They cannot bury your children. You will not allow it
or accept the flung coins,
the indemnity offered by the new government.
There will be no trading of flesh or sorting
of bones. When the city of La Plata celebrated
its centennial in '81, all the vultures
preened in the central square: the mayor and the bishop,
the generals with their empty, glittering faces.
They wouldn't let you join the parade
and when you finally entered, the police
surrounded you. They wanted to silence you,
to bury that banner with the names of your children
still burning like wounded flesh. You'd always
refused to bury them. Suddenly your leader snatched
the balloons from the startled vendor, tied the banner
of names to the string and launched them into the air.
As the police closed in, they floated above
the colonels' stunned eyes.
They scudded through the sky's blue-gray ocean.
Your raised arms soared like spires,
and beside you, the cathedral shrank back into its stones.

CHAPTER 4

Resistance Mounts

Their hectic pace of writing, meeting, and demonstrating left the Mothers little time to brood about the tortures their offspring were enduring, their activity giving them both a sense of hope and the feeling that they were not abandoning their children. They were surprised to discover that in the midst of such horror they were experiencing a surge of happiness as their group provided them with new ties of affection, serving as a refuge against a society and, in many cases, an extended family that rejected them. They identified strongly with each other and began to think of themselves as more than Mothers looking for their *disappeared* children.

After two years of work they realized that they had acquired a stature and an identity. They were now faced with the question of whether to continue being a gathering of tireless Mothers or to give more definition to their struggle. A strong argument for formalizing their cooperation was to gain the support of many Mothers who felt they would be safer if they were represented by an organization. There were six human-rights associations in Argentina with which the Mothers frequently cooperated, but the women wanted to create their own body where they would feel comfortable and be in charge. They had no intention of diluting their goals and were uninterested in seeking power.

The human-rights groups active in Argentina at the time included the Families of the Disappeared for Political Reasons, which would become a Latin American movement in 1980; the Communist League for Human Rights; the Christian Service for Peace and Justice (SERPAJ), founded by Adolfo Pérez Esquivel, a sculptor, professor, and fervent Catholic concerned about the poor throughout Latin America; the Ecumenical Group for Human Rights; and the Permanent Assembly on Human Rights, which included a number of people who had been active in politics. The Center for Legal and Social Studies (CELS) was established in 1979 by Emilio Mignone, a lawyer whose daughter was *disappeared*. Two other fathers joined Mignone— José Westercamp and Augusto Conte MacDonnell, whose son was *disappeared* while serving in the military. CELS attempted to deal with the *disappearances* by providing legal advice, drawing up writs of *habeas corpus*, and taking up individual cases when there was evidence that security forces were involved. It was CELS that coined the phrase *detained-disappeared*, implying involvement by the security forces. Emilio Mignone joined the International Commission of Jurists and gave testimony before the United Nations Working Group on Disappearances, an act of bravery that resulted in his own brief detention. [1]

Another group was the Grandmothers of the Plaza de Mayo, formed at the time the Mothers formalized their society. Though they collaborated with the Mothers, their goals were to find their grandchildren who either had been born in captivity or who were *disappeared* along with their parents, and this would remain their primary objective.

The Association of the Mothers of the Plaza de Mayo was registered on August 22, 1979, commemorating the place where they had first met. When they had initially begun to demonstrate in the Plaza in Buenos Aires, groups of Mothers had also started meeting informally in the city of La Plata and in the provinces. By the time the Mothers had formalized their organization they had developed a vast network of communications and cooperation with the Mothers in the interior. After the fall of the junta a number of other groups sprang up until there were fourteen chapters spread throughout the country.

The principles in their founding document establish their independence from all political parties and groups, not only outlining their goals but also legitimating values such as peace, justice, brotherhood, and a democratic system that respects human rights. The document categorically rejects the junta's practices of torture, kidnapping, arrests without due process, and any form of religious, racial, or political persecution. In a statement they would repeat through the years, the Mothers insisted, "We don't judge our *detained-disappeared* children, nor do we ask for their freedom. We want to be told where they are, what they are accused of, and ask that they be judged according to legal norms with the legitimate right of defense if they have committed any crimes. We ask that they not be tortured or kept in inhumane conditions and that we can see them and assist them."[2] They have never relinquished their demand for a reply concerning the whereabouts of their children.

What was extraordinary about the establishment of the organization was that it proclaimed principles totally at variance with the political system and that it did so openly, just as its marches and protests occurred in the streets and on the Plaza in public view. To those who live in free societies this may not seem remarkable, but the creation of an association aiming to achieve justice within a repressive dictatorship took great courage. The Mothers were easy targets and their homes could be bombed and sacked at any time. Even in 1979, however, at the height of the political repression, they opted for openness as a fundamental principle because of their democratic values and their belief that only the truth could heal a country that had been ravaged by state terror. Proclaiming the truth in a regime dedicated to systematic lies and cover-ups may have been dangerous, but it was also an important source of power.

After signing their founding document the Mothers officially elected an eleven-member commission that had in effect been functioning informally. Hebe de Bonafini, who had emerged as the leader among them, was elected president and María Adela Antokoletz vice president. María Adela was the divorced wife of a diplomat, and, unlike the majority of the Mothers, she enjoyed a high standard of living. Her son was a lawyer who had often represented political prisoners and had refused to listen to her warnings that he should give up his work or leave the country.[3] Despite his international reputation and strong connections with both the Organization of American States and the United Nations, he was *disappeared* in November 1976. From the day they had decided to raise funds and place an advertisement in the newspapers Juana de Pargament had served as treasurer, and María del Rosario de Cerruti had kept the vouchers, carting a bag with the paperwork—writs of *habeas corpus*, letters, petitions, and forms—to the cafés, homes, and churches where they met. The organization solidified a division of labor that had emerged spontaneously. Formalizing their group strengthened the Mothers and gave them a sense of distinction. They were now more than desperate Mothers and proudly sent letters around the world announcing their establishment.

In the fall of 1979 the Inter-American Commission on Human Rights of the OAS finally came to Argentina on a fact-finding mission, the result of a year of maneuvering between the United States and Argentina as the latter consistently refused the commission's formal request for a visit. An agreement was reached when an American firm requested a loan from the Export-Import Bank to finance a project that would supply turbines for a dam to a company owned by the Argentine navy. The request had sparked a heated tug-of-war within the State Department between those who were concerned with the economy and jobs, and Patricia Derian, who was concerned with human rights. Finally, it was decided that EXIM funding for the project would be approved if the junta invited the commission to visit before October 1979. The lengthy discussions allowed the junta time to clean up some of its worst detention centers and thus eliminate incriminating evidence.[4] The number of prisoners in the ESMA was drastically reduced: some of them were taken to an island by police launch, while others were transferred, dismantling the information network the Mothers had carefully constructed.[5] In anticipation of the visit, the offices of human-rights groups were sacked and the secretary of the Families of the Disappeared for Political Reasons was *disappeared*.

The Mothers had pelted the commission with letters and cards for a year, determined to testify before it regardless of the consequences. The first day the commission met, the junta sponsored a famous singer to hold a concert in the Plaza de Mayo in order to divert the public's attention, also hiring groups of young thugs to taunt and harass the Mothers as they stood outside the doors of the commission.[6] Nonetheless many people were puzzled by the line of silent older women and went to ask questions. They left deeply disturbed by what they heard.

The result of the commission's inquiries was a 374-page indictment of the junta's practices. Although the junta refused to release the report, Emilio Mignone was in the United States when it was published there and smuggled five hundred copies into Argentina. The junta angrily rejected the results, but the fact that the *disappearances* diminished by the end of that year testifies to its impact. Unfortunately, the Mothers later would regret their testimony before the commission. Much of the information they gave found its way back to the military. The international repercussions of the report were also less than hoped for. Under the Carter administration a country that was the subject of a special Inter-American Commission on Human Rights report usually was featured in a resolution by the OAS Assembly. The delegation of Mothers who went to the OAS meeting in November 1980 was sorely disappointed when the Mexican ambassador prevented the passage of a resolution, claiming that harsh criticism would have no impact on such regimes.[7] The Mothers learned an important lesson about the behind-the-scenes bargaining that occurs in diplomacy, and they roundly criticized the OAS for its insensitivity.

The Mothers were also facing increased pressure from the government. Because the violence meted out to them was so flagrant that they could no longer meet regularly in the Plaza, they began to stage *lightning marches*: one week they would enter the Plaza on Wednesday morning, another on Friday evening, always changing the hour and the day.[8] By the time the police arrived they were already gone. They soon had to resort to meeting in cafés and in the few churches that still tolerated them. In 1980, SAAM suggested they establish an office, sending them a check to finance it. The Mothers found a little place on Uruguay Street that needed only a coat of paint and some cleaning to make it comfortable. Juana de Pargament and Hebe de Bonafini hardly slept for excitement the night before they moved in. They embraced each other when they met there, exclaiming, "See how far we have come!"[9] Their husbands brought in some second-hand furniture they had managed to find, and they soon had an office that looked like a home and that would be the seat of a distinctive political style where the private and public intermingled. In that space the Mothers carried on a frenetic agenda of planning political strategy and maintaining relations with foreign embassies and journalists, while at the same time strengthening the bonds of friendship and affection that united them. Without conscious effort they were developing a political style that combined the attitudes and practices of the private space of home and family with the space of their public lives. A huge poster with the pictures of the *disappeared* children greeted visitors, and from there on guests had the feeling of being in a home as well as in the midst of a vibrant political organization. They were given lunch or tea and not only heard the Mothers' tragic stories but also witnessed the continual weaving of the intimate and the public as the Mothers' conversations jumped from politics to the practical details of their lives in the new setting.

SAAM sent the Mothers a telegram announcing that they were arriving with a group of television reporters who wanted to film them. In order to celebrate this event the Mothers planned a party that would include the ambassadors from Sweden and the Netherlands and a march headed by SAAM.[10] When they requested permission for the march a police officer reminded them that the country was in a state of siege and that no political demonstrations were permitted. The Mothers insisted on reading the fine print of the decree, then retorted that they would be able to hold the march because it would be a march of pain and silence, therefore falling outside the decree's purview. They had begun to explore the cracks in the junta's armor.

That same year they decided to return to the Plaza to reclaim it from the government, even if it meant being killed. The first Thursday of February 1980 they converged on the area with their white scarves. Four of the Mothers went into the Casa Rosada to present a petition for an audience with the president while the others circled outside. Caught off guard when they saw the Mothers, the police were outnumbered and were unable to stop them as they circled the pyramid in the center of the square for forty minutes. The following Thursday, however, security police were waiting in full force, some even perched in trees. They set their dogs on the Mothers and wielded their truncheons.[11] A group of Mothers was arrested and detained for thirty hours, but after that no demonstration of force would ever again dislodge them from what they had come to regard as their sacred territory. The Mothers continued coming to the Plaza in increasing numbers, often accompanied by other human-rights groups. Relentlessly, they appeared at the Casa Rosada with letters and petitions demanding that the government publicize the list of *detained-disappeared*, their locations, and the reason for their detentions.

Now internationally known, they started to receive invitations from around the world to attend human-rights conferences. A group of socialists in the European Parliament suggested that the Mothers be nominated for the Nobel Peace Prize. The prize was awarded to Pérez Esquivel of SERPAJ, who fit the male model of protest as opposed to the Mothers' radical and collective model. However, the Mothers received a check from Stockholm so that two of them could accompany Esquival when he accepted the prize.[12] They also traveled to the United States to participate in a special ceremony for him attended by, among others, Theo Van Boven, Jacobo Timerman, Patricia Derian, Edward Kennedy, Amnesty International, and a number of ambassadors to the OAS.

Shortly thereafter the Mothers received the Peace Prize of the People, given by the Norwegian government to those who qualified for the Nobel Prize but who did not receive it. This recognition initiated a round of invitations and honors from various organizations throughout Western Europe. Political leaders in France publicly expressed their support for the Mothers, Italian president Sandro Pertini spoke about them in his New Year's message, and a number of Italian political parties took out an advertisement in the Argentine paper *El Clarín* to publicize their revulsion at the *disappearances*.[13] A group of prominent French personalities, which included Mme. François Mitterrand, Catherine Deneuve, Yves Montand, and Pierre Joxe, a journalist from the newspaper *L'Express*, began demonstrating in front of the Argentine embassy in Paris, and a support group for the Mothers was founded in Paris by Ada Alessandro, an Argentine exile. The government in Buenos Aires was dismayed by the Mothers' growing recognition and by their efforts to urge foreign governments to pressure the junta. It instructed its delegates to human-rights conferences to defame the Mothers and circulated the rumor that they were being exploited by leftist organizations. When Pedro Esquival received the Nobel Prize the junta claimed that his activities were being manipulated by terrorist groups and described the prize as a provocation.[14]

Despite pressure from the government and very real financial limitations, the Mothers maintained ceaseless activity. In 1980 they began to publish their own bulletin—not a slight undertaking given that some of their children had been abducted for passing out political leaflets as well as for their reformist activities. The Mothers had no machines and did most of the layout and design by hand, which was but a minor detail. The pamphlets aimed to explain their organization and its goals, and to reach an international audience. Theo Van Boven was one of the first to receive a copy, and he asked to remain on their mailing list. The first bulletins were produced in Hebe de Bonafini's house in La Plata, and when police caught wind of the publication they visited Hebe's house in order to intimidate her. Unimpressed, Hebe handed each one a copy as if she were conferring a favor.[15]

The bulletins were headed by the Mothers' insignia—Truth, Justice, Peace, and Love—and were sprinkled with quotes from the Universal Declaration of Human Rights and from the Bible. These standards may not seem startling to people in free societies, but in the Argentine setting, where injustice, fear, persecution, and violence were rife, they were daring. The bulletin featured the Mothers' activities within the country and abroad, and provided an outlet for their anguish. A number of pages were devoted to poems the Mothers wrote for their children as well as to essays expressing their anger and grief at the *disappearances*. In a country that sought to make them invisible, the Mothers kept finding new ways to become a significant presence.

That presence was enhanced by Hebe Pastor de Bonafini's powerful personality and her gift for language. She was chosen to succeed Azucena de Villaflor de De Vincente as the president of the Mothers' organization because of the energy and decisiveness she had displayed during the early years of the Mothers' struggle. She had organized a chapter of Mothers in her home city of La Plata as well as traveled to Buenos Aires to participate in the Mothers' activities. She was particularly close to Azucena because they came from similar backgrounds; she admired Azucena's spirit and drive. Although the Mothers' organization was run as a direct democracy, Hebe's keen intelligence began to pervade the group from the time she assumed the presidency, her leadership enhancing the organization's political style of spontaneity and defiance. Hebe, however, was and is only the first among equals. When they engage in political acts, the Mothers are a flock of geese rolling into a headwind with a seamless movement. The bird leading the angle and breaking the impact of the air is Hebe.

Hebe de Bonafini is one of those extraordinary people who have lived an ordinary life and whose innate strength and capability blossom when tragedy strikes. In a picture of her taken when she was four, dressed as Madame de Pompadour for the yearly carnival that celebrates the end of Lent in Argentina, she stands with her hands on her hips, staring defiantly into the camera. That defiance would reemerge in the face of the middle-aged woman holding a placard with pictures of her two *disappeared* sons and her *disappeared* daughter-in-law.

The house where Hebe grew up was built of corrugated iron and located on an unpaved street in front of the factory where her father worked. He made hats, and because of the wet and steamy conditions in which he shaped the wool brims, he eventually became disabled from arthritis. Nevertheless, Hebe recalls a rich family life with work and thrift the center of her parents' concerns. She learned how to fish and hunt for small game, how to bake bread and use edible plants. She learned weaving from the nuns, and she and her mother wove the strips that circled the hats. Despite their difficult circumstances her family was always active in community affairs, and Hebe grew up with the love of a large extended family on one hand, and the reality of economic hardship on the other. Both taught her to live intensely.

Despite her dreams of acquiring an education, Hebe never went beyond primary school because her tiny neighborhood did not have a secondary school and her family could only afford one bus fare to another district. When a choice had to be made in the patriarchal Argentine society, it was Hebe's brother who went to high school. Hebe resigned herself, but she never gave up her love of reading and was a regular visitor at the library. She married her sweetheart, Humberto de Bonafini, on November 12, 1949, remaining near her family. Her husband had a small mechanics workshop where she helped him clean carburetors and adjust valves even though women were not supposed to do those kinds of things.[16] But Hebe never believed there were things she could not do; it was only a matter of wanting to learn. Because there was little money in the household she also worked, sewing ponchos and school uniforms, or knitting.

The births of her three children were joyous events and absorbed all of Hebe's attention. She liked children so much that there was always an extra child or two who needed temporary shelter living with them. Somehow she managed to place these children with families wishing to adopt. Her husband teased her that because of her longing to become a teacher, she was turning the household into a school. Later, the roles were reversed as her children brought her books and explained the contents to her. By that time she found the education she had hungered for remote from her daily concerns, and she had to struggle with the material her sons urged her to read. Still, she harbored the ambition of acquiring a secondary education when her children were in high school and even hoped she might go to the university and study medicine. Such aspirations were unheard of in those times, and her husband feared that they might create a scandal in the family.[17]

Although her ambitions were blocked, Hebe accepted the traditional Argentine values that kept women focused on household and family. She was happy in her marriage and poured her expansiveness, strength of character, and energy into rearing her children. As they grew, she supported their many activities with enthusiasm. When her older son married she saw her family life enriched and never dreamed of rebelling or extending her horizons beyond her circle of family and friends. Hebe now regards that peaceful period, when it was sufficient to be useful to her family, as the time of her naïveté.[18] The military coup of 1976 shattered this private and contented life and catapulted Hebe into the circle of Mothers, ultimately landing her the role of an internationally respected leader.

At the time of the coup her older son Jorge was a teacher studying for a degree in electronic engineering at night, and her daughter-in-law María Elena was studying psychology. Like so many of the young adults who were *disappeared*, Jorge also taught Sunday school, worked with children in poor neighborhoods, and was an active member of the Third World church. He was attracted by the message of the new theology, with its focus on the need for social change to bring about equality and genuine community. From the time he was in high school he had urged his mother to extend her mind to the world of politics. Hebe now believes that the government considered his activities dangerous because "what they wanted was people with no access to education so they cannot reason, or fools that don't care about anything, and that's why a whole generation disappeared."[19] Jorge had spoken to her a few times about the *disappearances* that had occurred in his university, about the detention of his fellow students and even some professors. He had explained to her that this was a totally

different phenomenon—these were clandestine prisoners. Nobody could
bring them clothes or food, or even visit them. Hebe advised him not
to become involved and to be cautious, but the worst she feared was
that his thesis would be turned down.

She remembers the last time she heard his voice. On February 8,
1977, Jorge called his mother from a public telephone on a crowded
street to tell her that he was planning to spend the afternoon at the
hospital with his ailing uncle so that Hebe could stay home with his
younger sister. As Jorge recounted to a prisoner who was later released, they were waiting for him when he rushed home from his
classes to have something to eat before going to his uncle. Five cars
loaded with armed men circled the block and then idled in front of his
home. When Jorge opened the door to leave he was struck with a rifle
butt. He collapsed under the force of the blow, unable to get up. Ten
men dressed in civilian clothes started smashing the furniture and then
attacked him again. A neighbor heard him screaming but turned the
radio up so that his abductors would believe she had heard nothing.
When they took him away she closed her window. That evening,
Jorge's wife María Elena found a trashed and empty apartment. She
immediately contacted Hebe, and they went out on a desperate search,
first to his school, then to his friends' houses. Finally they managed to
reach the owner of the small grocery story on the corner of Jorge's
street. He told them that Jorge had been dragged away, trussed up, and
thrown into a car.

Hebe despaired; she could not understand why five cars had come
to drag him away if he had done nothing. She was stunned and
perplexed, convinced that a mistake had been made and that he would
be returned to her. Her younger son Raúl was terrified and wanted to
hide in a friend's house. "Why in the world should you hide if you
have done nothing?" his mother cried. She woke up her husband
Humberto and her eleven-year-old daughter Alejandra and began a
frenzied and heartbreaking journey. The family went from one police
station to another, only to be told that there was absolutely no
information about Jorge. At the time they did not understand that they
were caught in a net of lies and deception. They believed that eventually
they would find Jorge.

Raúl had the idea of resorting to a writ of *habeas corpus*, but they
did not know how to draw one up. They decided to contact María

Elena's brother, who was a lawyer, but found him in a state of panic about the safety of the rest of the family. He refused to help them. "Forgive me," he burst out, "but I can't! I'm too afraid." Hebe's husband retorted, "If you won't do it yourself, at least tell us how to do it ourselves." Remembering a distant cousin who was an official in another town, they piled into their car for yet another journey. When he had listened to their story he replied that they were dealing with either the army or the police or a combination of these forces, but that there was nothing he could do because even those who were raising questions were being taken away. He also told them that the *habeas corpus* would not be much help. It was better just to wait and hope for the best.

On the ride home, images whirled through Hebe's mind while Alejandra wept in the back seat. Hebe thought of María Elena, who was expecting a baby within a few months, and feared that in her anguish she might lose it. When they reached their home in La Plata, exhausted and discouraged from their fruitless efforts, they went to the hospital to visit their uncle, who was dying of cancer. They had decided not to tell him about Jorge. When they arrived, however, he greeted them with an account of a strange dream. All through the night, he had dreamed that Jorge was lying on the ground bleeding.[20] The uncle died two days after they published the *habeas corpus* for Jorge.

Hebe replayed these events as if she were watching a film, trying to understand a reality that eluded her. She encountered disbelief and closed doors. She lost some of her old friends, and she began to learn about the fear that gripped the whole country when she contacted friends of friends in the legal profession. They dismissed her with vague courtesies and a few platitudes, letting her understand that they did not intend to endanger themselves on behalf of her son. She spent her time writing letters and searching for Jorge. Sometimes that meant waiting entire days at an army barracks or police headquarters. Barely two months after Jorge's *disappearance*, she started to display an uncharacteristic boldness. Once, when she had become tired of her day-long vigil without facilities, food, or water in the waiting room of the barracks of the First Army Corps in Palermo, she entered one of the offices and shouted at the military officers. One of the parents drew her back into the room with a warning that she herself was in danger if she behaved in that manner. Then in April she drafted a brave and impassioned letter to President Videla asking for news about her son. The courage that had always been there flashed out in streaks through her terror and confusion. She was capable of recklessness and possessed an anger that would become a significant source of her strength.

During June, Hebe learned the truth about Jorge. Someone contacted her, leaving a brief message that a person who had seen her son wished to speak to her. She and her husband arranged to meet with him in a local bar in the city of La Plata. He was a childhood friend of hers who had been imprisoned on false charges and then released. "Do you want to know the whole truth?" he asked. Characteristically, she exclaimed, "Yes, I want to know everything!" His account began the transformation of Hebe de Bonafini. She and her husband listened to the description of the brutal torture her son endured, to accounts of how he begged Hebe's friend to tell his mother to get him out, to tell her everything because she was the type of person who would want to know. Afterward she and her husband went for a silent walk, then separated for a bit of solitude. Without thinking, Hebe marched to the Fifth Police Headquarters where her son was being held, strode into the office, and shouted at the top of her lungs all she knew about her son. She screamed at the police, crying that they were assassins, criminals, and degenerates who did not deserve to be alive.[21] Four armed men threw her out on the streets.

Hebe has continued this charge vigilantly. Though outraged, she also has revealed the depth of her humanity, especially when she has encountered Mothers whose children have been released and who refuse to share information because of their fear. She has learned compassion and understanding for those who are less brave and is determined not to give in to the terror and apathy fostered by the government. She has come to resemble the resistance fighters during World War II, people whose qualities blossomed rather than collapsed under the weight of circumstance.

Like his older brother, Hebe's son Raúl had developed a social conscience and the heart of a reformer. After his brother was abducted his joyous spirits vanished. He continued his pursuits with passion, but he had changed. Although he did not speak much about it, he was frightened that he would be the next candidate for abduction, and he grieved for his brother silently. While studying ecology at the university, he held down two jobs, one at the same firm that employed his father and another selling wine to retailers and loading crates in a candy factory. An active member in the local chapter of his trade union, Raúl was twenty-three years old.

Hebe planned to go to bed early one night rather than wait up for Rául because she was exhausted from housekeeping and her activities with the other Mothers. She had prepared Raúl's dinner, leaving it out so that he could reheat it when he returned. When he had not appeared by two o'clock the following afternoon, she called her daughter-in-law María Elena, who told her that there had been a meeting of the local chapter of the union in Berazategui. A group of cars had converged in front of the house, and, afterward, all the people at the meeting were taken away. Hebe and a friend took the train to the house in Berazategui. When they knocked on the door, nobody answered. "Keep trying," a neighbor called out. "We know the woman is there because she has just come back from the police. They called her in." Hebe and her friend kept pounding on the door. Finally, it opened a crack, the chain still attached. The woman who peered out affirmed that the group had been taken away the previous afternoon. It was December 7, 1977, the same day that two of the Mothers were abducted from the Church of the Holy Cross.

After being transferred from one detention center to another, Raúl was sent to La Cacha in La Plata, where he would remain for two years. Hooded, the prisoners were chained together on the floor while tape recorders blared Nazi marches continuously, depriving them of sleep. Even more fearful were the terrible screams of those being tortured. Raúl de Bonafini kept up everyone's spirits by whistling and singing, despite the repeated beatings meant to silence him.[22]

Before he fled into exile a young man released from that prison wrote an anonymous letter to one of the Grandmothers of the Plaza de Mayo in which he described the unforgettable inner strength and spiritual force that Raúl de Bonafini had possessed. He told the story of how Rául took under his protection a young man who had arrived in their cell half mad from tortures and who stared at the floor without speaking. Raúl gave him half his rations, even though these were terribly meagre. While he was feeding him Raúl told the others, "We are here, but that doesn't mean we should stop behaving like human beings. Here where we are all equal and nobody has anything, we can't afford to be egoists." The young man eventually gained some weight and started to talk with the others. When he was in better shape, however, the jailors took him away, saying, "Now you are fat enough to be transferred." In prison jargon that meant he was to be executed.[23]

Jorge's *disappearance* had been a brutal blow. When Raúl was *disappeared*, Hebe reacted with aching sorrow instead of panic and confusion, a sadness that drained all of her energy. "Isn't this just what the junta wanted," she reflected, "to appear all powerful and make the people feel impotent?" By now she had changed profoundly. She understood the enemy. This time she grieved not only for her son but also for his friends who were taken away with him. A week later when Hebe returned home from the Plaza she noticed two thugs standing on the corner across the street from her house. Her immediate reaction was rage. Without considering that she was alone and could be dragged away from that empty street without any witnesses, she marched over and demanded to know what they were doing there. They told her they were waiting for someone. Hebe strode into her house without a backward glance, but as soon as she closed the door she telephoned one of Raúl's friends and asked him to look for María Elena. "Make sure she doesn't come home tonight," she urged.[24] Her warning was prophetic. On May 25, María Elena was abducted with a group of her friends while she was in a café. None of the young women was ever seen again, but Hebe has information that María Elena was in a detention center in Ezeiza for two years. She never learned what happened to her daughter-in-law or if the pregnancy came to term.

Hebe has repeatedly claimed that her sons' examples and moral stance awakened her to political realities. Their courage and compassion, however, reflected her own qualities. When Jorge and Raúl were abducted, these traits blossomed and a new Hebe was born, a Hebe who not only fought on their behalf but also took up their goals for social reform. In 1981 when her husband Humberto, who had been her staunch supporter during these difficult years, became ill with lung cancer, Hebe knew that she would be a widow shortly. By September 1982 she and her daughter Alejandra were the only ones left to gather up the threads of the family and keep its memories. But Hebe was undaunted. She had once reflected in the midst of her pain and out-rage, "As long as I am alive, my sons will also be alive."[25]

These tragedies have transformed Hebe de Bonafini into a powerful political leader. She no longer has the time to cook elaborate meals,
to tend her plants and her garden, or to sew ponchos. Although she
does not look like a heroine in her white shawl and cotton dress, there
is something distinctive about the way she holds herself when she is in
the Plaza addressing a crowd or leading a demonstration. Hers is a
stance of defiance and moral outrage, one that radiates both dignity
and power. When she speaks she is transformed, her message always
including a clear demand for justice. In the most benign political
system someone who speaks the truth with clarity and simplicity will
offend many people. In Argentina to do so is downright dangerous, but
she seems unconcerned with her safety. She travels continually
throughout Argentina and around the globe because she wants to not
only call the assassins to accountability but also prevent this kind of
genocide from recurring.

During her years of leadership Hebe de Bonafini has grown in
moral and political stature by virtue of her many confrontations with
governmental institutions, including the police and the security forces.
Her forthrightness has gained her enemies as well as admirers, and she
has been criticized for her combative and confrontational style by
those who fail to take into account her successes in pointing out the
web of connections between the military and the government. Hebe's
aim is not to be gracious or compromising but to bring about justice.
She has become the organization's chief planner, although she would
chafe at that description since she regards herself primarily as an
activist. She is the one who has taken the lead in designing the
Mothers' yearly slogans that challenge the government, and she is the
one who formulates strategies for action and analyzes the government's
latest moves. Because of her lack of formal education she is not self-
conscious about her mental acumen. Moreover, she has no desire to
promote herself, which is why her photograph will never appear on the
cover of a popular magazine. Hebe's moral strength comes from her
refusal to be swayed by the lures of power or to compromise her
principles. It also arises from her unique spiritual perspective. Having
waged a battle against the hypocrisy and complicity of the church
during the Dirty War, she lives the message of all religions, extending
her unconditional generosity not only to her work but also to all who

seek her help. Addressing a group of youngsters in a school, she told them, "I think the whole body is a heart."

Sometimes affectionately called *La Gorda*, or the fat one, Hebe is a large woman, and her imposing personality adds to her stature. She does not walk—she strides—and I have seen her march up to a plainclothesman disguised as a videocameraman and literally drive him off the Plaza, saying, "I know who you are, don't think you can fool me. You have no right to be here." She is the one who always manages to find a forum for the Mothers in a society that seeks to deny their very existence. The Mothers cannot afford to be choosy about their television appearances and accept all invitations as opportunities to explain their cause. Once Hebe appeared on a television program whose anchorman was noted for his barbed questions. At the end of the interview he asked her if she minded being called *La Gorda*. There are many people who have thin bodies and fat heads, she replied, and she herself would rather have a fat body than a fat head.

When she appears on television she refuses to wear makeup, insisting that her wrinkles and gray hair are a badge of her suffering. She always makes certain that the focus of the program stays on the topic of the *disappeared*, though this is not always easy. Once she was invited to appear on a Spanish television program that covered the problems of NATO and the ozone layer. All the other discussants were men who did not allow her to get a word in until she exploded. "Wait a minute!" she cried. "You are treating me like a woman from an underdeveloped country who can't talk." The moderator, embarrassed, questioned her about the Amazon, the rise in temperature, and whether this was happening in Argentina. "Yes," she replied. "The land over there heats up, but not because of deforestation, but because there is hunger and there is terrible injustice."

Her energy is phenomenal. She is in frequent demand for university colloquia on human rights throughout Argentina and Brazil, and it is not unusual for her to travel for hours by bus, sometimes throughout the night. She will then typically speak without notes and answer a barrage of questions for hours. The University of La Loma once asked her to help set up a course on human rights. "Human rights are not taught," she replied. "You practice them all day long from the moment you get up in the morning."[26]

Hebe's most remarkable talent is her ability to think rapidly. In 1981 the city of La Plata sponsored a centennial celebration with festivities that included a parade leading to the central square in front of the cathedral, the burial of a time capsule with documents, a huge cake, and celebrations in the streets. All dignitaries would be assembled in front of the cathedral—the city officials, the bishop, and representatives of the military junta. The Mothers saw this as the perfect opportunity to publicize the plight of their children. They arrived in full force holding a large banner with their children's names and the question, WHERE ARE THE DISAPPEARED? The Mothers tried to join the marchers, but because they did not have a permit they were turned away. Finally, Hebe became impatient, and when the Mothers were asked if they had their identifying number allowing them to enter she snapped, "Is thirty thousand *disappeared* enough?" As the Mothers joined the march the onlookers clapped and cheered while the police unsuccessfully tried to block the view of the banner as the women passed by. When they arrived at the reviewing stand where a man announced each group as it came up, he took one look at them and disconnected the microphone. At that moment the police moved in on the Mothers, trying to form a ring around them. Hebe left the march, sped over to a balloon vendor, and hurriedly bought out his entire stock. The Mothers quickly attached their banner to the balloons and launched it in the air. It sailed high above the heads of the stunned officials.[27] As the police closed in, the Mothers made a tremendous outcry, screaming their names and the numbers of their identity cards.

Hebe is always one step ahead of her harassers, and her verbal ripostes are humorous and well-aimed. Once she was interviewed by an Argentine journalist who was determined to slight her. The journalist said that she wanted Hebe to limit her discussion to recipes because she had heard that Hebe was a good cook. "That's fine with me," Hebe said. "I am going to show you how to socialize a chicken and also how to make militant veal osso buco."[28] She proceeded to describe the preparation of both in minute detail, interspersing comments on how to assure the equitable distribution of resources in Argentina. Another time, Hebe recalls going to a party at an embassy. When officials asked her to take off her shawl as she entered, she replied that they had not invited her because she was Hebe de Bonafini—nobody knew her. They had invited her because she was the president of the Mothers of the Plaza de Mayo and she had three *disappeared* children. That was what the pañuelo meant, and if she could not go in with it, she was not going in at all. She added, "The military come with their uniforms. Why don't you tell them not to come with their uniforms?" She was allowed to retain her shawl.[29]

In 1980, when the pope visited Pôrto Alegre in Brazil, the Mothers traveled thirty-six hours by bus, determined to seek an audience with him. When they arrived, though worn out by the journey they did not stop even to take a shower or rest but set right to work. They first went to find a newspaper that would cover their activities and then moved to the cathedral, where they settled outside with a big sign: FOR THE DISAPPEARED IN ARGENTINA. As soon as he caught sight of them the local archbishop hurried over and admonished the Mothers for engaging in political activities in front of the cathedral. Hebe retorted that the worst political action was the one he was engaging in by trying to move the Mothers from the cathedral door, adding that they intended to meet with the pope. "That's impossible!" he exclaimed.[30] Undaunted, the Mothers headed off to approach members of the Brazilian legislature.

On the night of the pope's arrival, while people congregated in the square in front of the cathedral to catch a glimpse of him, the Mothers were on top of a twenty-story building installing their sign. Hebe claims that the pope knew where they were, but he did not look up. The Brazilian police ejected the Mothers from their post, though a legislator, moved by their efforts, drew a huge poster for the Mothers with the help of his children and hung it from their balcony: THE MOTHERS OF THE PLAZA DE MAYO ASK THE POPE FOR HELP. The pope finally relented and said he would see one of the women. Hebe insisted that twenty Mothers had come and that twenty Mothers would meet with him. After a great deal of negotiation over this point—the Mothers refused to give in—they managed to prevail. When the archbishop accompanied them to the pope he told them, "You see how well the pope has received you?" "Yes," Hebe retorted, "but not because of you. He received us because we worked very hard for it."[31]

Hebe never prepares her speeches; she simply tells the truth about the Mothers, how they decided to go out into the streets to find their children, what they think and what they feel. On the eve of an important appearance or sometimes barely an hour beforehand, she will meet with the board of directors of the Mothers' organization to discuss the main points she will make, to listen, and to incorporate everyone's views. Whenever I have heard her address a gathering, I have felt as if I were hearing her for the first time. One of her constant refrains is that "the Mothers don't give up. They will never shut up, forget, or forgive, but will continue to struggle against injustice."

This refrain characterized the Mothers' growing resistance to the junta. They had broken the denial surrounding the *disappearances* by their ubiquitous public presence, and by the end of 1981 they had passed the test of fire. They had survived as an association despite physical threats and despite the death of four Mothers, including one of their leaders. Three Mothers were *disappeared* in Argentina; and one who fled to exile in Peru, Noemi Esther de Molfino, was abducted there by a group of Argentine officers and later was found dead in Madrid under suspicious circumstances.[32] Nevertheless, the organization continued to grow, achieving recognition around the world and access to government ministries abroad. The Mothers gained admittance to the halls of the OAS and the United Nations, meeting with ambassadors and members of the Working Group on Disappearances. In addition, a number of support groups were formed in Western Europe, and Pax Christi, a nongovernmental organization accredited to the United Nations, offered its seat to one of the Mothers.

In keeping with their policy of proclaiming their goals and their presence with openness, the Mothers reclaimed the Plaza. Once they repossessed that territory nothing could dislodge them, not even repeated instances of brutality by the police and security forces. In December 1981 they began the first of their annual twenty-four-hour marches to celebrate Human Rights Day. By this time the Mothers were no longer alone during their marches; the Plaza was swarming with journalists from abroad who had come to cover the strange phenomenon of middle-aged women marching in defiance of a state of siege. That same year, when the Mothers celebrated the fourth anniversary of their marches in the Plaza, they were accompanied by well-wishers from France, Chile, Bolivia, Spain, Brazil, Sweden, Britain, Holland, Venezuela, Italy, and from many cities around the United States. Despite the junta's attempt to silence them, the Mothers had gained international recognition for their relentless pursuit of the truth about the *disappeared*.

NOTES

1. Guest, *Behind the Disappearances*, 212, 272–74.

2. Madres, *Boletín*, no. 1 (no date). See also *Acta constitutiva asociación Madres de Plaza de Mayo*, La Plata, Argentina, August 22, 1979.

3. Simpson and Bennett, *The Disappeared and the Mothers of the Plaza,* 154.

4. Guest, *Behind the Disappearances,* 175, 184–86.

5. Sánchez, *Historias de vida,* 197.

6. Guest, *Behind the Disappearances*, 184–86.

7. Ibid., 177, 239.

8. de Cerruti, interview, August 1989.

9. Sánchez, *Historias de vida,* 192.

10. Ibid., 193.

11. Madres, *Boletín*, no. 1 (no date).

12. Ibid., no. 4, January 1981.

13. Ibid., no. 5, March 1981.

14. Guest, *Behind the Disappearances*, 239.

15. de Bonafini, interview.

16. Jo Fisher, *Mothers of the Disappeared* (Boston: South End Press, 1989), 46–48.

17. Sánchez, *Historias de vida,* 65, 74.

18. de Bonafini, interview.

19. Ibid.

20. Sánchez, *Historias de vida,* 80, 85–87, 90–93, 97.

21. Ibid., 100, 123–25.

22. Ibid., 132–34, 144, 201–3.

23. Ibid., 201–3. Zulema Leiva, who was released from the concentration camp La Cacha in 1978, identified one of Raúl de Bonafini's torturers as an official who is presently a government employee in the city of Florencio Verala. Another, driven insane by his role in burning the bodies of executed prisoners along with automobile tires to mask the smell, is currently in a psychiatric hospital. Once these men were identified, Hebe de Bonafini was able to trace their movements through inquiries at their places of employment. These men know that Hebe has identified them—and that she will work to bring them to prison until the day she dies. Letter from Hebe de Bonafini to Marguerite Bouvard, February 15, 1993.

24. Ibid., 146–47.

25. Sánchez, *Historias de vida,* 75.

26. de Bonafini, interview.

27. Ibid.

28. Ibid.

29. Ibid.

30. Ibid.

31. Ibid.

32. Guest, *Behind the Disappearances,* 207–8.

EDUCATION

You never went to high school or read Plato.
But you have learned about the Sophists:
you read the newspapers,
talk with government officials.

You who were taught to *cook, sew and shut-up*
have learned the most important
lesson, that what seems like personal tragedy
is not an isolated fact.

You see patterns, make connections.
You have learned who your friends are,
learned to call out the names of your enemies
and the friends of your enemies.

Evenings you hold *teach-ins* at the university.
The students ask for courses
on human rights. But you don't believe
the bibles, the books

of philosophy apply. *"Let's have a dialogue,"*
you say, *"human rights
can only be practiced."* In the country
of pampas and cordilleras,

learned citizens are mute.
They are in Plato's cave,
necks fastened to the wall, gazing
at shadows from reflected lights.

CHAPTER 5

The Junta Falls

The international setting changed drastically in 1981. Human rights were no longer on the U.S. foreign-policy agenda as Ronald Reagan had defeated President Jimmy Carter in the November 1980 elections and began a rapprochement with the junta. He invited Roberto Viola, who had replaced Jorge Rafael Videla as president of Argentina, to visit the White House and issued orders to U.S. representatives in the World Bank and other international financial institutions to stop opposing loans to that country.[1] His secretary of state, Alexander Haig, undertook the job of persuading Congress to lift the prohibitions against military aid to Argentina that were imposed by Carter in response to human-rights abuses.

President Reagan had his own views about the United Nations and intended to curb that body by reducing its finances and weakening its powers in the area of human rights. He appointed as the U.S. representative Jeanne Kirkpatrick, who upheld the United Nations' principle of noninterference in a country's internal affairs and sided with the junta. Kirkpatrick was a former political scientist who had published books on Argentina and who believed that Carter's policy on human rights had undermined U.S. national security. She put forth a redefinition of human rights by claiming a distinction between authoritarian and totalitarian regimes that enabled the United States to resume close relations with governments that routinely violated their citizens' rights. Her tenure also meant the end of Theo Van Boven's Working Group on Disappearances.

The Working Group had broken with UN tradition in the way it gathered information from groups and individuals who did not have consultative status with the organization and in its decision to review individual cases, but it nevertheless enjoyed the support of Kirkpatrick's predecessor and his superiors. In December 1980 the Working Group presented an exhaustively documented case against Argentina with testimony from former ESMA inmates. It revealed the existence of detention centers, asserting that even if the *disappearances* had slowed, there could be no question of improvement until they had been explained, a point the Mothers had insisted upon all along.[2] When the report was released it caused an uproar throughout Europe and was included in the records of the March 1981 congressional hearing on Argentina. The Working Group's mandate was extended for another year, and in 1981 it took up the issue of the Grandmothers of the Plaza de Mayo, its last vigorous effort in this direction.[3] Van Boven's career was on the decline with the change in the U.S. administration and the appointment of Javier Pérez de Cuéllar as secretary general of the United Nations. The two had clashed over Pérez de Cuéllar's visit to Uruguay in 1979 to report on the fate of political prisoners when he took the side of the Uruguayan government.[4] On February 8, 1982, Van Boven announced that he had been dismissed because of policy differences with the new secretary general. Gabriel Martínez's long efforts had finally paid off, depriving the Mothers of an important friend.

Jeanne Kirkpatrick's attitude at the United Nations was mirrored in her behavior toward the Argentine government and the opposition. When she traveled to Buenos Aires the Mothers wrote to her asking for a meeting. She declined the Mothers' request, and her public comments revealed neither understanding nor concern for their problems. The U.S. embassy, which previously had maintained a warm relationship with the Mothers, now turned its back on them. The new ambassador, John Bushnell, was a former State Department official who had fought Patricia Derian over the issue of the *disappearances* and had consistently expressed sympathy for the junta.[5] In late July 1981, Hebe de Bonafini and María Adela Antokoletz visited the United States, where they received a peace prize on behalf of the Mothers from the Rothko Ecumenical Movement and inaugurated an American support group founded by Patricia Derian and Senators

Edward Kennedy and Patrick Moynihan. Upon their return they were picked up at the airport by the police despite the fact that the human-rights organization, America's Watch, had asked U.S. embassy officials to meet them.[6] It was a telling comment on the new attitude at the U.S. embassy in Argentina.

Nineteen eighty-one was a momentous year for the Mothers and for Argentina. The Mothers' reputation among the population was steadily rising, their self-confidence was bolstered by support from West European political leaders and personalities. The junta, on the other hand, faced increasing problems within its ranks. Divisions arose between the senior staff of the army and navy and their junior officers; as a result, the air force became disaffected from the other two services. Although the junta had been wracked by factional disputes over economic policy and the conduct of the Dirty War, President Videla had managed to retain power for the five years of the Proceso by a skillful exploitation of the military's opposition to privatization of state corporations that had fallen into the hands of military administrators and by retaining control of foreign policy.

When General Roberto Viola replaced President Videla in March 1981, however, the Proceso was coming apart. While repression had waned, the trade deficit resulting from an overvalued peso soared, reaching an all-time high of $500 million.[7] During the previous summer several large banks and financial institutions had declared bankruptcy, creating financial panic. President Viola's economics minister reversed the liberal economic policy established by Martínez de Hoz and ordered devaluations of the peso, destroying local investor confidence and leading to a run on the banks and flights of capital.[8] Argentina's foreign debt had risen from 14 to 42 percent of the gross national product since 1979, and servicing this debt now accounted for more than 30 percent of exports. Economic collapse was complicated by continual squabbling within the junta as Viola confronted his army commander, General Leopoldo Galtieri, over the president's plans for concessions to the Peronists and the opening of a dialogue with the political parties. As a consequence of the falling value of the peso and his overtures to the political parties, in December 1981 President Viola was in turn replaced by General Galtieri, a military hardliner and an anti-Peronist. A few weeks before coming to power General Galtieri had visited Washington and offered the United States military bases in Patagonia in return for investments in a new gas pipeline and in the oil industry.[9] When he assumed office he further developed cordial relations with the United States, training the Contras and the Salvadorian security forces on behalf of the U.S. administration, which legally was forbidden to become militarily involved in these areas.

The diplomatic gains of the junta failed to stem the incessant jockeying for position within its ranks; thus, President Galtieri turned to foreign affairs as a path to maintaining power and unifying the armed forces. Compounding the issues of its external image and its internecine quarrels were the disastrous consequences of the junta's economic policies, which provoked waves of domestic unrest. Increasingly embattled on a number of fronts, the junta decided to permit the reactivation of political parties in December 1981 with the stricture that they behave responsibly. The parties refused to accept any conditions, however, and initiated a movement to reconstitute themselves in a collective association called the *Multipartida*, or all-party coalition, which included the Peronist party, the Radical Civic Union, the Christian Democrats, and a number of smaller parties.[10] It would prove to be a significant move toward the restoration of civilian government.

The Mothers had no intention of being left on the sidelines. They immediately pelted the all-party coalition with letters warning against any pressure from the armed forces to overlook the problems of the *disappeared*. By now the Mothers had changed their tone. They were no longer making requests with humility but demanding attention as well as a seat at the coalition's first gathering. To further this goal they placed an ad in *La Prensa* reminding the church and the political parties that the country's crisis was above all moral and that national reconciliation could not be achieved by forgetting the *disappeared*. Their first attempts to gain admittance to coalition meetings were unsuccessful; they were barred by the security guards of the Peronist party and by the police. They kept insisting, however, until the commission of the *Multipartida* finally invited them to discuss the problems of the *disappeared* at one of its meetings.[11]

During this period of ferment the Mothers stepped up their activities, sending petitions to President Galtieri and Cardinal Francisco Primatesta, holding roundtable discussions, and handing out their bulletins. They were present at important Masses and religious events, distributing their material and talking to anyone willing to listen. Frequently, they were joined by the other human-rights groups and by those few members of the church who supported them—the bishops of Neuquén, Nevares, and Quilmes; and Father Rubén Capitanio. During one march more than two thousand people circled the pyramid in the Plaza de Mayo with the Mothers, first in silence, then singing the national hymn despite the cordon of hundreds of police and plain-clothesmen and the noisy clatter of helicopters hovering overhead.[12]

The Mothers were no longer respectful in their petitions addressed to the president and church officials and in their frequent newspaper ads. After one of their interviews with the pope the Mothers had written, "We are convinced that the church is strong enough to solve our problem. If the Holy Father demands that our government return our children, we are certain to have an immediate reply." As if they were giving seminars on governmental institutions, the Mothers lectured the church, the courts, and the political parties on the proper functioning of democracy. In April 1981 they sent a letter to the Argentine Council of Bishops, a body that had studiously ignored their pleas for help during the Dirty War. "To deny human rights is a compromise with God and men. Once more we ask for a clear statement, definite and substantial, that will bring a solution to the anguishing and terrible problem of the *disappeared*."[13] The Mothers were waging a relentless battle to keep their goals in the public consciousness and to prevent behind-the-scenes maneuvering for power at the expense of their children.

The junta's response to its growing domestic problems was a last-ditch effort to divert public attention by embarking on a dramatic foreign-policy gamble. With the easing of international pressure the junta felt confident enough to develop plans for invading the Falkland Islands, or the Malvinas, which had been disputed ever since the British had occupied them in 1833 and whose two thousand inhabitants were staunchly loyal to Britain. The decision to invade the islands was an act of desperation by a government facing billions in foreign debts and the first signs of disaffection among the formerly quiescent labor unions. A sign of unrest, the Mothers were now accompanied by ever-larger numbers of people until their marches included thousands, and the junta hoped that the invasion of the Malvinas would unify a country that was rapidly unravelling.

The attack had been designed by Admiral Jorge Anaya in late 1981 and was originally planned for May 25—the anniversary of the May Revolution—or for July 9—Independence Day. But popular pressure on Galtieri continued to mount.[14] In late March 1982 the unions organized a mass demonstration to protest economic conditions, and the junta speeded up its plans for the invasion. On March 25, Captain Alfredo Astiz landed with Argentine marines on the South Georgia Islands to test world reaction. A week later Argentina launched a full-scale attack, calculating that the United States would not object and that the British would not be interested in waging a war across the Atlantic. Galtieri's cordial relations with the Reagan administration had led him to believe that the United States would support him in this offensive. He also estimated that Britain's commitment to the islands was too slight to provoke a strong protest. The junta, then, was totally unprepared for the U.S. position or for Prime Minister Margaret Thatcher's determined response.

Public sentiment in Britain viewed the invasion as a contest between democracy and a despicable Latin American dictatorship. Within two weeks of the assault Britain had mobilized a large naval force that headed toward the Falklands. Simultaneously, it launched long-distance bombing attacks on the islands' main airfield from a mid-Atlantic base and imposed a two-hundred-mile "exclusion zone" around the islands. As the hostilities increased, the United Nations initiated a series of diplomatic efforts toward mediation. The General Assembly passed a resolution calling upon both sides to withdraw and begin negotiations, and although each party seemed ready for a cease-fire, they failed to agree on an agenda for negotiations. UN Secretary General Javier Pérez de Cuéllar and Fernando Belaúnde Terry, the president of Peru, also unsuccessfully sought to bring the two sides together. While supported by Latin American countries and by Spain, the junta incurred condemnation from the United States and members of the European Economic Community. In addition, the United States imposed economic sanctions against Argentina and offered Britain arms and technical support.[15]

By the end of May the British had almost surrounded the islands and secured a bridgehead on shore. The first major land battle between the two forces resulted in the surrender of Argentine troops and gave Britain virtual control of the islands. Seventy-two days after its ill-fated invasion, the Argentine forces suffered a humiliating battlefield defeat, and on June 14, 1982, General Benjamin Menéndez surrendered, agreeing to an "unnegotiated cease-fire."[16] Argentina's much-touted armed forces were revealed as underequipped and ill-prepared, emerging from the incident with a badly tarnished reputation.

While the Argentine people had initially supported the invasion with enthusiasm, many now regarded it as a cynical manipulation of patriotic sentiment. Instead of turning to its trained regulars the junta had relied upon ill-equipped and raw teenage conscripts, a number of whom now complained of widespread abuse and corruption.[17] As these demoralized forces returned home they added fuel to the growing outrage against the junta, which consequently lost both its will and its ability to hold onto power. Leopoldo Galtieri was removed in disgrace and power was handed to General Reynaldo Bignone, who acted as transitional president, overseeing the return to civilian government. Bignone faced a crumbling political situation plagued with rampant inflation, collapsing business, and angry unions demanding wage increases. On July 17 the minister of the interior, General Alfredo St. Jean, lifted the ban on political rallies and recognized political parties. That same day five thousand people gathered in a soccer stadium to hear an address by Raúl Alfonsín of the Radical party. The tide had turned against the armed forces as Argentines prepared for a new episode in their political history.

The military leaders, nevertheless, were determined to continue covering up the facts of the *disappearances*, and President Bignone was under heavy pressure by the upper echelons of the armed forces to avoid any public discussion of the Dirty War. In August 1982 an under secretary at the Ministry of the Interior announced there would be no list of *disappeared* published, no explanations. Instead, the armed forces intended to declare an amnesty for itself before the transfer of power to civilians, the first of several attempts by the army at self-exoneration. Led by the Mothers and the Center for Legal and Social Studies, human-rights groups persuaded the political parties not to accept such a move. The all-party coalition agreed to delay elections until October 1983 but refused to promise the military an amnesty. On December 5 the unions declared their first general strike, and ten thousand people joined the Mothers for a massive protest to mark the beginning of their heyday.[18] The Mothers were now a powerful group

The Mothers in their first office, on Uruguay Street, in 1982

The Mothers are charged by the police during a demonstration in 1982 (*photo by Eduardo Longoni*)

with branches all over the country and hundreds of members. Whether or not the United States or the United Nations sided with the junta made no difference to them.

When Hebe de Bonafini and María Adela Antokoletz arrived in Europe to gather support in early 1983 they were received as though they were heads of state. In Madrid they met with Prime Minister Felipe González, and in Paris with President François Mitterrand. In Rome they visited the pope as well as their friend and supporter President Sandro Pertini, handing over a list of Italian nationals who were *disappeared*. They insisted that the *disappearances* had to be explained during the transition to democracy and that pressure should be maintained on the junta. Just before their visit the Mothers raised an anguishing question in an open letter to the pope published in *La Prensa*. "Holy Father," they asked, "what is our place in the church?"[19] Their message to the pope was unsettling, for they claimed they had been betrayed by the church in Argentina.

While abroad the Mothers were surrounded by journalists, and when Hebe de Bonafini returned to Argentina she was greeted at the airport by over one hundred Mothers wearing white scarves. No longer content to wait patiently in the antechambers of the government or the church, the Mothers were a ubiquitous and assertive presence with their marches, their leaflets, and their rallies. Most of all, they were triumphant because they were able to claim that they had raised the banner of freedom and human rights during the Dirty War, when the rest of the country was cowed into submission. As the long-silenced population was finally able to find its political voice, it paid homage to the Mothers. People applauded them from balconies, storefronts, and sidewalks as they marched by, shouting, "Mothers of the Plaza de Mayo, the people embrace you!"[20] When the Mothers initiated their annual twenty-four-hour march to celebrate Human Rights Day, they were met by a group of police and plainclothesmen who had cordoned off the Plaza. The large group of people accompanying the Mothers cried out, "Let them pass!" and the Mothers continued marching in the Plaza until 3:30 the next afternoon.[21]

That the transitional government persisted in harassing them was an indication of the importance of their voice. The security forces splashed graffiti and obscenities on the walls of the Mothers' homes, criticizing them as terrorists and anti-Argentines. The Mothers also continued to endure tear gas and nightsticks in the Plaza, and many of them were charged by policemen on horseback. They were frequently interrupted by groups of young toughs shouting, "Argentina, Argentina!"[22] The police and security forces, however, could not contain the crowds that now accompanied the Mothers and that surged through police barriers shouting, "Liberty!" and, "The military dictatorship will fall."

Fighting with pointed public statements, the Mothers called a press conference. "Our peaceful movement and our denunciation of what has happened is the reason why we have experienced such violent repression," they announced. "If our voice was not so strong and profound, we would not have elicited such a reaction." They sent a telegram to President Reynaldo Bignone, asking, "Do you imagine that you enjoy absolute impunity?"[23] The Mothers were making it clear that nobody could silence them and put an end to their demands. They continued to press their cases and met with Thomas Enders, the under secretary of state for Latin American Affairs in the State Department, during his visit to Argentina. That meeting seemed to bear fruit when the minister of the interior, Alfredo St. Jean, announced a few days later that he would give some information to the relatives of the *disappeared*, his statement published in Argentine and U.S. newspapers. Spokesmen for the State Department received the news with the comment that it would improve relations between the two countries, and many people called to congratulate the Mothers. It was all a ruse, however, and the Mothers were once again shunted from office to office. The minister of the interior responded to their visits by telling them that they should contact the judiciary. The minister of justice, Jaime Lennon, told them that the problem did not lie in his jurisdiction, and, in an interview with the *Buenos Aires Herald*, President Bignone claimed that it was impossible to publish lists of the *disappeared* because the government did not know what had happened to them, a statement that set a pattern for later denials.[24] All the while the Mothers were publicly claiming that the clear responsibility for illegal detention rested on the commander in chief of the army and the members of the military junta.

The Mothers recorded the daily events of the return to democracy in their bulletin, documenting the military's destruction of important records and the attempts of several key officers to leave the country.

While people celebrated, in a country electric with euphoria as more and more took to the streets to express their new-found freedom, the Mothers continued to march and remained focused on their goals.The military sought to exonerate itself of the atrocities, and there was tension between it and the political parties. Argentina was like a country in the aftermath of a bloody war.

In the fall of 1983, Raúl Alfonsín conducted a successful campaign for the presidency, promising to restore respect for human rights and rejecting the military's attempts at self-amnesty. During the time of the junta he had been a member of the Permanent Assembly of Human Rights and was not compromised by connections with the military. In October he won the election easily, gathering 52 percent of the popular vote. His Radical Civic Union received support from sectors that had not previously voted for the party, which enabled it to bypass a Peronist party suffering from the diminished influence of the unions under the junta and its association with Isabel Perón's government.[25]

On December 9, 1983, the Mothers called out their sympathizers for a last protest march against the military, brandishing thirty thousand silhouettes of the *disappeared*. They were joined by Patricia Derian, who had come to participate in the inauguration ceremonies, and by Aryeh Neier and Michael Posner of America's Watch and the Lawyers' Committee for International Human Rights, respectively. Representatives of all the political parties were present as were well-wishers from countries around the world. Minutes before General Reynaldo Bignone left the Casa Rosada for good, a Mother wrote a message on a piece of paper and stuck it behind the windshield wiper of his car: "Cain, where is your brother?"[26] When his chauffeur tried to remove it an angry group surrounded him. The Argentine people had had enough.

December 10, Human Rights Day, was also the day of the inauguration of the new president and the return of constitutional government. The Mothers were seated in the gallery wearing their white shawls when Raúl Alfonsín was sworn in, and they were invited to meet with foreign delegations who were present for the ceremony. They were no longer referred to as "the crazy women"—they had achieved national and international recognition for their courage and persistence. That same day the newly elected Chamber of Deputies abolished the junta's self-amnesty as its first official act. Like rats scuttling from a sinking ship, prominent members of the armed forces fled to countries elsewhere in Latin America and to Europe.

With the installation of a democratic government people rushed forward to denounce the atrocities that had occurred under the junta. Now that it was safe again the Mothers were joined by others who had been only too happy to leave that task to a group of crazy women. It was a time of both euphoria at the end of military rule and of shock at the revelations, but everyone believed that Argentina was once more on the path to democracy. For the Mothers the period preceding Raúl Alfonsín's ascension to power was also a time of transition. As the group of followers who had gathered around them at the time of the Falklands War swelled, they were suddenly catapulted into the limelight, attracting large crowds of supporters when they marched around the Plaza de Mayo. Instead of being ignored or vilified by the press, their activities received sympathetic and wide coverage. The Mothers had become a symbol of resistance in a country that had lost its voice.

NOTES

1. Guest, *Behind the Disappearances*, 290–96.
2. Ibid., 232.
3. Madres, *Boletín*, no. 5 (no date).
4. Guest, *Behind the Disappearances*, 141–45.
5. Ibid., 249–53.
6. Madres, *Boletín*, no. 7 (August 1981).
7. Rock, *Argentina 1516–1987*, 373.
8. Lewis, "The Right and Military Rule," 175.
9. Rock, *Argentina 1516–1987*, 374–75.
10. Madres, *Boletín*, no. 7 (August 1981).
11. Ibid.
12. Ibid., no. 8, November 1981.
13. Ibid., no. 10, May 1982.
14. Rock, *Argentina 1516–1987*, 377.
15. Ibid., 379.
16. Ibid., 380.
17. Ibid., 381–82.
18. Guest, *Behind the Disappearances*, 337–44.
19. Madres, *Boletín,* no. 10 (no date).
20. Ibid., no. 13, January 1984.

21. Ibid., no. 9 (no date).
22. Ibid.
23. Ibid.
24. Ibid., no. 11 (no date).
25. Calvert, *Argentina: Political Culture*, 270–71.
26. Madres, *Boletín*, no. 13 (no date).

POWER

Two abreast, the Mothers alight at the door
of the Casa Rosada. As usual, they arrive with the precise
consonance of migrating birds. But the President's secretary
wrings her hands, "*El Presidente is away. We do not know
when he will return.*" "*We have an appointment,
we will wait,*" the Mothers reply. "*Señoras,*" the secretary protests.
The Mothers can't hear her. There aren't enough chairs
in the waiting room and they are busy ferrying some in.
Unlike Odysseus, they know where they are going
and what a straight line is. The day wears on.
Evening, the palace empties. The Mothers feel
quite at home, but the night cleaners cannot come in.
Morning comes and the Mothers are barricaded
behind the front door. The government officials,
their assistants and their sub-assistants must enter
through the back door. Everyone is embarrassed.
After lunch, an emissary of the President
comes out to ask the Mothers if they will speak with him.
The Mothers understand the political process.
They will take a vote and then they will announce their decision.

CHAPTER 6

$\int$peaking Truth to Power

One of the things that I simply will not do now is shut up. The women of my generation in Latin America have been taught that the man is always in charge and the woman is silent even in the face of injustice. Outside of the house, she couldn't speak of this. Now I know that we have to speak out about the injustices publicly. If not, we are accomplices. I am going to denounce them publicly without fear. This is what I learned. This is the form the struggle takes.

María del Rosario de Cerruti

At the end of the transition period, a long-silenced and frightened population recognized the bravery of the Mothers of the Plaza de Mayo and cheered them as they continued their daily rounds in the Plaza in Buenos Aires. Now that it was less dangerous the Mothers were accompanied by thousands as they circled the pyramid. A characteristic of such a transition period, however, is that a long-suffering population will think only of its dreams, failing or refusing to see the new obstacles that can arise after the demise of a tyranny.

The Mothers were not so naive. They had been educated by fire and had learned that politicians often lie and must be prodded continually to keep their promises—that politicians often turn their backs on the people and rely on the support of special interests to keep them in office. The Mothers' frustrating experiences with the church had taught them that power can be manipulated behind the scenes and helped them understand the distinction between the formal structure of government and the informal structure of influence. Their years under the junta had also shown them that the Argentine population preferred to ignore unpleasant realities. Thus, the Mothers feared that in the euphoria which resulted from the junta's demise the fate of their children might be forgotten, or, worse, might become a bargaining chip in the adjustment of interests.

By the time President Raúl Alfonsín came to office the Mothers had changed profoundly. They had not only acquired political sophistication, but they had also formulated a vision of the kind of political system they wished to see in Argentina, a system that ultimately would pit them against the realities of the country's history and the exigencies of the new political regime. Until the restoration of constitutional government the Mothers had been one of the groups that opposed the military regime and its lawless repression of dissent. Once a new government was elected, the issue for all reform groups was how they could pursue their goals without jeopardizing the fragile democracy that had been reinstated. This issue caused a rift between the Mothers and the other groups that had been working toward reform and eventually a rift within the Mothers' organization itself. On the one hand, groups like CELS, SERPAJ, the Assembly for Human Rights, and some of the Mothers felt that it was necessary to support the government and to withhold criticism of its policies in order to ensure its survival. These Mothers eventually left the organization, and in their desire to support the new government, a few of them joined political parties such as President Alfonsín's Radical party. The aims of most of the Mothers, however, were now much more far-reaching. Their immediate goal continued to be that of securing the release of the *disappeared* who might still be alive and accounting for all the *disappeared*. They also sought the punishment of those who were guilty—from the members of the junta to the middle-ranking and junior officers who were implicated in the abduction, tortures, and murders of the *disappeared*.

Beyond these issues of political policy, however, they had acquired yet another purpose, a purpose would entail no less than a complete transformation of Argentine political culture. The Mothers wanted to eliminate the scourge of the military presence in the country and its impact on the political system. They believed that the military had been the chief source of repression and that no less than a complete dismantling of its power would ensure a true democracy. While the other reform groups shared the Mothers' intent of calling the military to account, they did not seek such a radical reorganization of power and feared that such efforts could backfire. From their point of view and from the government's perspective, too much pressure on the military would cause it to revolt and take power. In the Mothers' opinion insufficient pressure on the military would create the same result.

From the beginning of the new regime the Mothers continued to raise their voices, calling out not only the truth of their own situation but also the truth of the behind-the-scenes maneuvering of the government. Like the child in the fairy tale who piped up that the emperor had on no clothes, they collectively shouted their political perceptions in the Plaza and the streets and published these views in their newspapers and pamphlets, proving that language can be used by the powerless to jolt and engage the powerful. They crafted their slogans to express complex situations in ways that most people could easily grasp. Their leaflets and banners demanded CARCEL A LOS GENOCIDOS, or, PUT THOSE WHO COMMITTED GENOCIDE BEHIND BARS, thus equating the deeds of the military junta with those of the Nazis in the extermination camps of World War II.[1] They continually referred to the military as *assassins*, *torturers*, and *oppressors*, and unmasked what they saw as the true intentions of a government that would call for reconciliation, pacification, and the healing of wounds. Language became their nonviolent weapon to capture the public consciousness. They chose simple words with deeply emotional resonance to clarify political events and to give presence not only to the *disappeared* but also to political problems that were being swept under the carpet. Their slogans clarified their goals and, like well-aimed darts, unmasked government policies. Rather than contending for power the Mothers wished to claim an ethical, political, and historical presence by continually speaking out.

The new moral and political situation left the Mothers with a fresh set of challenges. The population that was so supportive of them in the transition period and in the flush of a restored democracy eventually turned against them because many people interpreted any dissent or criticism as tantamount to destabilization of the new and fragile democracy. Because the Mothers' demands were so ambitious, the government's attitude toward them soon turned to one of enmity and criticism. It sought to discredit them by characterizing them as intransigent women who were pursuing fruitless goals and who refused to accept their children's deaths. Instead of *Las Locas*, or, the crazy women, they were now referred to as "the nervous and confused women" who had little judgment and who were being manipulated by the Left.[2] Before long President Raúl Alfonsín was also trying to silence them. Even before Alfonsín had assumed power the Mothers had raised their new battle cry in the form of the blunt slogan JUDGMENT AND PUNISHMENT OF ALL CULPRITS, which indicated their determination to call to account all those guilty of the *disappearances*. Their incessant demand placed the president in an awkward position as he sought to reestablish a democratic system without provoking the military to another coup. The military's image may have been tarnished by its defeat in the Falklands War, but the armed forces still presented a problem and retained enough power to foil the government's attempts to rein it in.

While he was running for office Alfonsín appeared as a champion of human rights, pledging to introduce new antiterrorist legislation, ban secret detentions, reintroduce *habeas corpus*, and free detainees held without trial.[3] He also acknowledged, however, that the military had faced extreme provocation and that the guerrillas bore a substantial share of the guilt. Once installed in the Casa Rosada, Alfonsín governed with two faces, trying to placate both the armed forces and the general population while ultimately satisfying neither. He immediately retired one half of the generals, one third of the admirals, and drastically cut total troop strength as well as the armed services' budget. Fundamental military reform proved elusive, for although the president sought to confine the army specifically to military intelligence gathering, commentators indicated that the armed forces' intelligence officers continued to receive reports on what they regarded as subversive activities—including forms of loyal opposition. Although the president selected civilians to head the Ministry of Defense, they preferred to deal directly with military commanders rather than create a nonmilitary bureaucracy beneath them.[4] They were no match for an officer corps unused to obeying civilian authorities and convinced that it had saved civilization during the 1970s. Hydra-headed, the armed forces continued to operate behind the scenes, confounding the government's attempts to control them and drawing upon the Catholic circles and economic interests that traditionally had supported them.

Their opinions and pronouncements still occupied prominent space in the large daily newspapers. As a result, throughout his tenure President Alfonsín was criticized for proceeding too cautiously in dealing with the military and for responding with a series of half-measures rather than an overall strategy.

The fact remains, however, that the president made history by his decision to bring members of the junta to trial, an unprecedented move in Latin America. At his inauguration on December 10, 1983, Raúl Alfonsín had promised to prosecute both military and guerrilla leaders. Three days later, in a dramatic announcement that startled the world as well as the Argentine people, he ordered the prosecution of the nine members of the juntas that had governed Argentina between 1976 and 1983—including Generals Videla, Viola, and Galtieri, and Brigadiers Ramón Agosti, Omar Graffigna, and Basilio Lami Dozo—for the crimes they had committed in their war against subversion. He also ordered the arrest and prosecution of prominent ERP and Montonero leaders, including Mario Firmenich. In one statement he condemned both state terror and antistate political violence, a linkage that would later be labeled the "theory of two devils."[5] In addition, the government ratified several international human-rights conventions, including the UN Covenants on Civil and Political Rights and on Economic and Social Rights, as well as the UN Convention Against Torture. It also agreed to be bound by the decisions of the Inter-American Court for Human Rights.

The Mothers regarded the theory of the two devils as ominous because it provided implicit justification for the junta's repression and evidence of military pressure on the new president. They were outraged that their children could be once again linked with terrorist groups and portrayed as subversives. Indeed, President Alfonsín soon revealed himself as a pragmatist when he conceded to the armed forces and modified Argentina's code of military justice to allow any cases arising from the Dirty War to be judged by military rather than by civilian courts. In a newspaper interview he made a telling comment. "I have decided to make sure that the bulk of the cases remain within the competence of military justice," he said. "I believe that the civil judgment of the armed forces would create a wedge in Argentine society and that the military would defend itself in a melancholy ghetto."[6] The new legislation, Law No. 23.049, mandated that all cases of human-rights violations be tried initially before the Supreme Council of the Armed Forces. The same bill included a controversial clause stating that defendants would be presumed to have acted "in error about the legitimacy of their actions," for obeying orders unless they had exceeded them.[7] The prescription did not apply to so-called atrocious acts, but its general effect was to legitimate the excuse of acting under orders, or due obedience. Further, the new law effectively broadened the defense by giving judges discretion to decide if it applied. Law No. 23.049 was enacted even though it undermined the principles expressed in the Nuremberg Trials and established in international law, according to which obedience to orders is no excuse for committing such serious abuses as crimes of war or crimes against humanity. President Alfonsín sought to walk a tightrope between alienating the military, which could topple him at any time, and honoring his program for the restoration of democracy.

In Madrid, Hebe de Bonafini held a press conference challenging President Alfonsín's modification of the law, demanding judgment and punishment not only of those who gave the orders but also of those who carried them out and those who kept silent. President Alfonsín had argued that Law No. 23.049 would fix a hierarchy of responsibility—senior officers who gave the orders, middle-ranking officers who committed excesses, and junior officers who followed orders—thus avoiding a wholesale prosecution of the army. But the Mothers wanted them all brought to trial. In what would prove to be a prophetic statement, Hebe de Bonafini worried that "if Alfonsín does not impose his power in the first few days, it will be difficult to solve those cases later."[8]

The first day Raúl Alfonsín was in his office the Mothers arrived at the Casa Rosada with boxes containing thousands of testimonies of *disappearances* and a reminder that they would not cease their activities until justice was done and all the guilty were punished. They also asked him to sanction a commission composed of senators and congressmen with power to investigate the *disappearances* and punish the guilty.[9] Immediately they began to apply pressure on the political parties in the Congress to back the creation of such a body, receiving support from sections of the Peronist, the Christian Democratic, and the Intransigent parties. The establishment of the National Commission on the Disappeared (CONADEP), though, was one of the president's many compromises among the various interests. Instead of appointing a parliamentary commission with substantive powers he created an advisory panel that merely would review the testimony and send criminal cases to the courts. He appointed ten prominent citizens as members, leaving six other positions open for the House of Deputies and the Senate to appoint, though only the House named its three members. Alfonsín selected a well-known writer, Ernesto Sabato, to head the commission. Housed in the cultural center of San Martín rather than in the government, it was not given subpoena powers or the ability to compel testimony.[10]

The Mothers were bitterly disappointed. At the national meeting of their chapters in Mendoza they emphasized their refusal to participate in any of CONADEP's activities or to attend human-rights meetings that categorized the *disappeared* by nationality, ideology, or religion. Instead, they planned to devote their efforts to publicizing the names of the repressors and the dates of their presence in the detention centers. They distributed pamphlets explaining their position among trade unions, student groups, and artists' organizations. Rifts between the human-rights groups began over this issue and over cooperation with the Sabato commission. The Mothers recalled that Sabato had attended a luncheon convened by President Videla in 1976 and afterward made a public statement describing the president as cordial and cultivated, which they published in their bulletin.[11]

CONADEP began its painful task of receiving testimony from thousands of witnesses, beginning with a list of *disappearances* provided by the Permanent Assembly on Human Rights and CELS and building up the file as new evidence was provided. It established branches in several major provincial cities and both staff and commissioners traveled to various areas to receive testimony. Statements were also taken in consulates and embassies in Mexico City, Caracas, Los Angeles, New York, Washington, Paris, Madrid, Geneva, and other cities that harbored Argentine exiles.[12] Anyone who had information about a *disappeared* person was invited to find the person in the file, and the commission would then check a claim against other evidence and follow it up with an on-site investigation. CONADEP gathered testimony for 8,960 *disappeareds*, a number that fell far short of the information gathered by the Mothers and other human-rights groups, but what they did find was so harrowing that some CONADEP officials resigned, unable to tolerate the stress, and others sought psychiatric help.

While it gathered fifty thousand pages of evidence from the victims and their families, the commission elicited none from their tormentors. A number of the most notorious military personnel were asked to testify, and not one of them replied. Members of the military often refused to cooperate with on-site visits of detention centers. In one of many such instances General Paz, the head of the Second Cavalry regiment, refused to allow representatives of CONADEP to inspect a detention center outside Olavarría that had been identified by former prisoners.[13] When commission personnel did visit detention centers, the former victims who accompanied them often found that the centers had been completely transformed.

Although CONADEP did not have the legal force or constitutional stature that the Mothers had hoped for, its work did help publicize the facts of the Dirty War—the locations of detention centers, their commanders and personnel, the tortures and assassinations that occurred there—evidence that the truth, however horrible and terrifying, can never be buried. It published some of its findings in a book entitled *Nunca Más*, or *Never Again*, revealing that the victims belonged to all social classes and that many had no links with guerrilla organizations. The omissions in the report were significant, however, particularly the list of security officers directly implicated by witnesses. The book also failed to address the question of the fate of the *disappeared*; it conceded that there were many more *disappeared* than the names on its list, yet it offered no estimates. Notwithstanding, copies were snatched up eagerly by the public, and *Nunca Más* became the subject of a two-hour television program so powerful that the government debated whether or not to allow it to be aired. Minister of the Interior Antonio Troccóli made an introductory and closing statement aimed at muting the impact of the documentary by repeating the theory of the two devils. Nevertheless, it provoked the first threats of military insubordination that eventually led President Alfonsín to dismiss the chief of staff of the army.[14]

The Mothers took serious issue with *Nunca Más* because of its emphasis on mass extermination and the disposal of corpses and because they felt it meant to show that the *disappeared* were dead. They felt that the report's objective was to close the case on all of the *disappearances* at a time when the Mothers were still concerned with finding some of their children alive. They had no intention of allowing either the government or the commission to turn the page. They criticized the report for its omission of the names of the torturers, for the fact that it contained information that had been known for years, and, most important, for not stressing in its categorization of the victims that the vast majority consisted of the political opposition while only a very small number were actual terrorists. [15] When Troccóli described the repression as a consequence of subversion in his introductory remarks, the Mothers felt he ignored the fact that few of the thousands of innocent victims were actually engaged in subversive acts.

For all its shortcomings the report appeared at a time of revelation in Argentina. Mass graves were being uncovered and formerly silent victims were coming forth with accounts of their own sufferings or the torment of family members. The nation was descending into its own entrails, the caverns of nightmare, sadism, and cruelty opened, and testimony that had been too dangerous to present finally was given because it was now safe and would be believed and recorded by the press. Names were aired, names as notorious as those that emerged after the Third Reich collapsed: General Ramón Camps, the chief of police of the province of Buenos Aires; Antonio Bussi, the former governor of Tucumán who ran La Perla detention center in Córdoba and who was also responsible for the disappearance of Guillermo Vargas, a former provincial senator; the junta's minister of the interior, Albano E. Harguindeguy; Rubén Chamorro, director of the the Naval School of Mechanics (ESMA); and General Carlos Suárez Mason and General Benjamin Menéndez. Like the former Nazi torturers they fled the country, making certain beforehand that much of the documentation relative to their crimes disappeared. [16]

The long-quiescent newspapers were filled with stories provided by former inmates of detention centers and articles on the various task forces and death squads in which officers of all ranks participated. While these crimes may have been a revelation to the general population, they were not news to the Mothers, who had been gathering this information over the years and who would devote sections of the newspaper they founded in 1984 to what they termed the "Gallery of Repressors." Survivors of the detention centers had provided them with long lists of names and aliases of army personnel who were torturers and commanders in these centers as well as lists of doctors who had assisted in the tortures and priests who were present. The Mothers' bulletin provided articles about the destruction of documents ordered by the military hierarchy and the police. In their editorials they repeatedly demanded that the executive power establish a moral condemnation of those responsible for crimes against humanity and kept up a barrage of criticism of Alfonsín's legislation regarding judicial power. They maintained that the military should be tried in civilian courts because allowing them to be tried in military tribunals would both violate the spirit of the constitution, which admits no privilege, and lead to impunity and a travesty of justice. Ultimately, they were proved right.

In 1984 voices that previously had been silent demanded information about the *disappeared*. Parliamentary commissions from Israel, Spain, and Italy arrived to investigate the cases of *detained-disappeared* from their countries, and journalists' and lawyers' organizations, as well as the National Commission of Atomic Energy, clamored for information about those who were *disappeared* from their ranks. Families of *disappeared* soldiers came forward, adding their voices to the general outcry. For a time the much maligned Mothers were regarded as heroines. The public, however, while outraged, wanted to acknowledge and then bury the dead, while the Mothers worked to keep them alive. Initially, many of the women believed that their children might actually be living. A few of the Mothers had had telephone communication with their children before the transfer of power, and some had received tape-recorded messages, although they heard nothing more after that.[17] As a matter of policy, though, the Mothers refused to consider their offspring dead because they viewed this acceptance as a way of burying the past and, more important, giving up the pursuit of justice.

Thus, while the country was busily unearthing corpses the Mothers continued to demand a release of the living, choosing this unpopular stand not only because they wished to refocus attention on those responsible for the *disappearances* but also to ensure a social and historical space for their missing children. As Mercedes Mereno explained, "They took my daughter away when she was with her children. I ask my grandchildren, 'Did you see them take your mother away alive?' 'Yes,' they answer. I tell them, 'If you saw that she was alive, I am asking for her alive, because if she isn't, I want to know who killed her and I want that assassin to be put in jail. If I ask for her as a corpse, then I am killing her, not the one who assassinated her.' If my grandchildren can understand that, an adult can."[18]

Nevertheless, the Mothers were under unrelenting pressure to accept the deaths of their children. During the rule of the junta the government steadfastly denied the *disappearances*, but as evidence of the widespread abduction, torture, and executions accumulated, ministers began to talk about "mistakes" and "excesses." Responding to pressure for information from the families of the *disappeared*, the junta passed the law on presumption of death because of disappearance in August 1979 (Law No. 22.068) and a law granting economic reparation to families of the deceased (Law No. 22.062).[19] It authorized the families of the *disappeared* to exercise the right which laws regarding pensions and retirements would grant after the deaths of those persons were proved. This law established a quick route to obtaining a pension, which could be paid the day after the first six months of absence. After three years it was necessary to decree legally the death to continue collecting the pension, and anyone registered as missing between November 6, 1974, and September 12, 1979, could be declared dead by the state.

The intent of the legislation was to change the status of those who were *disappeared* to "presumed dead" so that the Mothers would stop pressing their cases. In fact, a law with provisions to cover problems arising from prolonged absence already existed, rendering the new legislation unnecessary. What it did do was allow the state to request a declaration of death against the wishes of the family; a judge could then declare a person dead without any attempt to investigate the circumstances of the *disappearance*. Moreover, the new law applied only to those cases of *disappearances* that occurred between 1974 and 1979 and thus appeared to have been created especially for cases of persons abducted by the military. The rationale for the legislation, provided by General Albano E. Harguindeguy, minister of the interior under the junta, was telling. "Though not a few of the presumed vanished continue in secrecy or have left the country secretly," he declared, "there exist reasonable possibilities that others have died as a result of their own terrorist activities." In other words, receiving a pension was inextricably linked with accepting the rationale that a loved one who had been dragged away by security forces was engaged in terrorist activities and had died as a result. When he came to power President Alfonsín replaced the presumed-dead law with two similar decrees. Law No. 22.062, regarding economic reparation, continued in force despite the Mothers' repeated attempts to have it repealed.[20] They maintained that President Alfonsín had caved in to pressure from the military, who wanted to put an end to the Mothers' demonstrations.

As a result of the new legislation on economic reparation, some Mothers received telegrams from the government in 1984 inviting them to pick up their children's remains along with an indemnity payment, or, worse, demanding that they sign a certificate stating that "the child had fought with the police and was killed as a consequence." Other Mothers simply received a box in the mail containing the alleged bones of their missing children. One morning in November 1984, the president of the La Plata branch of the Mothers' organization, Beatriz Rubenstein, received such a package containing a pile of bones identified as the remains of her daughter Patricia, who was *disappeared* on February 7, 1977, in La Plata, and a letter from a Commander Condor:

Dear Madam,

In response to your incessant search for your daughter Patricia, we have decided to send you part of her remains which should satisfy your anxiety to be reunited with your dear daughter. . . . This decision was taken after an examination of her conduct as a member of a camp of armed guerrillas. In case you were unaware of them, we are listing the crimes that she committed with her husband Carlos Francesco:

—Betrayal of her country
—Concealing the activities of the enemy
—Collaborating actively with Montonero assassins

For these reasons she was condemned to death. May God have mercy on her soul.

A forensic analysis of the bones revealed them to be those of a man between twenty and forty years old. In response Beatriz Rubenstein insisted that the armed forces had taken her daughter away alive and that she was not going to accept a few bones in exchange. The only crime committed, she maintained, was the arrest of her daughter Patricia.[21]

At the national meeting of all their chapters in April 1985 the Mothers formulated their retort to these new developments: NO EXHUMATIONS, NO POSTHUMOUS HOMAGE, AND NO ECONOMIC REPARATION, proclaimed their new slogan, floating in their banners during the weekly marches. They initiated a campaign to seek space on television for diffusing the photos of the *disappeared*, hoping this would help support the judicial investigations. The Mothers also joined with other human-rights groups and held a press conference to denounce the digging up of bones as a continuation of the terror the country had endured under the junta. They rejected categorically any possibility that the *disappeared* be considered dead as a result of armed confrontation and reminded people that many witnesses could attest to the fact that the *disappearances* had been carried out by heavily equipped members of the military and the security police.[22]

At a follow-up meeting of their national organization in Mendoza held in July 1985, the Mothers again rejected all forms of compensation that included economic measures or posthumous homage. They condemned the current practice of unearthing hundreds of bodies as a way of numbing popular sensitivities and closing the issue of the *disappearances*. The nation could not just identify cadavers as name unknown (NN), asserted a pamphlet they designed and circulated, while the assassins who created the terror remained NN. They insisted that there should be no scientific investigation of remains that was not preceded by an exhaustive inquiry to determine who gave the orders and who carried out the crimes of *disappearance*, which the civilized world considered crimes against humanity.[23]

At that time Lowell Levine, a dental forensic expert, declared that the identification of many cadavers was impossible because of the way the assassinations had been carried out. He recommended the creation of a single national center with multidisciplinary experts who would bear the sole responsibility for the exhumation, transport, and care of the corpses.[24] The Mothers fully agreed with this view and expressed their disgust with the chaotic manner in which exhumations were occurring. In fact, they had come to believe that the discovery of mass graves was being orchestrated carefully by the government to silence them and put an end to their search. But the Mothers had to wrestle with the problem of the bones since as Christians some of them found it difficult to refuse to bury them. It took many weeks of stormy, tearful meetings to come to this decision because so many of the Mothers had been brought up to believe that it was necessary to have a funeral and a Mass after a death. A few mothers who were not members of the organization did accept bones, knowing that they might not be the remains of their own children but wishing to give the person a decent burial. Since many of the *disappeared* were buried in mass graves, it was virtually impossible to identify the bones. "We want to know how our children were murdered," the Mothers consistently told the government, "but we don't want them moved or touched. Let them stay with their friends and companions."[25]

In December 1985 the Mothers reacted to a suit brought by the U.S. government on behalf of José Siderman, who was tortured in detention during the dictatorship and whose property was confiscated.[26] Speaking out against any form of indemnity of the victims of human-rights violations in Argentina, or any kind of legislation that would give material compensation as an insult to human dignity, the Mothers insisted that reparation for such crimes would constitute the legalization of torture and detention without charge. They made their position on economic compensation abundantly clear. "Would you be able to bring a morsel to your mouth, knowing that you bought it with the money they gave you because they killed your child?" Hebe de Bonafini questioned. "And if it isn't food, a pullover? That pullover is going to weigh like a steel plate or a mountain of bricks. It will weigh on you like death. The Mothers insist that they don't want that money because the life of our children has no price."[27] Because many of the *disappeared* were from the working class and their families were therefore in difficult circumstances, the promise of reparation seemed a way of abusing their poverty. The Mothers claimed that the government believed the poor to have no dignity but, by their refusal to accept a cent, asserted that they would prove the contrary.

The Mothers' Thursday afternoon march in the Plaza de Mayo (*photo by Gerardo Dell'Orto*)

The Plaza de Mayo with the Mothers' insignia, a white shawl, painted by the Support Group in preparation for the Mothers' twenty-four-hour march on Human Rights Day, 1987 (*photo by Gerardo Dell'Orto*)

A demonstration on behalf of *disappeared* members of the press corps

The Mothers marching with their banner, BRING THEM BACK ALIVE! (*photo by Gerardo Dell'Orto*)

The Mothers march against the passage of the full stop law, 1986

The Mothers demonstrate against the full stop law

The Mothers with their banner, WHY ARE THOSE WHO ARE RESPONSIBLE FOR THE DISAPPEARANCES STILL AT LARGE? (*photo by Gerardo Dell'Orto*)

The Mothers demand the return of the *disappeared* alive

Their role was not to mourn their children, the Mothers insisted, but to bring the assassins to justice. That is why in 1984 they adopted the slogan APARICIÓN CON VIDA, or BRING THEM BACK ALIVE. When the Mothers first voiced this cry many supporters of the government criticized them as crazy, obstinate women who refused to accept the reality of their children's deaths. The Mothers explained that their demand was in truth "asking a question of those who do not wish to answer it and questioning a whole system which generated a savage repression against the population."[28] The slogan was a response to the junta's mythologizing of reality, most especially to its campaign of denials during the terror. It was also a reaction to the legislation under Alfonsín transforming the *disappeared* into victims of murder and to the official pronouncement of the theory of the two devils. In demanding the return of their children alive, the Mothers insisted upon recreating and reasserting the complexity of reality, the shades of differentiation that the junta's reduction and simplification had sought to eliminate. "Our children are not dead," one of the Mothers insisted. "They are '*disappeared*.' Why should we accept cadavers, so the murderer can go unpunished? For my son to be dead, his murderer has to go to jail. People think that you have to have a tomb to go and cry in front of. I don't want to cry at a tomb because if I do, I am going to allow thousands of other youngsters to die."[29]

Since 1980 there had been a divergence among human-rights organizations in Argentina with respect to the demands regarding the *disappeared*. Hebe de Bonafini recalls going to a meeting in 1979 with representatives of the Permanent Assembly on Human Rights, the Families of the Disappeared, the Grandmothers of the Plaza de Mayo, the Ecumenical Movement for Human Rights, and the League for Human Rights. Hebe asked each one of the representatives, "How do you want my child to appear, dead or alive?" They all answered that they would like to see the Mothers' children returned alive but, when it came to the debate, showed no support for the women's position. At that time the Mothers had not acquired the political sophistication they reveal today. They could not understand why their stance was not supported when there was so much positive evidence that many of the *disappeared* were alive, especially in the ESMA, the notorious concentration camp in the Naval School of Mechanics. The Grandmothers' association, the Families of the Disappeared, and SERPAJ—

the Catholic organization—were the only human-rights groups that supported the Mothers' position. At its 1981 congress the Families of the Disappeared condemned the practice of creating laws applying the presumption of death to the *disappeared* as a way of covering up the crimes committed under the junta. The Mothers were present at that congress and were instrumental in including in its final communiqué an affirmation to continue the struggle until all the *disappeared* were accounted for.[30]

The disagreement among these human-rights associations was most pronounced immediately before the 1983 elections that would install a new constitutional government. Both the Permanent Assembly on Human Rights and the Ecumenical Movement for Human Rights refused to participate in the Mothers' demonstration under the BRING THEM BACK ALIVE banner.[31] The Permanent Assembly contained members of the various political parties, in particular the Radical party of the future President Alfonsín. They wanted to march under the Radical party's WE ARE LIFE, WE ARE PEACE, a slogan that, ironically, was an adaptation of the Mothers' FOR LIFE. The Mothers felt that since the Permanent Assembly had so many links to the political parties and the government of Alfonsín, it was uninterested in supporting their stand. They also believed that because the Ecumenical Movement had so many clergy as members, and because the upper clergy had always supported the government, that group would also refuse to join the Mothers.

During their interviews with government ministers and with deputies in the early years of the Alfonsín regime, the Mothers were subjected to intense pressure to accept exhumations. When they began to receive telegrams saying that the *disappeared* were buried in such and such a cemetery under the initials NN and that the bodies should be unearthed, they understood that the government wished to change them from Mothers of the *disappeared* to Mothers of the dead and thus close that chapter of history forever. One deputy claimed that there were more than one thousand unmarked graves and that he would see to it that they each received their proper name. "Yes," the Mothers answered, "but first tell us who turned them into cadavers."[32]

The Mothers regarded the press as an accomplice to this campaign because it treated the subject with sensationalism, publishing photos of people placing the bones of cadavers in boxes and providing running commentaries as if reporting a soccer match. The Mothers viewed that effort as part of the campaign to persuade the population that the *disappeared* were dead and therefore to allow all to wash their hands of the matter. The Mothers not only refused to accept the bones that were dug up from mass graves, but they also made certain that some exhumations did not take place and initiated a tug-of-war with the Alfonsín administration. To catch the Mothers off guard and prevent a demonstration, the government scheduled the first official unearthing on March 3, 1985, at the time of the Italian president Sandro Pertini's visit to Buenos Aires. The Mothers had scheduled a meeting with Signor Pertini, and President Alfonsín hoped that this would absorb their attention. But they were not fooled. They decided to split into two groups, one that would meet with the Italian president in the capital and another that would travel the four hundred kilometers to the Mar del Plata cemetery where the exhumation was to occur.[33]

Mar del Plata is a resort city with beautiful beaches and a glittering string of high-rises outlining the shore. It is a place where the wealthy congregate during the warm winter months—an unlikely setting for the horror that occurred there during the terrible days of the junta. The Mothers traveled by bus during the night and arrived at the Cementerio Parque in Mar del Plata at 6:30 A.M., just in time to begin circling the three graves scheduled to be opened. Two of them were the subject of a request by families of *disappeared* who belonged to the Grandmothers' organization. A forensic anthropologist from the United States, Clyde Snow, had arrived at their invitation to determine whether a Liliana Pereyra, who was presumed to be buried there, had given birth before she died.[34] The third grave was purported to be the resting place of the daughter of Mrs. Torti, a member of the Mothers' organization who did not wish to have the grave opened, and the Mothers had filed a request to cease those operations on her behalf. When the authorities called in a judge to prevent the Mothers from interrupting the proceedings, Hebe de Bonafini confronted him, saying, "If you touch one of those corpses, I am going to throw you in the grave head first."[35]

As a result, Hebe was hauled off to court and almost sent to prison. But instead of being cowed she confronted the judge, exclaiming, "What have you been doing all of those years when you were supposed to be investigating what happened to our children? Why are you ordering the exhumation of remains to find out to whom they belonged instead of finding out who ordered their burial?"[36] The unearthing did not take place. The judge who had ordered the proceedings acceded to the Mothers' requests and the women scored another victory in their fight to keep the memories of their children alive. After that, the only exhumations that occurred in Argentina took place because they were requested by families of the deceased.[37]

Although many people abroad believed that the forensic experts flocking to Argentina were on a humanitarian mission, the Mothers regarded the whole process of examining bones as macabre and beside the point. They believed that the sight of the remains on television and in the newspapers reflected the government's intention to frighten the public and send a message to potential dissenters as well as to bring about closure to the problem of the *disappeared*. They were tireless in their insistence that the only valid response and the only possible reparation would be to bring those responsible for the terror to justice. (Nevertheless, the Mothers did not take issue with the Grandmothers of the Plaza de Mayo, who are dedicated to finding the children of the *disappeared* and who view the opening of graves as a way of helping to identify and find their grandchildren. In fact, the Grandmothers' organization supports the Mothers' position against exhumation without the express consent of the family.)

While many people believed that opening graves was an important step in uncovering the crimes of the junta, the Mothers asserted that it was only a diversionary tactic and would not lead to the identification and prosecution of those responsible. They saw the guilty remaining in positions of power in the armed forces and the security services while public opinion around the world applauded Argentina's return to democracy. Despite this, the issue provoked a dispute within the Mothers' organization, and several members eventually broke away to form a separate organization.

The Association of Ex-Detained, Ex-Disappeared, created in 1984, supported the Mothers' position on the exhumation and identification of remains. They also questioned the ethics and sensitivity of forensic anthropologists who helped identify bones. Like the Mothers, they felt that it was more important to identify the assassins rather than the victims. The whole phenomenon of *disappearances* involved a legal and political reality that could not be equated with simple homicide, and the concept of individual guilt did not even begin to cover the meaning of the genocide committed by the armed forces.[38] Both groups felt that genocide was a crime against humanity and should be dealt with on the national level rather than on a case-by-case basis.

The Mothers' attitude toward the experience of pain is also connected to their political goals. Their pain, a source of their spiritual strength, drives them, and while many people in Argentina were practicing denial during the days of the junta, retreating into their private concerns, the Mothers wanted to face the situation head-on and examine the reality that their children were experiencing. They began to read about concentration camps and queried their network of *ex-disappeared* about the tortures taking place in the detention centers, leaving themselves open to the terrible sufferings their children experienced. Hebe claims,

> If you don't feel other people's sufferings and you start covering up, you don't have strength because you start accepting things and you are being crushed. Becoming aware of all the terrible things the young people were enduring made us see the ferociousness of the enemy clearly. The ferocity of the enemy gives us the strength to face him. I mean, how are you going to allow him to go on? The other very important step is to go on fighting even though we may not find our children so that it will not happen to someone else, so that another mother and another child will not have to suffer. This is a step that not every mother wants to take. There are mothers who feel that because they didn't find their child, they will not go on with the struggle.[39]

Contrary to the normal process of grieving, during which the agony of loss slowly moves away from the center of one's concerns, the Mothers have made a deliberate decision to keep the wounds open, in order to help them maintain their purpose and momentum. Given the universal penchant for avoiding suffering, and the enduring pain of seeing reality in all its dimensions, the task the Mothers have set themselves is unusual. It is not that they do not wish to heal; rather, they see their healing as a result of the significance of their mission. But one cannot equate the Mothers' work with efforts to keep alive memories of genocide through memorials and memorial services. The Mothers will have no part of such ceremonies, not only because they insist that their children are alive but also because they want their children's dreams of reform to remain an active part of the political dialogue. As one Mother told me, "I was a housewife. I never mixed with politics or studied. I was simply raising my family the way I had been brought up to do. My son always used to tell me that we were in this world for something beyond ourselves. Later on, I learned what he meant by that."[40]

Keeping their wounds open is also a political statement. In the interests of political stability President Alfonsín hammered at the need to *heal the wounds of the nation*. The Mothers interpreted this statement as a sign that the crimes committed under the junta would be forgotten. But they believed this was a dangerous policy. Because the military officers responsible for the terror were able to continue in their jobs with impunity, they were thus free to resort to terror once again when they saw fit. For the Mothers, it was important to keep alive the memory of those times so that they would never recur. "Let there be no healing of wounds," they argue. "Let them remain open. Because if the wounds still bleed, there will be no forgetting and our strength will continue to grow."[41] As the Mothers have faced fear head-on by taking the risk of possible arrest and torture that their former president and some of their members have endured, they have overcome fear. By facing the dreadful sufferings of their children in detention centers, they have transformed their attitudes toward death and survival.

The French sociologist Raymond Aron has pointed out two meanings to death.[42] One refers to biological death, the other includes the death of a culture. For the Mothers the physical annihilation of their offspring does not mean the death of their dreams. They believe that their children live on inside them, which is why they see no contradiction between their slogan, BRING THEM BACK ALIVE, and the fact that most of the *disappeared* have been assassinated. "We have given another meaning to death," the Mothers have said. "To die for a cause has a different meaning, because it's a death that kills the body, but it doesn't kill the feelings, the idea. Then it is as if one remains. That is why we are not afraid of death." A few Mothers do still nurture the hope that someday they will see their children; some will not change their residence in case a child returns, and some still keep clothes or personal possessions. The organization does not take a stand on that question because the Mothers believe that such feelings are intensely personal. However, the Mothers realized their children had been assassinated when they learned about the nature and ferocity of a military regime, according to Hebe de Bonafini. "We knew that our children were fighting against all that, that they wished a world without injustice or exploitation, and we realized that they [members of the military] had to assassinate them precisely because of that."[43]

Before I visited the Mothers and witnessed their extraordinary vigor and the support groups of young people that gather around them, I wondered if their struggle would be abandoned because of their age and ill health. Daily they face their increasing years and the illness of many of their members. Hebe shrugs off those who plan for tombs and headstones. She tells me that the Mothers are concerned with a different kind of finale. People may die, but the dream of justice lives on. She speaks of a project to have a home for the Mothers, "not a geriatric unit but a matriarchy," so that they can continue working and maintain the solidarity that is the source of so much of their strength. "We know that is what we all want; to die in the Plaza, to die working."[44]

When the University of La Plata wanted to name a classroom after Hebe de Bonafini's son, she refused because to do so would have been tantamount to a posthumous homage. She told me, "It's very easy to say, 'Here so and so studied,' instead of saying, 'We are going to commit ourselves to doing the same thing he did.' "[45] She believes it is too easy for people to relieve their consciences by paying respects with some material sign. Because of Hebe's position on the matter, some students came up with a novel idea. They placed her son's name inside a crystal, and the day his murderers go to prison and social justice prevails, the crystal will be smashed.

Likewise, the psychology department where Hebe de Bonafini's daughter-in-law studied placed plaques with the names of the *disappeared* in every classroom. Hebe refused to attend the ceremonies for their installation, saying, "I want them to say, 'This classroom commits itself to do what María Elena was doing, to fight for the country the way María Elena did.' "[46] The students responded by writing that message with black paint on each plaque. What the Mothers want are not accolades for their children but rather to have others step into their footsteps and resume their efforts for reform.

The Mothers disagreed with the government and much of the population not only by refusing to bury the dead but also by upholding their own view of democracy. While they welcomed the return of constitutional government, it was soon clear that they cherished a very different view from either the government or those sectors of public opinion that supported the president. From the beginning the Mothers' public statements characterized a true democracy as one that ensured the active participation of all sectors. They anticipated public criticism of their activism by protesting that they would be the first to fight any threat of destabilization. "We respect the government but we won't shut up," they asserted. Dissent was one of the underpinnings of democracy, and human-rights groups had played a dominant role in bringing about its return.[47]

A tug-of-war ensued between the Mothers and President Alfonsín over the substance of democracy, the Mothers holding a view that was closer to the more tolerant and socially concerned models practiced in countries such as France or Sweden than the one that had surfaced intermittently in Argentine history. Although the Mothers hardly considered themselves theoreticians and were acutely conscious of their lack of education, the program they developed presented a view of democracy very much at odds with Argentine political culture. They were demanding a genuine pluralism and a wide respect for all shades of opinion. President Alfonsín, on the other hand, spoke of the necessity for national unity and the need to pursue the national interest.

Supporters of the government adopted the attitude that "either you are with us or against us." The Argentine people, it seemed, had not learned much about the concept of a loyal opposition and continued to feel that those who dissent hardly deserved the protection of the constitution. Various groups in the center and in the right of center began to condemn the Mothers for their supposed intransigence. They criticized the Mothers not for their goal of promoting justice but for their political style and their tone: the women failed to support the president, and they asserted their positions too forcefully for a country that still measured women against the standard of the gentle, long-suffering housewife.

Nevertheless, the Mothers continued to evolve. Not only did they keep up the pressure for information about their children, but they also unleashed a barrage of criticism against the government for promoting former members of the military involved in the Dirty War and for retaining many of the judges who were active under the junta. They continued to present new demands, including the release of political prisoners jailed under the junta and the development of a more equitable economic distribution. They hoped that their program would be reflected in public policy and that their voice would be welcomed among the welter of voices that surfaced in the euphoria of the new constitution. Soon, though, they found themselves not only ignored but also maligned by the Alfonsín administration. When constitutional government was first restored the Mothers focused their activities on the Congress and gained some support among the parties in the opposition. But President Alfonsín soon developed the practice of rushing bills through the Congress, riding roughshod over even his own Radical party, and resorting to decrees. The Mothers once again found themselves disregarded by governmental institutions.

In 1984 the Mothers began to publish their own newspaper, which would become the instrument of an often acrimonious dialogue with the government. Their first editorial remarked that although democratic institutions had been reestablished, a democratic reality had not yet taken hold. They used their paper to criticize the slowness with which the government was pursuing the trial of the nine former members of the junta and the cordial ties that were developing between the military and the president. Political institutions were unable to contain the cross fire of interests, they pointed out, and the military still wielded power behind the scenes. "Alfonsín has the government and the armed forces have the power," one headline asserted. The newspaper served as an alternative press, documenting the persistent harassment of human-rights groups and the failure of the government to dismantle the intelligence apparatus as well as providing lists of names and aliases of those involved in these activities. When President Alfonsín referred to the federal police as "guardians of democracy," the Mothers countered with an article revealing the uninterrupted existence of illegal detention centers in police stations and disclosing the fact that the federal police continued to keep minute records on trade unions and political parties.[48] While the world saw one image of the president as a leader struggling to restore democracy, the Mothers presented another one.

The differences between the Mothers and the Alfonsín administration over the trials, the exhumation of corpses, and the need for a reconciliation of the nation continued to widen until the government began to criticize them both at home and abroad. While the Mothers were touring Europe and publicly complaining about the slowness of justice, President Alfonsín sent a telegram to the Foreign Ministry in France claiming that Hebe de Bonafini was a liar paid by international Marxism. When he appeared on German television in September 1985, Alfonsín claimed he had serious differences with the Mothers. "It was bad for democracy to defend those who caused all the bloodshed with conceptions that led to terrorist subversion," he said, thereby blaming the young victims rather than the task forces for the terror. A bishop who was one of the Mothers' supporters asked, "Is Alfonsín poorly advised? It's as if in 1947 a German politician had attacked the White Rose, the purest movement that opposed Nazism."[49]

The attempts to destroy the image of the Mothers gathered steam in 1985. The minister of the interior, Antonio Troccóli, reinforced the image of the women as mothers of terrorists while President Alfonsín claimed that "the political objectives of the Mothers do not coincide with the national interest."[50] After the government began a campaign to portray the Mothers as helpless, grieving women who were being manipulated by leftist political forces, they responded in their own newspaper. As they become more and more isolated by a press that followed the leadership of the president, the Mothers turned to press conferences abroad to defend themselves as true democrats and to remind the Argentines of their struggle for human rights under the junta and of the democratic principles embodied in their founding document. "After our struggle for love, liberty, and human rights, is it still necessary for us to prove that we are democrats?" they queried in one of their editorials.[51]

A war of words began between the Mothers and the large daily newspapers, which referred to the Mothers as "grumblers, the impatient ones, the insulters." The morning paper, *Río Negro*, claimed that "their style is less than elegant" and that they were "professional malcontents." One of the largest newspapers, *La Nación*, proclaimed that the Mothers were exercising another kind of terrorism—"sentimentalism"—and described them as dangerous. An article in that newspaper criticized them because "beyond their illusory demands to see their children alive, is an attitude of vengeance."[52] One after another the *Buenos Aires Herald, Nueva Provincia*, and *La Prensa* claimed that the Mothers were being used by leftists and revolutionaries and even suggested that the women were manipulated by groups outside of the country. After *La Prensa* published a cartoon of the Mothers with a woman telling Hebe that she could not go to the Plaza because her son was using her white shawl to go to a meeting of the Montoneros, the Mothers immediately dispatched an angry letter to the paper.[53] These salvos were intended to isolate the Mothers from the rest of the population and to characterize them as out of step with the majority of the Argentines and the national interest.

The Mothers interpreted these barbs not only as an attempt to silence them but also as a manifestation of remorse and shame on the part of the newspapers for having contributed either by their articles or by their silence to the crimes of the junta. In their own editorials the women questioned whether the press had stopped believing in democracy. Under the junta those who dissented, the Mothers in particular, were criticized as social misfits and treated as pariahs. The proliferation of stinging articles about them and the new boycott of their activities by television channels and radio stations reminded them of those times.

A confrontation that occurred in Buenos Aires in June 1985 highlighted the rift which had now opened between the Mothers and the government. At the national meeting of the fourteen chapters of the Mothers' organization, they decided to request an audience with the president, the purpose of which was to voice their growing disquiet over the promotions being granted to members of the military who had been implicated in tortures and deaths during the Dirty War. One of the Mothers from the Concordia chapter was concerned that the head of a regiment who was responsible for the *disappearance* of a conscript had just received a promotion and an award from the government, despite the protests of the various human-rights groups in that city.[54] Although they had been given an appointment, when the Mothers arrived in full force with their white shawls at the Casa Rosada, they were told that the president was not available. They replied that they would stay at the palace until Alfonsín received them, even if it took two or three days, and, gathering chairs, installed themselves in the entrance hall. When government employees left at the end of the day the Mothers' supporters arrived carrying blankets, chairs, and sandwiches, and they all settled in for the night. The cleaning personnel were unable to come in, and the following day, employees had to enter through the back door because the Mothers were still at their posts in full force. The hall was bustling with newspaper reporters and young people who came to support the Mothers. At the end of the day, government employees once again had to leave the presidential palace by the back door.

Finally, an agreement was reached between Dr. Rabossi, one of the president's advisers, and Dr. Ravenna, a government official and a friend of the Mothers who served as a mediator. When Dr. Rabossi offered to see the women,[55] they held a vote to decide whether to meet with him as a way of pressing their claim for a presidential audience. As they had demonstrated under the junta, the Mothers were once again proving that they could not be dismissed easily. They insisted on their rights to be heard and continued to press their demands—their persistent, bold political style earning them the charge that they were difficult and ill-advised.

One of the chief sources of friction that developed between the Mothers and the government had to do with the impending trials of members of the military for their role in the Dirty War. The Mothers were close to the truth when they claimed that the president had the governmental institutions behind him while the military retained the power. The military continually attacked the government in retribution for the trials, and clandestine gangs organized a bombing campaign in protest when leaders of the junta were brought into court.[56] Yet, unlike other human-rights groups the Mothers refused to accept any political compromise that succumbed to this reality.

"What good is an army like ours which turned the country into a concentration camp, robbing, torturing, assassinating, taking money out of the country?" Hebe de Bonafini asked in a newspaper interview. "When it was time to really defend the country, it couldn't do it!"[57] The Mothers were dismayed at the complex political maneuvering, the slowness with which justice proceeded, and the frequency and ease by which it was detoured. They feared that all the talk of reconciliation and healing the nation's wounds was a prelude to impunity for the worst offenders. Watching the maneuvering between the government and the military with concern, they were prepared to launch public campaigns against any measures that would exonerate those responsible for their children's *disappearances*. In anticipation of legislation that would provide a statute of limitations on the military trials, the Mothers raised their banners with the new slogan No to the Full Stop

AND DUE OBEDIENCE as they circled the Plaza. On the eve of the trials they were on the streets handing out photocopies of faces, eyes, and mouths to remind people of the victims of repression while their support group drew pictures of the *disappeared* on the sidewalks.

The case against the members of the junta went to trial in April 1985. It lasted five months and consisted of a succession of open hearings. The prosecutor, Julio César Strassera, had sifted through the information, including that provided by CONADEP, and called many CONADEP witnesses to testify. Strassera and his assistant prosecutor, Luis Moreno Ocampo, offered evidence on 711 cases of illegal abduction, torture, and murder, providing witnesses as evidence.[58] The defense also provided witnesses—prominent Argentines who spoke about the violence that prevailed at the time of the coup. Lawyers for the defendants cross-examined most of the prosecution's witnesses, trying to undermine their credibility and establish their association with guerrilla organizations by innuendo.

The trial had important political significance. On the one hand it represented a dramatic departure from current political practice in Latin America, where amnesty for the armed forces is the price insisted upon by the military in permitting a transition to democratic government; as such, it raised the hopes of human-rights activists around the world. On the other hand, the trial was a result of a long series of political compromises between the government and the military, and its outcome would have a significant impact on the functioning of democracy in Argentina.

After Strassera's summary of the case and the reply of the defendants had been completed, the court recessed while the six judges retired to consider the case. Hebe de Bonafini, who had sat in the gallery during the trial, had been forced to make a choice between being present and wearing her white shawl. The court characterized the shawl as a political gesture and refused to begin proceedings until she removed it. Eventually, she agreed, but as she realized the direction the sentencing was taking, she put her shawl back on her head. When the court president once again asked her to choose between her presence and the scarf, she left abruptly. She had seen enough. Similarly, the Mothers had difficult relations with the prosecutor, who openly criticized them for becoming more and more isolated from the rest of the population. The Mothers replied by asking where he was when they were facing police armed with clubs and guns. They accused him of giving a double message, one to the military—"not to worry"—and one to the public—"this is all you are going to get."[59]

The judges agreed with the prosecution that there was a deliberate, concerted plan to carry out a policy of covert repression and that this was the dictatorship's main weapon in its campaign to defeat subversion. They also ruled that the policy was carried out in a decentralized fashion but that the high command had maintained a significant involvement through its supervision and specific orders. General Videla was found guilty of 66 counts of homicide, 306 counts of false arrest aggravated by threats and violence, 93 counts of torture, 4 counts of torture followed by death, and 26 counts of robbery. He was sentenced to life imprisonment, perpetual disqualification from holding public office, and loss of military rank. On hundreds of other counts involving similar crimes, however, he was acquitted. Admiral Massera was also sentenced to life imprisonment. Brigadier Ramón Agosti, because he was found guilty on only eight counts of torture and three of robbery, was sentenced to just four and one-half years in prison. General Roberto Viola received a sentence of seventeen years. Admiral Armando Lambruschini, who succeeded Emilio Massera as high command of the navy, was sentenced to eight years. The air force commander of the second junta, Brigadier Omar Graffigna, was acquitted, as were the three members of the third junta, General Leopoldo Galtieri, Admiral Jorge Anaya, and Brigadier Basilio Lami Dozo.[60]

While the sentences were well received abroad, their leniency provoked serious disappointment in Argentina. Although the fact that the trial and the sentencing occurred was a condemnation of the military rule and evidence of judicial independence, the light sentences and acquittals of the defendants of so many serious charges frustrated and angered the junta's many victims. The results of the trials were a particularly bitter pill for the Mothers and would turn them into radicals. Though they had greeted the coming of democracy with enthusiasm, they now felt betrayed and no longer believed it was possible to hope for redress from the political system.

After the completion of the trial against the commanders in chief of the junta, public attention turned to the additional criminal complaints filed by the Mothers' organization and other private parties for human-rights violations during the Dirty War. Along with many of the victims' families, the Mothers had brought criminal complaints alleging illegal arrest, torture, and murder against members of the military. Two thousand criminal complaints had been filed by private parties in the federal courts rather than before the Supreme Council of the Armed Forces despite the promulgation of the law placing these cases under the jurisdiction of the Supreme Council. The Council ultimately established control of all these complaints, and while it proceeded with deliberate slowness, seeking to stall trials, it was vigorous in demanding that civilian courts stop proceedings against military officers.[61]

While jurisdictional issues were debated, several civilian courts had taken preliminary steps to investigate the charges against military men and required prominent generals to come forward as defendants or witnesses. These proceedings received wide press coverage. In one typical case a judge confronted General Reynaldo Bignone with two former draftees who themselves had been imprisoned and tortured and who accused him of the *disappearances* of two other conscripts. The Supreme Council obtained jurisdiction over the case and released General Bignone on the same day.[62] Dismayed at these developments, the Mothers began a hunger strike in protest, joined by an Israeli member of parliament who was visiting Argentina and supported by the bishop of Viedma, women's groups from the Peronist party, and human-rights groups.

Twenty-five percent of those cited for criminal acts were being considered for promotion by the executive branch, and they included Mohammed Alí Seineldín, who would later foment two attempted coups against the government.[63] A race ensued between the human-rights groups' presentations of testimony and the military's proposals for promotion. At the same time, human-rights activists were being threatened as fleets of Ford Falcons fanned out through the Buenos Aires area distributing pamphlets from a *Commando Argentino*, which condemned to death political personalities and even members of the Congress. The Mothers concluded that the security forces were still intact.

One of the cases that drew international attention and that concerned the Mothers most deeply was that pending against Captain Alfredo Astiz for the kidnapping and murder of the young Swedish woman, Dagmar Hagelin. He was also accused of infiltrating the

Mothers' organization and kidnapping the two French nuns, Sister Alicia Doman and Sister Léonie Duquet. Early in President Alfonsín's administration, Dagmar's father had initiated a criminal complaint in the federal courts with the support of the Swedish government. When the civilian judge ordered Astiz's arrest, the Supreme Council demanded jurisdiction over the case. Meanwhile, the high command of the navy informed the government that it intended to prevent the arrest on the grounds that it would provoke a revolt among Astiz's fellow officers. The arrest warrant was quashed, the case assigned to the Supreme Council. A few months later, it acquitted Astiz of the charges regarding Dagmar Hagelin on the grounds that he had been investigated in secret proceedings and cleared in 1981.[64] The case was appealed to the Federal Court of Appeals for Buenos Aires, but Alfredo Astiz refused to subject himself to identification in a lineup of prisoners and appeared in court in navy uniform. The federal court nevertheless retried the case, and Astiz was acquitted on December 5, 1986, because of a statute of limitations.[65] The charges regarding the French nuns were consolidated with other cases of kidnapping, murder, and torture in the ESMA camp.

It has been alleged that President Alfonsín met with the heads of the armed services in October 1985 and pledged that the human-rights trials would end. In any event the military was placing increasing pressure on him to declare an amnesty. The high command was especially concerned about complaints pending against members of the armed and security forces.[66] Many of the armed forces who were named defendants in these charges were still on active duty, and the military made it clear to the government that younger officers had become a symbol to their comrades, who threatened to revolt if the accused were handed over to the courts.

The radicalization of the Mothers' goals and their attitude toward the trials created strains within the organization that led to a split in 1986. A dozen Mothers, who referred to themselves as the Línea Fundadora (Founding Line) of the Mothers of the Plaza de Mayo, departed, their chosen name reflecting the fact that some of them were in the original group of Mothers. Among them were María Adela Antokoletz, and Renée Epelbaum, who has acquired an international reputation for her efforts against anti-Semitism and makes frequent guest appearances in the United States. Reasons for the splintering began to appear when President Alfonsín came to power and converged at the time of election for the presidency of the Mothers' organization. Feelings ran so high then that the Mothers hired a lawyer to supervise the elections, which took place on January 17, 1986, among two hundred members who gathered from the chapters. Two lists for the presidency were presented, one representing the disaffected Mothers, the other representing the rest of the organization. Midway through the elections the dissenting Mothers withdrew and departed, and a number of the remaining Mothers were so torn by what was happening that they turned in blank ballots.[67] Some left the organization, but the federation and the Buenos Aires chapter remained intact and vigorously opposed the government's attitude toward the trials.

The Mothers who formed the Founding Line were disenchanted with Hebe de Bonafini's leadership. They disagreed with the Mothers' stand against exhumations and applauded the work of Clyde Snow as providing proof that the exhumed were indeed tortured and assassinated, supporting those exhumations that were ordered by judges and carried out by forensic experts. Aside from policy differences was the issue of political style. The Mothers who left to form the Founding Line intended to work within the political system as an interest group rather than as a radical opposition group that continued demonstrating and marching against the government.[68] Although they disagreed with the law of due obedience and the *punto final*, or statute of limitations, they wished to express their support for the government. A number of them were from the upper and middle classes, a distinction adding an element of bitterness to their departure since the majority of Mothers were from the working class.

The Mothers who left expressed considerable irritation with Hebe de Bonafini's combative style and felt that she exercised undue influence over the association. They opposed the group's stand against memorials, believing there should be a plurality of approaches to this issue and ultimately planting a row of trees on the road to Tel Aviv in Israel to commemorate the *disappeared*. While the Mothers' organization believes that the memory of their children is best served by their political activities and by working toward their children's dreams of social reform, Renée Epelbaum commented on behalf of the breakaway group that "the resurgence of Nazism in Germany is proof of the need for memorials."[69] The Línea Fundadora ultimately established an office in the building owned by the Ecumenical Movement for Human Rights and holds its weekly meetings there. Its members continue to march in the Plaza, and during the last week of May they gather to commemorate the *disappeared* with the Federation of Families of Detained-Disappeared in Latin America, the Grandmothers of the Plaza de Mayo, and the Families of Detained-Disappeared for Political Reasons.

The minister of defense, Raúl Borrás, coined the term *punto final*, or full stop, for the legislation that he advocated to place a time limit on the prosecutions. He felt that the longer the trials lasted the more restive the armed forces would be, thus threatening the democratic government. Throughout the trials members of Families of Those Killed by Subversion (FAMUS) held Masses to commemorate the victims of guerrilla squads, at one Mass crying for Alfonsín's resignation.[70] Other close advisers to Alfonsín suggested an amnesty law, which the president refused to consider.[71] In April 1986 the Ministry of Defense sent instructions to the military prosecutors regarding the application of the due obedience clause. The orders were disguised as an administrative mechanism to bring together disparate cases and speed up the process.[72] The main message, however, was that the prosecutors should drop charges in those cases where due obedience could be an exculpating factor. As a result, one judge resigned and two others gave their resignations but agreed to stay only after President Alfonsín had assured them that he did not intend to undermine the court.[73] The subsequent public outcry was fueled not only from human-rights groups but also from many members of the Radical party. In a press conference President Alfonsín told the country that the instructions were not an attempt to undermine justice; charges would not be dropped in the cases of atrocious acts. Yet, the text of the instructions was not changed, and they were not withdrawn. Once again President Alfonsín had resorted to a double message. Officers on active duty were signaled that the government was moving to ease their situation, while the public was told that the president intended to assert the rule of law and continue prosecuting crimes of the Dirty War.

Caving in to military pressure in the autumn of 1986, President Alfonsín submitted a bill for a full stop law to the Congress. Although many Radical leaders disagreed with the proposed law, Alfonsín held a series of meetings with them and managed to crush dissidence within the party and rush the bill through. Though he continued to deny any military pressure his arguments for passage were based on the need to preserve democracy, and a number of legislators voted to uphold party discipline although they disagreed with the bill. Alfonsín received the support of the party in the House, and in the Senate the party was supported by right-wing Peronists and some conservative party members.[74] On December 24 the law was passed. It stated that no new criminal complaints could be brought against anyone for crimes committed during the war against subversion after the expiration of a sixty-day period following enactment. During that term all complaints previously filed would be considered moot unless the courts had heard the defendants or attempted to hear them. The previous day the Supreme Council had dropped charges against fifteen admirals in the ESMA case and stated its disagreement with the Court of Appeals conviction of Massera and Lambruschini, insisting there had been no kidnappings, murder, torture, or sexual abuse in secret detention centers.

The government expected that when the term expired only a small number of retired officers would continue to face charges. However, human-rights organizations worked feverishly over the next two months to file new charges or to submit more evidence in support of previously filed complaints. The courts ensured that they had complete records before allowing charges of serious crimes to be dropped, and many judges canceled vacations in order to complete their work. By the end of the term about three hundred officers continued to face charges, including generals and admirals.[75] The new law failed to improve relations between the government and the armed forces, costing Alfonsín politically.

The law also posed serious problems for the Mothers in their attempts to achieve vindication from the courts. After the *punto final* was passed, judges began to affirm that the *disappearances* constituted instantaneous crimes and that the principle of prescription began the day of the imprisonment of the *disappeared*. (If prescription is applied, the state renounces its punitive power when a specific amount of time has passed without judging the guilty.)[76] If victims had not appeared and no bodies were identified as evidence, the courts would not consider that a homicide occurred. The court, therefore, requested the Mothers to provide dental records of their children. Because they did not want to establish the death of their children or to categorize them as simple homicides and thus open their cases to the use of prescription, the Mothers refused. They continued to insist that the crimes committed during the time of the junta were acts of genocide and should be treated as such—not as simple homicides. They also reaffirmed their policy of not putting their individual desires to give their children a resting place before the needs of thirty thousand. They considered each child as belonging to them all. Since from the very beginning the Mothers had worried about efforts to clear the military for its repressive actions, they were not surprised when the full stop law was proposed and rushed through the Congress. Instead, they initiated a campaign to sensitize public opinion at home and abroad against the passage of these laws, traveling throughout Europe and, with the help of their many support groups, holding press conferences and meeting with government officials to persuade them to apply pressure on the Argentine government.

At home their newspaper kept up unremitting pressure to call to account those responsible for torture and murder. The Mothers went out in the streets with their banners, which proclaimed their new and blunt slogan DOWN WITH THE MILITARY as they marched through the city, accompanied by thousands of people including young members of the Radical party. They raised the slogan in their annual twenty-four-hour march celebrating Human Rights Day; Hebe de Bonafini described its purpose as "clarifying what is going on behind the scenes and what everyone wishes to conceal, what stinks." People were outraged that a large number of officers responsible for heinous crimes were now beyond the reach of justice. Personalities from abroad came to join them in this effort, including the Nazi hunter Beate Klarsfeld, who published a joint statement with the Mothers pledging "to awaken a consciousness in society about what human beings are capable of doing to each other and thus prevent genocide from occurring again, not to limit ourselves to struggling against atrocities in one's own country, and finally to never shut up or keep quiet."[77]

The Mothers' continual clamor in the Plaza irritated the president. At the time the full stop was rushed through they staged a mass demonstration there, launching thirty thousand balloons containing the names of the *disappeared*. It was an attempt "to reach the indifferent with their cries of life, justice and liberty," they proclaimed.[78] In June, President Alfonsín threatened to move the capital to the distant city of Viedma in Patagonia. To show him that they would continue demonstrating and crying out for justice regardless of geography, the Mothers traveled twelve hours by bus to demonstrate in the plaza where the government proposed to install its new offices. Members of the organization from all over the country converged there and were warmly received by their good friend, the bishop. After their march they placed two plaques in the square in Viedma, one with a white shawl and the date, and another for the organization with the names of all the branches. Hebe gave a stirring speech in which she referred to the *punto final* law, saying, "There will be no magic republic without guilty people. We are here in the projected capital to shout out that nothing and nobody, neither time nor magic, can silence our claims. Wherever the government will go to try to put an end to the inquiry, we will be there, raising the flag of clear principles, in spite of those who wash their hands and enjoy the pride of power."[79] After they returned to Buenos Aires the municipal council of Viedma wrote to the Mothers to inform them that it had removed the plaques as part of its duty to maintain order. But the Mothers had won the more important battle: the government offices remained in the Casa Rosada in the Plaza de Mayo in Buenos Aires.

Neither the leniency of the sentencing nor the *punto final* law placated a military that was still smarting from its humiliating defeat and its futile attempts to vindicate its behavior during the Dirty War. Officials of the armed forces were refusing to hand over personnel who had been served arrest warrants for instances of murder and torture. One of the officers in question was Major Ernesto Barreiro. Since 1984 he had been charged with torturing prisoners while he, then a captain, had served as a principal interrogator at La Perla detention center. When the Federal Court of Córdoba ordered his arrest on April 15, 1987, he sought refuge in his army unit.

On Palm Sunday the pope preached a message of peace and reconciliation before a huge crowd in Buenos Aires. Meanwhile, military chaplains were holding Masses for the victims of subversion, and Army Chief of Staff Héctor Rios Erenu called for an understanding of the military's role during the Dirty War. The army's insistence on its own version of its conduct under the junta would soon become violent;

the following Tuesday, the airborne infantry regiment in Córdoba initiated a revolt in support of Major Barreiro. Thus began the first rebellion against the new government whereby many younger officers demanded an amnesty law as well as the dismissal of all the generals on active duty. They resented the lack of civilian respect for what they viewed as their struggle against subversion during the Dirty War and felt that they should not have to appear in civilian courts to defend that role. The president reacted by calling the people to the streets and asking them to defend the democratic institutions. Two hundred thousand people appeared in the square, where Alfonsín told them that no concessions would be made to the rebels. The revolt soon fizzled out.

A week later, however, a more serious uprising erupted among officers at the infantry school at the Campo de Mayo just outside Buenos Aires. The rebels were special forces referred to as *carapintadas*, or blackened faces, a reference to the camouflage used during the Falklands War. They were led by Lieutenant Colonel Aldo Rico and represented a cross section of the Argentine army, drawn from bases all over the country. The president ordered General Héctor Rios Erenu to take matters in hand, and, after an unexplainable hesitation, he managed to muster enough troops to put down the revolt. At 3 P.M. on Easter Sunday, April 19, 1987, Alfonsín told the nervous crowds assembled in front of the Casa Rosada to wait for him while he went to the Campo de Mayo to meet with the rebels. Three hours later he returned to announce that the rebellion had been quelled. For once, the Argentines put aside party disputes and marched together down the Avenida de Mayo with a banner proclaiming, "THANK YOU MR. PRESIDENT."[80]

While the government proclaimed its victory it soon became clear that Colonel Rico's stand had been successful. The protracted period of inaction against the rebels was explicable only in terms of negotiations, and the rebels gained almost all they had demanded, including pay increases and modernization of equipment.[81] Even though General Héctor Rios Erenu was dismissed and the majority of the army's generals went into retirement—some for supporting the rebellion, others for not being able to control it—military trials were postponed and the law of due obedience was enacted the following June. Resistance to it was weaker than to the full stop, and the right wing of the Peronist party, as well as the smaller conservative parties, joined the

Radical party in supporting it.[82] Only the Mothers spoke out against the adoption of the law, and they were out on the streets in full force, passing out leaflets.

The law amended the due obedience clause in Law No. 23.049, according to which the presumption of innocence could be overcome. In the new law the presumption was irrefutable and no exception was made for atrocious acts. The version submitted by the president was intended to benefit everyone under the rank of colonel, though the Joint Chiefs of Staff asked the government to extend the protection to many who were generals. The House initially objected, but when the Senate version responded to the army's wishes it eventually concurred. The Supreme Court found the law constitutional, and when it was passed prosecutors were instructed to ask the courts to drop charges. The lower courts applied the law, although some expressed their disagreement. As a result, most of the defendants in the ESMA case, including Colonel Astiz, had their prosecutions terminated.[83]

When Raúl Alfonsín came to power the Mothers and the Argentine people in general had high hopes that there would be a calling to account for the horrible deeds carried out during the Dirty War. A few years later bitter resignation had set in as people realized that the army and the security forces were still important arbiters of power. The Easter Rebellion had once again proved that in Argentina violence is a semilegitimate means to attain policy goals, and that instead of moderating the goals of competing groups, the government was unable to bridge the vast gulfs separating differing interests. By the passage of the due obedience and full stop laws, the violent policies of the junta, far from being stigmatized, were now viewed as the organized product of the military government.

The Mothers were dismayed by the growing ties between the military and the democratically elected government. As they marched down the streets they carried banners proclaiming the slogan AGAINST MILITARY CIVIL AUTHORITARIANISM, thus castigating the government's complicity with the military that was so apparent in the new legislation. Not only did they insist on remaining within the political dialogue, but they also intended to retain the initiative and continue unmasking the reality of political developments. Hebe de Bonafini described the Mothers' role in the political dialogue as educational. "The Mothers are free to call out what they see happening and to repeat it again and again," she explained.[84]

The Mothers had been vigorous in their efforts to focus attention on the trials and the necessity of punishing the guilty, tirelessly pointing out that impunity was politically and socially dangerous. Eliminating the existence of culprits was also an insidious way of insisting that there were indeed no victims and thus continuing the historical obliteration of their children. Although they were not political theorists, the Mothers clearly perceived that the gap between formal democracy and actual political practice would create lowered expectations and further undermine the legitimacy of the democratic system, leading to increasing encroachment of the military. By now the Mothers' popularity had diminished, but not so their voice, which continued to raise the issue of human rights. Their new role, it seemed, would be similar to the one they had forged under the junta, a lonely, courageous, misunderstood appeal on behalf of the individual beleaguered by a system motivated more by raison d'état than by individual rights. They were self-proclaimed critics evaluating recent events against a standard that had once again become unpopular and dangerous to uphold.

Ironically, many people both at home and abroad continued to view them as a single-issue organization dedicated to finding their children and wondered why they did not cease their efforts and accept the new situation as well as their children's deaths. There was no lens through which people could perceive or understand a totally new phenomenon in Argentina—the intrusion of a group of older housewives in the political arena. The general public continued to view housewives and the aged as both powerless and socially marginal, and the substance of politics as public, not private. Because of this, it interpreted the Mothers' slogan BRING THEM BACK ALIVE literally rather than as a way of politicizing language and challenging the government. Many people believed the government's depiction of the Mothers and concluded that the women's refusal to remain in their traditional roles was indeed proof of their "craziness" and intransigence.

Once a constitutional government had been restored, however, the Mothers had no intention of retreating to their homes and to silence. They were in the Plaza to stay and had broadened their goals, demanding that justice be served. They would not achieve justice, they knew, while the very forces that were responsible for their children's *disappearances* were in place, and their powerful language reflected this perception. They now saw themselves as the opposition in a country that once again feared confronting the political equation which lay behind its constitutional structure. Their organization would continue to point out unpleasant truths to a population that historically had sought refuge in illusions and would provide radical solutions to political problems.

NOTES

1. Madres, *Boletín*, no. 19/20 (September 1984).
2. Ibid., no. 14 (February 1984).
3. Rock, *Argentina 1516–1987*, 389.
4. Poneman, *Argentina: Democracy on Trial*, 87–88.
5. Madres, *Boletín*, no. 19 (July 1984).
6. Ibid., no. 22 (October 1984).
7. Ibid., no. 19 (no date).
8. Ibid.
9. Ibid., no. 12 (December 1983).
10. Guest, *Behind the Disappearances*, 382–86.
11. Madres, *Boletín*, no. 17 (April 1984).
12. America's Watch, *Truth and Partial Justice in Argentina* (Washington, DC: America's Watch, 1987), 20–24.
13. Madres, *Boletín*, no. 15 (March 1984).
14. America's Watch, *Truth and Partial Justice*, 22–24.
15. Madres, *Boletín*, no. 19 (no date).
16. Ibid., no. 17 (no date).
17. Ibid., no. 12 (December 1983).
18. Madres, *Monthly Newspaper*, March 1985.
19. Ibid., July 1986.
20. Ibid.
21. Ibid., March 1985.
22. Madres, *Boletín*, no. 19 (no date).
23. Ibid.
24. Ibid.
25. de Pargament, interview.
26. Madres, *Monthly Newspaper*, December 1984.
27. Ibid., July 1986.
28. Ibid.
29. de Cerruti, interview.

30. de Bonafini, interview.

31. Madres, *Boletín*, no. 13 (no date).

32. Madres, *Monthly Newspaper*, March 1985.

33. de Pargament, interview.

34. "Controversia por la actitud de Bonafini," *La Razón*, March 13, 1985; "Extrañeza por la actitud de Bonafini," *Diario Popular*, March 13, 1985; "Incidente en Cementerio: Hebe de Bonafini impidió la exhumación de tres cadáveres," *Diario Cronica*, March 11, 1985; "Exhumaciones: Debate las Madres ratificaron su posición tras los sucesos de Mar del Plata," *La Voz*, March 13, 1985.

35. de Pargament, interview.

36. Madres, *Monthly Newspaper*, April 1986.

37. An interesting twist to the event has to do with Judge Pedro Hooft, who ordered the proceedings and then suspended them at the Mothers' request. The Mothers identified him as a judge who was active during the days of the junta and who had failed to investigate the death of a lawyer from La Plata when the lawyer's family came to him with a writ of *habeas corpus*. The lawyer in question was *disappeared* by the military and tortured to death in a detention center. Ibid., March 1986.

38. Ibid., April 1986.

39. de Bonafini, interview. I remember spending the night at Hebe de Bonafini's home. I slept in the living room, and because the streetlight was shining through the window, I wore an eye mask I had picked up during an overseas flight. I woke up with Hebe looking at me, saying that she was upset with the mask. I didn't understand. "Take it," I said, thinking she wanted it. "No," she answered. "My son spent months in a hood in the detention center, and it is very difficult for me to see one of those things."

40. de Petrini, interview.

41. Madres, *Monthly Newspaper*, October 1985.

42. Raymond Aron, *Peace and War: A Theory of International Relations* (New York: Doubleday, 1966), 71–93.

43. de Bonafini, interview.

44. Ibid.

45. Ibid.

46. Ibid.

47. Madres, *Boletín*, no. 13 (no date).

48. Madres, *Monthly Newspaper*, December 1984.

49. Ibid., September 1985.

50. Ibid., October 1985.

51. Ibid., September 1985.

52. Ibid., February 1985.

53. Ibid., May 1986.

54. Ibid., July 1985.

55. Héctor and Primi Mohina, *Video History of the Mothers of the Plaza de Mayo* (Buenos Aires, 1985–). Héctor Mohina is a supporter of the Mothers and an amateur filmmaker who has taken videos of all the Mothers' political activities.

56. Rock, *Argentina 1516–1987,* 400.

57. Madres, *Boletín,* no. 15 (no date).

58. America's Watch, *Truth and Partial Justice*, 31–33.

59. Madres, *Monthly Newspaper*, October 1986.

60. America's Watch, *Truth and Partial Justice*, 36–37.

61. Ibid., 40–41.

62. Ibid.

63. Ibid., 41–44.

64. Ibid.

65. Madres, *Monthly Newspaper*, January 1986.

66. Guest, *Behind the Disappearances,* 390.

67. de Pargament, interview.

68. Letter from Renée Epelbaum (Línea Fundadora) to Marguerite Bouvard, January 21, 1993.

69. Ibid.

70. Rock, *Argentina 1516–1987*, 401.

71. Guest, *Behind the Disappearances,* 390.

72. Madres, *Monthly Newspaper*, July 1986.

73. America's Watch, *Truth and Partial Justice*, 78.

74. Calvert, *Argentina: Political Culture,* 273–74.

75. America's Watch, *Truth and Partial Justice,* 63.

76. Madres, *Monthly Newspaper*, July 1986.

77. Ibid., December 1986.

78. Ibid., October 1986.

79. Ibid., June 1986.

80. Calvert, *Argentina: Political Culture,* 272–75.

81. Ibid., 276.

82. America's Watch, *Truth and Partial Justice*, 68–74.

83. Ibid., 70–74.

84. Madres, *Monthly Newspaper*, November 1987.

ETIQUETTE

for Hebe de Bonafini

When you spend the night at a Mother's house,
you must learn new rules of etiquette,
observe each object as if it were breathing.

The odd pieces of china in the cupboard
are not for tea. They are all
that's left of a son's home

after the abduction, after the police returned to pillage.
You must never wear an eyeshade
when you sleep, even if the street lamp

shines through the window.
A son of this house spent months
strapped to a chair with a hood tied over

his head. If you are served meat
for dinner, eat slowly and with reverence.
You come from a country

where only the surplus is shared.
Honor all the inhabitants of the house.
The mother talking on the telephone,

the daughter reading the newspaper in the kitchen
are not the only ones. The younger son
still gives his valedictory speech

from the graduation picture on the wall.
The older son and his wife
still lead us towards a more just world.

CHAPTER 7

Socializing Maternity

*I have one sister and she has three children.
Some time ago she asked me, "But why are you
continuing this struggle if you know that your
son is not coming back?" She thinks I am only
fighting for my son, that nothing is going to
happen to her children. So I told her, "I am
fighting for your children and for other children
also." "Why?" she countered. "My children
are not going to be involved in anything." I feel
sorry for her because she has not gone through
the process I have gone through. She still lives
only for her children, like all mothers, each
mother for her own child. So I feel sorry for her
because I have learned something. I have
socialized my maternity.*

María del Rosario de Cerruti

The Mothers' profound inner trans-
formation fueled their political activism and led them to analyze their
situations through new lenses. Because they had no previous political
education or affiliation, the analyses they made came out of their own
experience. They found a similar thread in their stories, perceiving a
pattern of lies and deception on the part of the government and those
interests such as the church that supported it. What they experienced
conflicted with the slogans offered by junta leaders and the media, and
as they began to clarify this disparity, they discovered explanations for
what had happened to their children and why it had occurred.

One of the most important changes they experienced was in their
attitudes toward their children. When their children were *disappeared*
the Mothers were unable to fathom the reasons for the tragedy. They
kept telling themselves and their friends, "My child was always so
good. How could this have happened to him?" The government-

controlled media tried to convey a completely different message and to induce a sense of guilt among the families of the *disappeared* by a barrage of slogans such as, "Do you know where your child is?" or, "How did you bring up your child?" By repeating that "they must have been mixed up in something," the government intended to create a link between political dissidence and social deviance in public opinion and to isolate the families of the *disappeared*. The church seconded this campaign; Monsignor Antonio Plaza claimed in a radio program "that there are children who are abroad and have changed their names. Their mothers, if they are truly mothers, are responsible because they agreed with this."[1]

At first, these attempts to smear the reputations of their children enraged the Mothers. Later, they concluded that the young people must indeed have been involved in something—that regardless of their varying affiliations, their children were political reformers who wished to create far-reaching social changes. In Argentina any thought of social change smacked of left-wing activity and revolution. Despite Juan Perón's efforts to incorporate the working class into the nation, society remained divided and burdened by a large, poverty-stricken population. Most Argentines were not troubled by this, but many of the *disappeared*, whether they were Peronists, Socialists, followers of the Third World church, or simply apolitical, were dedicated to improving the lot of the poor. The Mothers' discovery of the true nature of their children's activity brought them to a new level of political awareness, and they began to penetrate the kind of regime they were up against.

The young adults who were *disappeared* were different from their counterparts in democratic countries. First of all, in Argentina people marry at a much earlier age than in some other countries; it is not unusual for a couple in their early twenties to have been married for three or four years and to have two children. Moreover, youths in Argentina often become politically active in high school. While their U.S. counterparts are absorbed in sports and dating, high-school students in Argentina frequently become active Peronists, Socialists, Communists, or members of the Youth Group of the Radical party. Not all teenagers are so engaged but many of the Mothers' children were, and they had a number of traits in common that were more important to the Mothers than their differing political affiliations. Like the youths who work for the Mothers' organization today putting in long hours after work or school, they placed their social goals above their personal lives and pursued them with a missionary zeal, which is what it means to be an activist or a militant. The Mothers' descriptions of their *disappeared* children are of people who combined work or studies and parenting with a tireless activism.

The Mothers' stories of their children typically center around a person who had revealed a passion for justice at a very early age and who thereby had distinguished himself or herself from the other siblings. The Third World church and Liberation Theology, which stresses the importance of liberation in this life as well as the next, attracted many who wished to improve the lot of the poor. Members of the Third World church were considered dangerous revolutionaries by the government because of their use of Marxist terminology, and indeed some of these people often considered themselves proponents of social revolution. A number of the *disappeared* children were involved in that church and spent all of their free time after school or work teaching catechism in the slums and working with youngsters. I heard countless stories about a son or daughter who brought food and clothes to shantytowns and took an active part in helping people there. Some of the *disappeared* were doctors, like Juana de Pargament's son, or lawyers, like Josefa Donato de Pauvi's son, who gave their services freely to those unable to pay. A number were members of the Socialist or Peronist parties, such as Elsa de Mansotti's son Daniel Aldo and his wife. Many of them had no political affiliations but were strongly motivated to improve the lot of the forgotten and the misunderstood. Over and over again I heard statements such as "His one fault was worrying about other people. He was always asking me to gather together clothes I didn't use because there were so many people without even enough to eat."[2] One after another the Mothers told me that the government had taken away the best child, the one who had always cared for others.

María del Rosario de Cerruti's son is representative of the young adults who were *disappeared*. As a teenager, he distinguished himself in the family by guiding his younger brother and settling disputes among his friends. Before he was *disappeared* he studied economics and worked for a company that manufactured auto parts. When he was given a raise after a year, he complained to his manager that he had received the raise instead of his coworker, who had three children and had been there for seventeen years. He quit and became a union activist in a bottling company, where he persuaded the management to give workers gloves so that they would not cut their hands on the bottle tops. After the military abducted him, his boss told his mother that he had never had such an exceptional worker.[3]

When these children were still at home the Mothers fretted about their activity and their lack of attention to their own interests. After they were abducted by the military the Mothers began to understand that it was their social concerns which had earned them their cruel fate. This sensitized them to the economic problems in the country and would inspire them to become activists themselves. "Our children begot us," they claim. "You stop being a conventional mother when you give birth to children who think and work for something beyond their narrow personal goals."[4]

As the traditional family was torn apart by state terrorism, the Mothers reinvented the concept of family in the unique blend of public and private that characterized their political style. Each family with *disappeared* offspring became subjected to severe strains in the aftermath of the tragedy. Some husbands were supportive as their wives went out to march in the Plaza de Mayo, but several marriages broke up because of different reactions to the *disappearances*. A number of Mothers were politically active in the organization while their own parents stayed home, weeping, praying, or pretending that nothing had happened. Many family members kept away from the Mothers out of fear, and families separated into those who were political activists and those who maintained their distance.

The transformation of the Mothers' view of maternity occurred gradually as they confronted their shattered family lives, especially the problems faced by the siblings and the children of the *disappeared*. Forced to deal with the sudden and brutal absence of a brother or sister, siblings essentially lost their childhood. Their mothers were marching, their fathers were working, and they were often left alone or with a relative. Older children frequently became the caretakers of the home and younger siblings. While their mothers' activism provided examples of strength that would ultimately inspire many of them, these youngsters lost their innocence and security. Some of the children of the *disappeared* witnessed the brutal beatings of their parents, and a number were dragged away with them, the lucky ones left with neighbors.[5] All the siblings and children of the *disappeared* live in the long shadow of absence, the crimes that caused it, and the silence and complicity that accompanied it. When they were young the shadow often manifested itself in a fear of adults, an inability to concentrate at school, and excessive shyness. They were thrust into reality too quickly, and the truth they had experienced often set them apart from their friends.

Hebe de Bonafini's daughter, Alejandra, recalls that during the period from 1978 to 1982 she experienced the *disappearances* of her two brothers as well as the loss of two uncles, her grandfather, her paternal grandmother, and her father. At school she was persecuted by teachers who treated her with cruelty, and she remembers the repressive atmosphere in the country. "It was hard to have friends because you had to be on guard all the time," she recalls, "watching what you said, to whom you said it, watching what you did and who saw you do it, always watching everything. It was easier not to talk and to shut yourself in so you didn't hear anything."[6] She remembers bouts with depression and insomnia when she would sit up all night drinking maté, the bitter Argentine tea. She still experiences panic when confronted with tense, risky, or frightening situations and is in therapy to overcome her paralysis in fearful situations and her periods of irritability and anger. Alejandra has difficulty listening to American songs because her brothers tried to teach her English through the lyrics of popular songs. Deeply attached to her mother, she knows that if anything happens to Hebe her last link with her immediate family would be severed.

A number of children were abandoned or brought to police stations after both parents were *disappeared*. In some cases they were reunited with their grandparents because a grandfather was a well-known professional—a doctor or a lawyer—and had some influence. They were fortunate because they escaped adoption by accomplices of the junta. The Mothers who had custody of their grandchildren educated them about what had occurred and included them in their political activities. Many of these youngsters began to march with the Mothers as they reached adolescence. Arturo de Pratti, one of the lucky ones, was brought to a police station after his parents were *disappeared* when he was six months old. His grandfather, who had influence and was able to find Arturo, is raising him. His grandparents have told him the truth about his parents, and Arturo spends time with the Mothers, marching with them, visiting their office, and even living with Hebe de Bonafini for a time. He told me that he was part of a group of young people who have suffered. "I have two friends whose parents also were *disappeared*, and others who have separated parents," Arturo explained. "We are all very close because we understand each other." Like the other children the Mothers have taken in, Arturo is drawn to the photographs of his parents on the walls of the Mothers' office. Although he is only thirteen years old he told me, "We are going to continue their struggle, and we will never forget them, as the Mothers say, and in this way, will move forward."[7]

From the beginning the Mothers have welcomed these children into their office and provided special activities for them. They started a fund to send them to summer camp, sent gifts to them on Christmas, and formed a group to provide them with social, medical, and educational assistance. The younger siblings of the *disappeared* also have found refuge and an extended family in the Mothers' organization. The Mothers have begun to see each other's children and grandchildren as belonging to all of them. They learned this lesson from Esther Balestrina de Creaga, one of the women abducted at the Church of Santa Cruz in December 1977. Her pregnant daughter had been *disappeared* but eventually was released. Esther sent her daughter out of the country for her safety, but she herself returned to the Plaza to march with the Mothers, telling them, "It's useless to fight for only one child. We have to continue to fight for all the children." Likewise, in 1978 the group of twenty Mothers who formed the first commission received an offer from the government to free as many as twenty *detained-disappeareds*. Some of the Mothers responded to the blackmail and sent money, but the majority refused on the basis that their goal was to see all the children alive, not just their own child.[8]

In the beginning each mother embroidered her pañuelo with the name or names of her *disappeared* children and the dates they were *disappeared*. The Mothers also carried huge posters with enlarged photographs of their offspring. In 1984 when they adopted the slogan BRING THEM BACK ALIVE, however, they replaced the embroidered names with only the slogan. Some Mothers who were not able to take that step left the organization but continued to return to the Plaza with photographs of their children.

The Mothers were realizing that their struggle was a common one, and as part of their growing social awareness and burgeoning solidarity they stopped talking about their personal tragedies because they felt to do so was overly individualistic. Many of them found that their previous lives, centered on concern for their families, were overly self-absorbed and had prevented them from looking at larger social issues. As they examined these problems they came to believe that only a collectivist solution would solve social and economic inequities. They began referring to each other as *Mother* and to themselves collectively as *Mothers*, a manner of address that was politically charged. They were comrades in a dangerous struggle and as such their ties ran deeper than mere membership in an organization.

As the bonds they forged among themselves strengthened, the Mothers came to include in their new view of maternity not just their *disappeared* children but all the present and future youths of Argentina. "The child of one is the child of all of us, not only those who are missing, but the ones who are fighting for their rights today," they claimed. "We learned this from our guts, not from philosophic concepts."[9] The change from fighting for the return of one's child to regarding everyone's offspring as one's own was a tremendous leap, not necessarily an extension of maternity. Around the world mothers also identify with their communities, cultures, and religions, and these identifications may place them at odds with other mothers. The Mothers of the Plaza de Mayo publicly announced their sympathetic concern for all the children of the nation and of victims everywhere, standing against those in power on behalf of the restoration of a just community. They thus embraced political concepts that were fundamentally at variance not only with those promoted by the junta but also with those of governments to follow.

In reinterpreting maternity the Mothers fought the values and discourse of the military and of authoritarian politics by using symbols that contrasted life and the integrity of the family with the control, coercion, and annihilation practiced by the government. The pañuelo is one of the Mothers' most striking nonviolent weapons. Under the junta the Mothers put up banners of their baby shawls during church services and in public squares to serve as searing reminders that the family that the regime claimed to protect had been brutally sundered. Today, the Mothers use the pañuelo to dramatize that connectedness and hope are primary factors in human life and the proper starting points of political systems. They frequently tie their shawls together to create a protective cordon around their young helpers, keeping the police at bay. In 1987, on the tenth anniversary of the pañuelo, hundreds of streamers made of baby shawls fluttered in the Plaza de Mayo while loudspeakers blared a song about the white scarves written by the popular Argentine singer Teresa Parodi. When Hebe de Bonafini was brought to court on charges of defaming the president in June 1991, the presiding judge demanded that she remove her pañuelo. As in the 1986 trial she refused, not only because her scarf serves as a symbol of love and unity but also because, as Hebe explained, "the pañuelo continues to be the condemnation of torture, rape, theft, and assassination in this country."[10]

Images of the pañuelo and of the pregnant woman are immensely powerful, conjuring up the exposed and vulnerable body as well as the intimate knowledge of our beginnings. When Hebe de Bonafini claims, "His absence has left me permanently pregnant," and, "If they are no longer, I have had to be them, to shout for them, to return them," she proclaims the presence of the *disappeared* children to a country that wishes to conceal them as well as the Mothers' role of caring. The image of pregnancy is a stark reminder of the state's brutal interruption of maternal tasks.[11]

Philosopher Sara Ruddick sees in the celebration of birthing the beginnings of antimilitarist, maternal thinking. Thrusting the pregnant body into the center of the political arena is meant to undermine the very basis of militaristic thinking, which emphasizes death as well as the dichotomy between reason—signifying control, autonomy, and the mind—and the body—signifying passion, lack of control, and femininity.[12] Although the dichotomy is an abstraction it has been used throughout history to justify the arrangement of political and social power. The body defined by reason becomes a mere instrument of military will; soldiers are trained to mold their flesh in authority's image. The maternal thinking represented by the image of pregnancy and birthing provides an antimilitaristic conception of the body, immediate in its joys and sufferings, signifying life and new beginnings. The pregnancy heralded by the Mothers in the public arena is an image of connection, their message that bodies are as important as the causes which use them. From their very beginnings the Mothers proclaimed in their slogan FOR LIFE the significance of the body against the government and the military who seek to destroy it. To a country that had drowned in the eroticism and sadism of violence in its detention centers, the Mothers presented the promise of maternity. "We are aware that before everything comes the defense of life."[13]

Hebe de Bonafini is the Mother who most forcefully articulates the concept of being permanently pregnant. While her son Rául was in La Cacha he wrote a poem for her on the lining of his jacket. A young pregnant woman in the same cell, who was released on the condition that she speak to no one about her experience, managed to visit Hebe in 1980 and give her Rául's poem, which is in the voice of a child in his mother's womb. Since that time Hebe has said she feels her children have left her pregnant forever. "It is a strange thing," she explains. "On the one hand, I feel that one day, they will return or they will enter the government building. One of my children, not Rául or Jorge, but one of the others who are growing up in the struggle. On the other hand, I feel this state of permanent pregnancy. I always feel my children inside me. Often it seems as if we are thinking about the same things. This gives me much strength and makes me feel that my life is being used for the gestation of a new person."[14] The Mothers have turned the sequence of generations upside down by claiming that their children live through them. While many of the children of the *disappeared* speak of taking up their parents' causes, the Mothers have inverted maternity by taking on their offspring's mantle. The Mothers' organization has also transformed the role of pregnancy, infusing it with eschatological meaning.

Today, the Mothers continue to speak of giving multiple births, of creating offspring who will continue the revolution their children have initiated, which is at once political, social, and humanitarian. A May 1990 editorial in their newspaper proclaimed, "Last Thursday, the Mothers in the Plaza felt as if they were giving birth again because of all the Latin American children who were present meeting with Argentine youth. Those young Argentines who march with us are the new children we are giving birth to. After thirteen years, the Mothers are giving multiple births."[15]

A number of feminists, such as María del Carmen Feijóo of Argentina, have criticized the Mothers for their stand on maternity because they feel it locks women into a traditional, marginalized, and passive role. She claims that "analytically, a defense of human rights based on women's reproductive roles reinforces the conventional sexual division of labor."[16] The Mothers have subverted the concept of motherhood as merely biological, however, and stepped out of their roles as passive and private persons. In so doing they also challenged the conservative Catholic heritage that provided support for the political system. "The Mothers of the Plaza de Mayo pervert the role of the mother," an army captain criticized. "I can't imagine the Virgin Mary shouting, protesting, spreading hatred when her son, our God, was snatched from her arms."[17] These Mothers neither weep nor turn the other cheek nor retreat before physical danger.

This transformation is all the more significant because the majority of the Mothers come from the working class rather than from the privileged classes, where women have enjoyed more freedom and have been able to penetrate previously all-male professions. Writers on women's resistance have noted that class and ethnicity intersect with gender in shaping action. In the Mothers' case, their class origins set them apart from the system and hence gave them a perspective from which to develop new modes of political action.[18] They entered the political arena as a collectivity, refusing to be co-opted into the prevailing values and power structure. The Mothers prize their hard-won autonomy, rejecting the culture of obedience and hierarchy upheld by the church and the cult of *marianismo*, which complements the cult of *machismo* in Argentina. As the secular expression of the homage rendered to the Virgin Mary, *marianismo* holds the woman as morally superior to the man on the basis of her humility and self-sacrifice. In popular culture she is portrayed as a grieving woman, draped in a black mantilla and praying for the souls of her sinful menfolk to whom she is nonetheless submissive.[19] The Mothers do not need feminist theory to understand how the traditional female role reinforces a repressive system. They have refused to mourn or weep for their children because they have concluded that such behavior helps the government dominate them by absorbing the energy that should be used for political struggle. The Mothers do not wish to be seen as grieving women—they are fighters. When a gathering of women from different political parties celebrated the Mothers' organization after the fall of the junta, the Mothers responded, "We want to say that finally we feel that the Argentine woman has woken up from the lethargy that the terror has plunged her in."[20]

After the junta fell the Mothers also took up the cause of thousands of political prisoners who were jailed under it. They infused their political activity with their more private acts, claiming that they were "Mothers of all the oppressed" while, for example, bringing specially cooked meals to the prisoners over the holidays.[21] From the very beginning, the Mothers combined love with anger: love for those on whose behalf they were fighting, anger toward a system that permitted such brutality. The Mothers have added to the traditional role of nurturing the concept of empowering—raising the political consciousness of young people and inspiring them to activism. They began holding their own celebration on Mother's Day, which takes place on November 18 in Argentina. Their festivity occurs in the square as a counter to both the commercialization of Mother's Day and its celebration of the traditional, politically quiescent woman. In a Mother's Day speech one of their young supporters claimed, "The courage of the Mothers of the Plaza de Mayo shows us a road that is neither easy nor comfortable. It is dignified, and life has no meaning without dignity, without justice, without liberty, and without love. The Mothers have shown us that to live is to struggle and to struggle is to dream."[22]

When they became active the Mothers worked for continuity and consistency between their private and public lives. That in itself was a drastic change, because throughout history many political reformers have behaved in an authoritarian way in their homes, and many feminists have gone to the barricades while neglecting the rights of their household help. The Mothers claim political space and radical goals while maintaining the more traditional values of caring that come from the household; they continue to insist upon their identities as housewives and Mothers. Humanizing political behavior is an important thread in the changes they seek to bring about.

The way the Mothers respond to the many groups and individuals who come to their office for help is an expression of their unique version of mothering. When I was with them in November 1990, a young woman burst into their office holding her baby and weeping

The Mothers celebrate Mother's Day in the Plaza de Mayo (*photo by Rafael Calviño*)

with rage and fear. The Mothers gathered around her, trying to make her comfortable, bringing her something to eat. One of them tended the baby as they listened to her account of how policemen beat her husband and then dragged him away from their home in the middle of the night. Because the young man was a former *disappeared* and a member of a leftist group working for social reform, he was vulnerable to the police's practice, since the late 1980s, of harassing and *disappearing* radical youths and adults for periods of time. After expressing their concern the Mothers took the young woman to the Plaza de Mayo, introduced her to the crowds, and put her before a microphone so that she could denounce what had happened. They enlisted the help of their team of lawyers to secure the release of her husband, but they also wanted her to express her outrage openly. As a result of the Mothers' efforts the young man reappeared in the Plaza with his family the following week, the burn marks over his arms and neck revealing the torture he had endured. The Mothers concluded that he might be a likely candidate for assassination by the police, but they insisted on the importance of fighting back. What they wish to transmit to future generations are not their own political ideas but the notion that each one of us must assume responsibility for our political destiny. "All the children are ours," they told me. "We teach them to defend their rights, to demand them and exercise them. We feed them with love, wash them with the Plaza, love them by showing them a path toward struggle and liberty. We teach them that the struggle for life, justice, and liberty begins every morning when you wake up, open the curtains, and look at the sun."[23]

Many feminist commentators who have criticized the Mothers for clinging to maternal images have perceived neither their transformation of maternity nor their roles as revolutionary women. Some have charged the Mothers with continuing to support patriarchal authority and a state responsible for gender discrimination, failing to differentiate them from women such as Eva Perón or Corazon Aquino, who have projected the traditional image of motherhood into the political arena and helped perpetuate the authoritarian state while they wielded power. The Mothers are not interested in eliminating maternity as gender identification, but rather in creating a political role for the values of love and the caring work associated with maternity. They have redefined the private and public spheres and sought to create a political space where the two combine in their organization and political agenda. As such they have transformed themselves from women seeking to protect the sanctity of the mother-child bond within the existing political system to women wishing to transform the state so that it reflects maternal values. While retaining the traditional expectations of femininity, such as motherhood, they have also transformed them by refusing to support a destructive nationalism or to express denial. This transformation has eluded many of their critics, who have not recognized how the Mothers' politics undermine militaristic thinking.

An even more misunderstood stance is the Mothers' unique organizational and political style. The Mothers run their association as a direct democracy, refusing to model it on either political parties or more traditional interest groups. This has prompted critics to claim that they lack organizational sophistication and are therefore unable to participate in a meaningful way in the constitutional government.[24] The Mothers are not interested in bargaining and negotiating in the traditional manner because they do not wish to participate in a state system that they view as inherently corrupt. Far from being ineffectual and irrelevant, they are frequently called upon to help various neighborhood and labor groups organize themselves. They have met with railroad workers and sanitation workers, with teachers and pensioners, with a myriad of different groups across the country who have felt that neither the unions nor the political parties they belonged to represented them. The women have approached this work as Mothers and as anarchists, seeking to guide others toward independence and effectiveness rather than to impose their own ideas. "Our main work is to awaken people's consciousness and show them how they can be free," they explain. "We don't believe in people who are going to work for the grass roots; the grass roots knows what it wants. They might need support, a workshop or a lecture. We want people to make their own cooperative. We guide those people who go out to the street, who demand, who want change. We let them know that first we mobilized ourselves, but that after we organized ourselves, which is the opposite of the political parties which organized themselves before they mobilized."[25]

This attitude is a reflection of the work of mothering, which combines nurture with preparation for separation. Because sheltering their children proved both dangerous and counterproductive, the Mothers' vision of maternity became one of mentoring rather than protecting. A revolutionary Mother instructs her children and all who come to her for support in the ways of political power. In Argentina, political mentoring has been reserved for fathers who either groom their upper-class sons for positions of power or their working-class offspring toward militancy. In both cases daughters have been excluded from power and participation. But the Mothers have no intention of leaving women out of the equation; they envision their children, both male and female, assuming power on behalf of all the dispossessed.

While Mothers maintain the traditional concept of maternity, they have infused it with new content. They believe that they must not only be politically active but also willing to go to the barricades and risk their lives in order to achieve a just community. "A Mother of the Plaza de Mayo goes wherever the action is despite the fact that she may be beaten. She confronts the policeman's nightstick and rifle, saying, 'I'm not moving from here,' and is permanently working, giving, participating, marking a path for youth, overcoming fear and confronting the enemy."[26] An important trait of a revolutionary Mother is her solidarity with her coworkers and with the people. Hebe de Bonafini projected this image when she spoke in the Plaza in the fall of 1990, calling for the creation of a new reality. "They say that to dream alone is only a dream, but to dream with others is revolutionary. I feel like a revolutionary Mother, a fighting Mother every day, resisting and combating."[27]

Giving with love is the other side of the revolutionary Mother and constitutes an important part of the Mothers' maternal vision. The feminists in Argentina criticize the Mothers on these grounds, claiming that they perpetuate the concept of the self-sacrificing woman. The Mothers, however, are not engaging in self-denial but in an attentive caring that recognizes the *other* and lets that person be, with all his or her differences. Such a perspective stems from a position of strength and self-confidence rather than from a feeling of emptiness and renunciation. The Mothers consider caring an essential trait of a new political activism and see no inconsistency between their identities as housewives and as politically active women. They devote as much of themselves to their political activity as the leaders engaged in the political system, and yet that effort is suffused with traits of the private sphere. The revolution they are seeking to wage is a humanistic one; they attempt to infuse their political work with love and respect for the person. As such, their movement is clearly in the Gandhian tradition, which also sought to conduct politics with values from other spheres. One cannot help but feel that because the private sphere has been scorned by men for centuries—and recently by some feminists—as the source of powerlessness and marginalization, the values emerging from the home are suspect. But the Mothers' values have begun to speak to others. "We have even managed to make men see things the way we do," María del Rosario de Cerruti proclaims. "We have men working with us who feel the way we feel. So it isn't a feminine thing; we have stimulated a love for others, and it was our children who brought this about."[28]

The Mothers' emphasis on the continuing relevance of the private sphere indeed sets them apart from the many feminist groups in Argentina, who are primarily middle class and who seek to redefine themselves outside of that sphere and to claim space in the arena of work and political parties. Some feminist writers see the public and private spheres as interconnected, reverberating upon one another. Martha Ackelsberg has observed that in the United States working-class women have entered the public arena not as individuals but as members of households and of communities, and that they often view politics as a means of linking the concerns and perspectives they share with their neighbors to those of the state.[29] Notably, the women's group that consistently accompanies the Mothers on their marches is the National Movement of Housewives, created in 1982 as an urban protest to cost-of-living increases and poverty. Like the Mothers they have achieved their political consciousness by making connections between the issues that personally affect them and public policies. As they have sought to overcome the fragmentation of the private/public spheres, they have distanced themselves from political parties and created their own style.

The Mothers regularly participate in the yearly national women's conferences in Argentina, though always under the banner of their struggle for human rights. Often their stands on political issues, especially against the military and police, are incorporated in the final statements of these gatherings. They are also yearly recipients of awards from the Alicia Moreau de Justo Foundation, which continues the work of the Socialist Feminist Center de Justo, founded in the early 1900s. While the Mothers are frequent guests on women's programs aired on radio or cable television, they view these appearances as opportunities to promote their political goals.

The Mothers are uncomfortable with some of the feminist organizations in Argentina because they see them as representing privileged circles: "We believe in women's struggle, but not in the women who have another woman cleaning their floors," they state.[30] While they support women's rights they are uninterested in promoting change that would unravel women from their maternal role. In Argentina as in other countries, many women who have joined feminist groups and worked toward feminist goals have done so as a result of their educational, professional, or work involvement. The Mothers' experience was telescoped as they were catapulted from the home or socially ascribed work into the battlefield against a dangerous authoritarian regime. They did not have the luxury of an education or of time in which to awaken their political consciousness. As a result, their perspectives are similar to those of women who joined the Resistance against Nazi occupation in Europe during World War II, or of oppressed minorities for whom gender takes second place to freedom for the community as a whole. In the Mothers' eyes the task of creating a new society requires the participation of both sexes. Their male and female children's political activism is a more potent factor in their motivation than the feminists' task of transforming views of gender.

Because they see themselves primarily as activists and have populist aims, the Mothers also are uncomfortable with theoretical descriptions of their work. When, in a television interview in Spain, she was queried about her role as a housewife-turned-leader, Hebe de Bonafini replied that she was still a housewife but also a person who chose life over death when confronted with the *disappearance* of her children, a person happy and fulfilled in her political work.[31] The Mothers see no contradictions between these roles because they have combined them successfully in their own lives. Their political activism is rooted in the concrete maternal thinking that arises from the complexities of their intertwined lives and continually changing situations. As such, it is much more passionately engaged than militaristic thinking, which imagines a truth abstracted from the body and a self divorced from feeling.

Revolutionizing and socializing maternity is a powerful political concept; it threatens the very basis of the Argentine state and its oligarchic foundations, its reliance on the military, and its perpetuation of class divisions. In promoting this new reality the Mothers challenge Argentine culture and contemporary realities, demanding a state that will both reflect and enhance the private sphere. The Mothers are not unaware of the issues of gender, but they regard those issues, with the eyes of thorough revolutionaries, on the level of the political system and the world arena. They want to change the way nations are governed—their emphasis on weapons and military preparedness at the expense of social policy. In the words of María del Rosario de Cerruti, the editor of the Mothers' newspaper, "There is a paternal style of politics. They improve the lot of the needy to gain power. That is what Hitler and Mussolini did, give the poor some benefits so that they could dominate the people and kill whoever disagreed with them. It is the same here; the government is corrupt, it wheels and deals and oppresses the people."[32] Maternal politics, on the other hand, envisions a just society with health, education, work, and shelter available to everyone. It regards maternity as an extremely important role, viewing it as a new form of political participation rather than an obstacle to such involvement. Far from being passive, the work of caring is vigorous, politically active, and open to both sexes.

In a unique transformation of the bonding that occurs in the home, Hebe de Bonafini opened up the Mothers' ninth march of resistance in celebration of Human Rights Day with her mother and her daughter on either side of her. The Mothers have given that bonding political significance, and they demand that the government acknowledge it as a factor in the equation of power.

NOTES

1. de Cerruti, interview.

2. Susanna de Gudano, interview by Marguerite Bouvard, November 1990; Aurora Alonzo, interview by Marguerite Bouvard, November 1990.

3. de Cerruti, interview.

4. Madres, *Monthly Newspaper*, January 1988.

5. Madres, *Boletín*, nos. 14, 15 (February, March 1984).

6. Alejandra de Bonafini, interview by Marguerite Bovard, November 1990.

7. Arturo de Pratti, interview by Marguerite Bouvard, November 1990.

8. de Cerruti, interview.

9. Madres, *Monthly Newspaper*, May 1988.

10. Ibid., June 1991.

11. Ibid., November 1986.

12. Sara Ruddick, *Maternal Thinking: Toward a Politics of Peace* (Boston: Beacon Press, 1989), 141–59.

13. Madres, *Monthly Newspaper*, April 1988.

14. Ibid., November 1986.

15. Ibid., May 1990.

16. María del Carmen Feijoó, "The Challenge of Constructing Civilian Peace: Women and Democracy in Argentina," in *The Women's Movement in Latin America*, ed. Jane S. Jaquette (Boston: Unwin Hyman, 1989), 88.

17. Madres, *Monthly Newspaper*, May 1988.

18. Martha A. Ackelsberg, "Communities, Resistance, and Women's Activism: Some Implications for a Democratic Polity," in *Women and the Politics of Empowerment*, ed. Ann Bookman and Sandra Morgan (Philadelphia: Temple University Press, 1988), 297–313.

19. Evelyn P. Stevens, "Marianismo: The Other Face of Machismo in Latin America," in *Female and Male in Latin America*, ed. Ann Pescatello (Pittsburgh: University of Pittsburgh Press, 1973), 91–101.

20. Madres, *Boletín*, no. 17 (no date).

21. Ibid., no. 9 (no date).

22. Madres, *Monthly Newspaper*, November 1990.

23. Ibid., April 1988.

24. Feijoó, "The Challenge of Constructing Civilian Peace," 84.

25. de Bonafini, interview.

26. Alejandro Diago, *Hebe de Bonafini: Memoria y esperanza* (Buenos Aires: Ediciones Dialectica, 1988), 168.

27. Madres, *Monthly Newspaper*, March 1991.

28. de Cerruti, interview.

29. Ackelsberg, "Communities, Resistance, and Women's Activism," 299.

30. de Bonafini, interview.

31. Madres, *Monthly Newspaper*, March 1991.

32. de Cerruti, interview.

EXHUMING THE FACTS

You have read about the uprising
at La Tablada in your own newspapers,
how a group of left-wing citizens stormed
a military barracks. Like everyone else
you didn't pause before the anomaly,
the absurdity of the equation. In Buenos Aires,
you exhume the facts through tangled
and malodorous layers. Even the bodies deny their own facts:
the fingers have been cut off
to obliterate prints. You query
the human-rights lawyers, the foreign journalists,
the stunned families of the prisoners
who came to the Mothers for help.
Who called that meeting to gather people
in order to defy an allegedly, *planned military revolt*?
The Mothers left that gathering in haste
because of a familiar smell. The planning
for the *attack on the barracks* moved with deliberate
speed. Arms appeared from nowhere.
The lawyers and the priests, the indignant
students proceeded with an inexplicable
efficiency. They surged forward
with unseeing eyes. The barracks
were more than prepared. Who sent the napalm
and the helicopters? Who photographed the tanks
ramming the barracks, who wrote the script?

CHAPTER 8

Revolutionary Mothers

We realize that to demand the fulfillment of human rights is a revolutionary act, that to question the government about bringing our children back alive was a revolutionary act. We are fighting for liberation, to live in freedom, and that is a revolutionary act. The day in which there will be no more hunger, that justice will be done, that the murderers will be in jail, then we will have accomplished a revolution. To transform a system is always revolutionary.

Mothers of the Plaza de Mayo

In the last years of Raúl Alfonsín's presidency the Mothers became self-proclaimed revolutionaries. They were immensely frustrated not only with the system's inability to deal with the problems of the military but also with the overwhelming economic difficulties that resulted from the junta's disastrous policies and then continued to plague the Alfonsín government. Outraged by the government's program, which was applauded abroad for bringing Argentina closer to recovery but which at home created increasing misery among the poor and the dispossessed, they chose the route that many Argentines had taken throughout history: they sought redress by attacking the system itself.

The Mothers' revolutionary fervor was fed by a number of sources. Perhaps most important, they were influenced by the Argentine political culture's lack of emphasis on compromise and its propensity for seeking change by transforming the political system. Having failed in their attempts to have an impact on the political parties within the Congress, they now believed that the parties' chief concern—the squabbles among themselves—had rendered them ineffective in solving the economic and political problems facing the country. The Mothers thus chose to operate outside of the party system, deciding to work toward their goals with the techniques of spontaneity and direct action they had adopted from their early years. "We are transgressors," they claimed. "We are revolutionaries because we don't accept things so easily. We are carrying on a different kind of revolution, of women with a different point of view who do not hide. We do everything completely the opposite way."[1]

Many people who supported the political parties and considered them avenues toward reform were alienated by the Mothers' confrontational political style. The Mothers, though, felt it was still necessary to confront in order to point out the truth about the political system as well as to educate and empower their friends and would-be followers. They could not adopt a temperate tone because their goals were non-negotiable. Bishop Kurt Scharf, a former member of the Resistance against the Hitler regime in Germany, commented about the Mothers that "people come to me and complain that the Mothers are too radicalized and I answer, 'How many imprisoned children have they found? The fate of how many disappeared have they clarified? Was Captain Astiz condemned and the perpetrators of the kidnapping condemned?' They should continue becoming radicalized."[2]

The Mothers' uncompromising stand was also influenced by their religious convictions. Although most of them had left the Catholic church because of its behavior during the Dirty War, they nevertheless clung to the tenets of Christianity, viewing their politics as rooted in nonviolence and in the practice of the Christian principles of love, charity, and brotherhood. If anything, their organization and practices reflected the message of collectivism and equality in the Sermon on the Mount and the principles of the Third World church that so many of their children espoused. María del Rosario de Cerruti explained the Mothers' position this way: "One day, a priest was saying at one of our roundtable discussions, 'I am a Catholic priest and yet they tell me that I am mixed up in communism. If what I do is Communist, then I am a Communist,' and I replied, I don't know if what you do is communism but if being Communist means doing what Christ said, that you should do unto others as you would have them do unto you, I want to fulfill this principle."[3] The Mothers presented not only new modes of being but also an alternative political style based upon equality and mutual respect—a revolutionary idea. Although they were criticized for not working within the established structures, they believed that working outside of them was advantageous. It gave them a greater perspective on political reality within Argentina and helped them view their organization as a way of life that would ultimately lead to a better political system, ensuring broad citizen participation both at the national level and the grass roots.

Yet another impetus toward radicalization came from their support group of young people, the Front for Human Rights, which began to accompany them when constitutional government was reestablished. The group was formally organized in 1985 to support the work of human-rights organizations, including the Grandmothers of the Plaza de Mayo and the Families of the Disappeared, in addition to the Mothers. Establishing branches in many of the provinces where the Mothers have affiliates, in 1987 it began holding yearly conferences to coordinate its efforts.

There is an element of irony and perhaps tragedy in the Mothers' link with the Front for Human Rights. From the time they first gathered at the Plaza the Mothers have insisted on their autonomy from political parties and groups. Even though they had no political experience, they understood that by tying themselves with other human-rights groups they might be used, their goals compromised. The Mothers felt protected from any such betrayal of their trust and principles by a rule they had established, which stated that any young adult wishing to join the support group be free of political affiliation. Each prospective member was required to undergo a trial period of six months to demonstrate both commitment to the Mothers' cause and a lack of political ties or links to the omnipresent security forces. In the early years after the restoration of constitutional government a few of the young people were found to have connections with the police and were asked to leave the Front. Yet, the Mothers are unable to perceive the actual nature of the Front for Human Rights. Its sophisticated young members voice support for the Mothers and uniformly repeat their slogans while pursuing their own agenda of creating a Cuban-style revolution in Argentina.[4] During my interviews with the Front's members, they told me they had joined the group because of its revolutionary potential and that they supported the Cuban model, all the while insisting upon their lack of political affiliation.

Because the Mothers regard their support group as their future and as an affirmation of the continuing relevance of their movement, they have refused to see the Front's political affiliation, brushing aside those who would point them out with, "They are young, they'll learn."[5] These young and not-so-young adults, some of whom are in their late thirties and mid-forties, fill the emptiness left by their *disappeared* children. They have capitalized on the women's affection, frequently bringing their own children to the Mothers' office. Over the years they have sought to insinuate Leninist principles into the Mothers' discourse and perspectives and were instrumental in arranging their visit to Cuba in 1988. Welcomed there with carefully orchestrated enthusiasm, the Mothers remained oblivious to the human-rights problems and political repression in that country. Subsequently, their newspapers gushed with images of rifle-toting, revolutionary fighters from Cuba and articles in praise of Fidel Castro.

Given the government's increasing pressure on the Mothers and their alienation from traditional political interests, the influence of these young people is considerable. They meet at the Mothers' office twice a week from 5 to 10 P.M., printing pamphlets, designing press releases, and making the banners the women carry during their demonstrations. Because of the media blackout on the Mothers, flyers are important ways of announcing upcoming events and clarifying the Mothers' political stances. Members of the Front are also important participants in demonstrations and marches, surrounding the Mothers with linked hands to protect them from assaults. In the early 1990s some of them were admitted to the Mothers' weekly commission meetings, where policy issues are discussed. The Mothers have failed to perceive not only their young supporters' ulterior motives but also the divergence of their political methods and goals from those of the Mothers' organization. Ironically, the Mothers are keenly aware of the Communist membership of the Latin American Federation of the Families of the Disappeared and have been outraged by that group's attempt to capitalize on their reputation.

While many people in Argentina claim that the Mothers have been co-opted by the Communists and the far left, the reality is more complex. The Mothers are clearly on the left of the political spectrum but the substance of their revolutionary vision is neither Communist nor that of the Cuban model, despite the efforts of their support group. Their travels abroad have sensitized them to repressive regimes such as those in North Korea and Eastern Europe before the fall of communism and have introduced them as well to the achievements of capitalistic welfare states such as Sweden and France. As a result, they envision a socialist system free of the domination of special interests. "Revolutions are changes," the Mothers believe. "There was a dictatorship and then a constitutional government took power, yet the same system continues intact, the same corruption continues, the regime is supported by the same military people who ruled before them. We want a change. Why can't it be a popular party of the masses that governs? We want a party that represents the people, not the class with power."[6]

The Mothers challenged not only the current political system but also the Argentine political culture, with its intolerance of pluralism, the collisions of special interests with constitutional government, and the propensity for violence as a basis for acquiring and maintaining power. Through their activism they uphold a vision of popular participation as a source of legitimacy. Unlike the elitist Leninist model the Mothers' vision of a just state includes political pluralism as well as economic justice and extensive welfare measures. They note that in West European democracies Communists and the center right coexist, in contrast to the Argentine political culture where its classes are sharply divided and contempt for diversity of opinion is strong. Although the Mothers are influenced by their political culture they have nevertheless been able to maintain a perspective on it.

While people abroad continue to view the Mothers as a group devoted solely to the pursuit of their children's assassins, the organization keeps evolving in response to the Mothers' inner transformations and to fresh challenges from the political system. With each passing year they expanded their political agenda and forged alliances with the grass roots of various labor unions, with teacher, student, and neighborhood groups, with the indigenous population, the retired, and the marginal. Their detractors, unable to recognize that the Mothers had adopted a totally new form of political participation, claimed that they were isolated because they had not established links with either the political parties or with the leaders of interest groups. Their growing political program and their influence among the dispossessed, as well as their relentless pursuit of justice, brought the Mothers into a head-on conflict with the government.

The Easter Rebellion of 1987 that caused President Alfonsín to confront an increasingly assertive military also represented a watershed in the relations between the Mothers and the government. The president launched a campaign to bring about national reconciliation with the military, and, at the same time, portrayed the Mothers as unpatriotic and manipulated by outside forces. Worse, the Mothers began to suffer acts of violence by the security forces with what they believed was the approval of the government. The attitude of President Alfonsín toward the Mothers betrayed his campaign promises and was an important factor in alienating them from the political system.

In July 1987, while the Mothers were marching to protest a Mass of reconciliation for members of the armed forces to be followed by a military parade, they were attacked with chains and clubs by the security forces. The night before the march the Mothers and their young helpers had painted the names of military leaders followed by the word *assassin* on the streets where the march would take place; their weapon continued to be the use of language to embarrass their enemies. They did not anticipate the brutal assault. When the Mothers protested the violence, the government only criticized them for their intransigent attitudes.[7]

The Mothers were adamantly opposed to the concept of reconciliation, which became one of the government's rallying cries, because they perceived it as part of a campaign to draw a veil over the past and, in effect, pardon those who were responsible for the horrors of the Dirty War. They also worried that it would pave the way for the armed forces to increase their space in the political arena. They therefore staged a daily round of marches.

A few weeks after their demonstration during the military parade, a patrol of mounted police descended on the Plaza de Mayo while the Mothers were marching. The police charged them with nightsticks, arresting a Mother and a young man from the Front for Human Rights who tried to protect her. Several Mothers were injured, including Hebe de Bonafini, who suffered a broken rib. The Mothers' journalists had taken pictures of the attack, which the women sent to the minister of the interior along with a letter of protest. The government never replied.[8] President Alfonsín had just managed to push a defense bill through the Congress that established a clear military role for the armed forces that specifically excluded them from participation in internal conflict with a view to terminating the national security justification for its interventions. It is unclear whether the attack on the Mothers was inspired by the government or by elements seeking to discredit the government at this critical juncture. Whatever the sources, the Mothers now began receiving telephone threats ordering them to halt their activity or suffer the consequences.

The Mothers' predictions about the dangers of an unchecked military came to pass when 1988 began with yet another military rebellion. In mid-January, Lieutenant Colonel Aldo Rico, the leader of the Easter week uprising, escaped from custody and staged a revolt around the town of Monte Caseros on the Brazilian and Uruguayan borders. It was accompanied by rebellions in the provinces of Tucumán and Santa Cruz, while the Buenos Aires civil airport was taken over by army and air force personnel. The purpose of the uprising was to vindicate the honor of the armed forces, which claimed that they "had done nothing other than serve their country in a just and necessary war," and to condemn the generals accountable for the mismanagement of the Falklands War that resulted in the military's fall.[9] Unlike the Easter week uprising, the military forces not participating in the rebellion were loyal to the senior command and to the government, thus allowing Alfonsín to secure the unconditional surrender of the rebels. This second major military crisis in less than a year, however, revealed the fragility of Argentina's democracy.

Despite a subsequent purging of extremist middle-ranking officers, currents still remained in the armed forces that favored legitimization of the military's performance in the Dirty War. On December 3, 1988, a third rebellion was mounted by mutinous troops headed by Colonel Mohammed Alí Seineldín at the Campo de Mayo barracks. Alfonsín's order to put down the uprising met with conditional compliance in the military. The "loyal" forces allowed the rebels to move to the Villa Martelli barracks outside of Buenos Aires. The army was not satisfied with the law of due obedience or the full stop law and now demanded a larger share of the budget for the armed forces, pay raises for the soldiers, and full amnesty "to recover the lost honor of the army."[10] The rebellious troops were the *carapintadas* (blackened faces), an elite corps of younger officers. This time the mobilization of the mutinous forces triggered mass popular demonstrations as well as denunciations of the rebellion by most major political parties. People came out in the streets to demonstrate in front of the barracks and thousands of youngsters tried to stop the rebels with bottles and stones while troops and tanks loyal to the government remained immobile not far from the rebels. An embarrassingly long interval passed before the government was able to muster loyalist troops, put down the rebellion, and announce to the population that the house was in order.

President Alfonsín refused to grant comprehensive amnesty to the rebels, but he did authorize both a salary increase to the soldiers and funds for the modernization of equipment, referring once again to the theory of the two demons. General Caceres, supported by Mohammed Alí Seineldín, was able to claim a moral victory by insisting that the government recognize the legitimacy of the armed forces' battle against subversion.[11] They were supported by the bishop of Buenos Aires, who insisted that national unity would be impossible without a reconciliation among Argentines, and by right-wing senators, who asked for a law of reconciliation that would characterize actions taken by the armed and security forces during the junta as acts of war and therefore justified repression. The latest mutiny made clear that the army was far from a depoliticized body loyal to civilian authorities.

Outraged by what they perceived as the government's capitulations to the military, the Mothers organized a series of marches and demonstrations under the slogan To RESIST Is to COMBAT, turning the armed forces' vocabulary against them and unmasking, as they called it, "a hypocritical government which bargains for its miserable life with an army of occupation." A committee formed by friends and relatives of the victims of the uprising accompanied them, and Hebe de Bonafini proclaimed in the Plaza, "When the most humble people lose their fear and come out in the streets to defend themselves, that is the significance of To RESIST Is to COMBAT."[12] In their editorials and speeches, the Mothers noted that as a result of the uprisings, the army had increased its hold on national politics with the blessings of the government. They were prescient in their predictions that these capitulations were only the first steps toward the ultimate granting of amnesty to the military leaders responsible for the excesses of the Dirty War.

These events formed the background of the Mothers' reaction to one of the strangest events of the Alfonsín presidency—the attack on the La Tablada army barracks in January 1989 by a left-wing splinter group. The events surrounding the attack are a case study in the layering of reality within the Argentine political system and the secret machinations misrepresented in the media. Only those directly affected by such events can attest to the struggles for power behind the democratic facade; many sectors of the public accept the official versions of terrorist plots and dangers to national security.

During his last year in office President Alfonsín was plagued by a restive military and a crumbling economy. As a last resort he introduced an economic program intended to decelerate inflation and attract financing from the International Monetary Fund, the World Bank, and the United States. Because of Argentina's failure to pay the interest on its enormous debt, it was unable to acquire new loans, and the value of the austral (Argentine monetary unit) plummeted, taking with it public confidence in the government.[13] The president was also grappling with the military's continuing pressures for a greater role in national concerns. In particular, the armed forces chafed at their restriction from intervening in domestic affairs and sought an extension of their role in the arena of internal security. It was in this atmosphere that the military barracks of the La Tablada regiment were attacked by a small group of leftists called the Movement for the Whole Country (MTP), allegedly to prevent what they perceived as an imminent coup from the right.

On January 23 a group of MTP members crashed through the main gate of the barracks in a convoy, catching soldiers by surprise and managing to occupy different parts of the barracks and take a number of hostages. The armed forces responded almost immediately, and the subsequent bombing and artillery barrages killed and injured both soldiers and MTP members. The surviving thirteen MTP leftists surrendered the following morning after nine soldiers, two provincial policemen, and twenty-three members of the MTP were killed, and four members of the police and security forces seriously injured. Five people who had not participated in the assault were captured the same afternoon.[14] A Capuchin friar who was a good friend of the Mothers, Father Juan Antonio Puigjane, was arrested after he presented himself voluntarily to the federal police.

It was difficult to unearth the facts in the storm of countercharges between the left and the right. People on the right believed that this was a terrorist plot while people on the left viewed it as an attempt to discredit President Alfonsín and force him into further capitulations to the military. Mysteries remain as to how members of the MTP had access to highly sophisticated weapons, how an extremely mobilized military unit appeared in formation almost instantaneously after the attack, and why a civilian judge had not been present outside the barracks to make formal calls for surrender, as had been the case during the past three military uprisings. Whether or not the MTP attackers had been given opportunities to surrender, which might have minimized the death toll, was also questioned. Many observers, including the chief of the federal police, commented that the recapturing of the barracks was unnecessarily prolonged and violent and could have been more safely achieved with the use of tear gas.[15]

Before the incident, members of the MTP had tried to persuade the Mothers that a rightist coup was imminent and to join them in preventing that attack, but the Mothers were skeptical and refused to go along. In fact, they were concerned that the whole affair might be a trap set by the government. Afterward, the handling of the affair brought up cases of serious human-rights violations, leading families of the MTP to contact the Mothers and Amnesty International for support. Evidence emerged that some of the MTP members listed as dead were summarily executed after having surrendered and that prisoners in military custody were tortured and held incommunicado.[16] Amnesty International sent observers to the trial of MTP defenders, while the Mothers' lawyers also lent their services to the defendants. Not only did the government fail to investigate complaints of extrajudicial executions and torture, but it also failed to ensure a fair trial to the defendants. The proceedings pitted two points of view against each other: order, on the one hand; and the MTP's ideas of revolutionary justice on the other. Both facts and due process were lost in the heat of the exchange. In the coverage of the testimony of the defendants the Mothers' newspapers recounted that MTP members were subjected to the same kinds of torture that the women's children had endured during the Dirty War.[17]

While the Mothers did not support the attack on the barracks, they experienced a sense of déjà vu in the treatment of MTP members, whose tormentors were also active during the Dirty War. As far as the Mothers were concerned, the enemy was still in place.

The MTP, a left-wing organization created in 1983, was known for its moderation and commitment to the defense of human rights. The year before the attack on the La Tablada barracks, however, it had split after members of the former People's Revolutionary Army (ERP) joined.[18] These newcomers insisted that a right-wing military coup was unavoidable and that the group should prepare itself to wage armed resistance. Some leaders of the MTP had friendly ties with high officials in the Alfonsín administration, especially with former Interior Minister Enrique Nosiglia, which were used by conservative politicians and newspapers to accuse Alfonsín and his friends of being involved in the attack. The charge, though, was never taken seriously.[19]

Although the complete facts of the incident have yet to be revealed, the attack on the barracks had far-reaching consequences for the role of the military in internal security and for the country in general. Following the attack President Alfonsín announced the creation of the National Security Council in which the armed forces chiefs of staff would participate.[20] He also issued a decree that allowed the intervention of military intelligence agencies in domestic affairs and granted unlimited powers to the heads of operation in internal military security work. He then proposed an antiterrorism law to the Congress that contained provisions limiting freedom of expression, which was widely protested by the Mothers and the other human-rights groups. Major newspapers supported the law, as did Carlos Saúl Menem, who would soon be running for president.

After the incident at La Tablada, the Mothers raised their new slogan THE RESISTANCE CONTINUES as they fanned out through the streets carrying white pasteboard silhouettes of the *disappeared*, chanting, "No to the repressive law." They set up mock ballot boxes in squares and parks around the city, urging citizens to cast their vote against the law and showering the country with leaflets explaining their position. Once again they designed a slogan co-opting the words of the powerful, using them as a means of defiance and a demonstration of their continuing strength. While the newspaper coverage of events stressed the danger of leftist terrorism, ignoring the implications of the proposed antiterrorism law for human rights and freedom of expression, the Mothers' dire predictions about the intentions of the military were becoming a reality. In April 1989 they organized a march to demand an investigation of La Tablada and to commemorate the thirteenth anniversary of the coup that had brought the junta to power. The object of the march was to teach people how to confront fear, as their slogan THE RESISTANCE CONTINUES proclaimed. Fewer people than usual accompanied them.

In their newspapers and in press conferences the Mothers denounced the way the government had handled the La Tablada incident, making a connection between what had happened to their children and the treatment endured by members of the MTP. They also criticized the military and the judiciary for their partiality during the MTP trials. While they admitted that their friends in the MTP had made mistakes, they insisted that "between the mistakes of their friends and the firing squads of their enemies, they would stand by the side of their friends." To those who criticized the Mothers for their support of the MTP defendants, the women replied, "When justice will be equal for all, the Mothers will also be able to be impartial."[21]

The aftermath of La Tablada included a renewed spate of threats against the Mothers as well as persecution of young people on the left. Beatriz Rubenstein, head of the Mothers' chapter in Mar del Plata, received a letter charging her with membership in the MTP and condemning her in absentia of treason, sentencing her to death by a firing squad in a location to be determined. It was signed, "Glory to those who died for the country, Commander Condor," an eerie reminder of the letter she had received in 1984 regarding her daughter's fate.[22] A number of Mothers from Mar del Plata who received similar threats traced them to an employee in the municipal government who, operating under a pseudonym, was also a member of the intelligence services. They brought complaints before a judge and sent letters to the president, the minister of the interior, and the municipal government, but to no avail.

Hebe de Bonafini received a similar letter: "Commander and Heroes of La Tablada inform you that as reprisals for the officers and soldiers of the Argentine army and agents of the federal and provincial police of Buenos Aires, fallen in defense of the fatherland, you have been condemned to death. The sentence will be carried out wherever you are found. Glory to the fallen of La Tablada! Long live the Fatherland!" Shortly after the letter arrived Hebe's daughter Alejandra saw a green truck parked at the end of the block as she was leaving the house. When she drew closer those inside threatened her, saying, "We are coming to get your mother."[23]

Hebe de Bonafini narrowly escaped death one night in August when she was returning from Buenos Aires to her home in La Plata, fifty miles away. As she was walking home from the bus stop a car came barreling down the street at top speed, then swerved onto the sidewalk attempting to crush her against a brick wall. By some miracle, it missed, and thereafter Hebe knew that she was a marked woman— the threats she received were not idle. Shortly after this incident reporters working for the Mothers' newspaper were roughed up by a group of civilians in Ford Falcons who insulted them as they beat them, each saying, "I am the police. I do as I please," and referring to the Mothers as "the cunt of subversion." The Mothers, however, refused to be cowed, maintaining a busy schedule of conferences and debates on the events of La Tablada. When Hebe and another Mother opened a public debate on the projected antiterrorist law, they were watched by followers of General Antonio Bussi, who had headed La Perla detention center during the Dirty War and was responsible for the *disappearances* of 428 and the deaths of 225 people. He was now running for governor of Tucumán. Hebe was introduced by a brother of a *disappeared*, who cried out, "Votes don't wash out crimes."[24] The threats and the confrontations the Mothers endured never received coverage in the major newspapers.

When the Mothers installed their customary stand at the yearly artisans' fair in Lomas de Zamora, a municipal official claimed they had to leave because the fair was closed to political parties.[25] After a week of sparring and a flurry of letters to the Ministry of Culture, the Mothers were allowed to return to the fair. Once there, however, they were confronted with a military stand peopled with soldiers from the regiment of La Tablada and fortified with a tank for good measure. Undaunted, the Mothers continued to point out the dangers of an unchecked military.

I was with the Mothers in August 1989 when their lawyers were speaking with families of the *disappeared* and detained members of the MTP, and there I experienced the surreal theater of Argentine politics. Many parents had been unable to locate their children among the corpses or in the prisons. After the assault of the military against the MTP a number of corpses were unidentifiable because their fingers had been cut off. The Mothers speculated that this represented an attempt on the part of the government to imply that more members were involved in the initial attack on the barracks, thus making the MTP appear a greater threat. Also, members of the MTP, who were seen by witnesses, had been *disappeared*. Yet none of these matters was discussed by the newspapers, which focused on the dangers of a terrorist plot. From the Mothers' point of view little had changed since the coming to power of a constitutional government.

Their pessimism and embattled stance remained undiminished even when, on May 14, 1989, the country managed an orderly transfer of power from one elected civilian president to another, the first to take place in sixty years. The May elections brought in Carlos Saúl Menem as the successor to Raúl Alfonsín, but the Mothers were not impressed with democratic procedures that continually yielded conservative economic and social policies. If anything, Menem, who won by a comfortable majority and also gained seats in the Chamber of Deputies, was more conservative than Alfonsín. According to the constitution he was scheduled to take office on December 1. Economic problems, however, including spiraling inflation and food riots in major cities where people were sacking supermarkets, forced Alfonsín to turn over the presidency on July 8. During the unrest the Mothers proclaimed in the Plaza de Mayo and in their newspaper, "When the poor rob to feed their children, they are described as leftists and subversives and treated with tear gas and prison; when the controlling classes rob us, they call it inflation."[26]

Although Menem received support from a broad spectrum of interests, including the labor unions, he veered to the right once in office and spent almost as much time with conservative politicians such as Alvaro Alsogary of the Union of the Democratic Center, a former supporter of the military junta, as he did with labor leaders. Because of an inflation rate that rose to 114 percent, a nearly bare treasury, a huge national debt whose annual interest was 6 billion dollars, and a virtually collapsed economy, he deferred populism and turned to the business community for advice. The result was a program intended to restore the health of the economy by devaluing the austral, freezing wages, raising public utility prices, and drastically reducing the size and cost of government by privatizing government enterprises plagued by huge deficits.[27] The president anticipated that these measures would spur economic growth by bringing in foreign capital and raising production for export.

This bitter medicine incurred tremendous social costs, falling hardest on the working class, which now faced massive layoffs and declining real wages. The Mothers criticized these measures in their weekly marches, demonstrations, and newspaper editorials. They suggested closing down military bases and selling military equipment as austerity measures. They also suggested privatizing words. "Making those who speak, the friends of the government, pay to use the national television and radio channels would not only help economically, we wouldn't have to listen to so many stupidities."[28] The Mothers were joined by the thousands of state enterprise workers laid off and by retirees who were struggling to survive on dwindling pension payments. The core of people who had voted for Saúl Menem now felt betrayed.

The next task President Menem faced was dealing with a restive military who vigorously opposed the prosecution of officers and soldiers accused of human-rights abuses. The Mothers anticipated his intentions in their slogan WE WILL NOT FORGET, WE WILL NOT FORGIVE. In October, three months after taking office, Menem startled the world and outraged most Argentines by granting a blanket pardon to all those who were tried and sentenced under President Alfonsín for their participation in the Dirty War, for misconduct during the Falklands War, and for their participation in the three military uprisings against the government—280 people in all. The pardoned military officers included Leopoldo Galtieri, a former president and army commander under the junta. Menem claimed that because he himself, like a number of Peronist politicians, had been imprisoned for five years during the junta, he had the moral authority to grant a pardon. He also insisted that the pardon would heal the rift between civilians and the military. In a speech describing his decision, he said, "There remain some wounds to close and as president of the Argentines, I dedicate myself before God and my people to heal definitively these wounds so that in national unity we can create a great country." The Mothers replied, "An assassin is an assassin despite any law or pardon. Such crimes, deliberately planned and carried out, can't be pardoned. They are crimes against humanity and the assassins will commit them again."[29]

The Mothers held press conferences, insisting that they themselves would continue to hunt down the criminals responsible for their children's *disappearances*. Supported by the Human Rights Commission of Chivilcoy, Hebe de Bonafini painted *Vergez Assassin* in front of the house and store of the former director of the concentration camp La Perla, who was the founder of the Córdoba branch of the AAA and a man known as one of the most vicious torturers. Héctor Vergez complained to the minister that the Mothers had publicly claimed, "If the assassins are not condemned by the courts, we will paint their houses and we will come and get them."[30] Unfazed, the Mothers sent letters around the world asking their supporters to identify former participants in the Dirty War in embassies and overseas residences for future reference. They were out on the streets in full force to oppose the pardons, joined by other human-rights groups and members of the political opposition. Their young helpers covered the Plaza with silhouettes of the *disappeared*. Trade union groups, the Grandmothers of the Plaza de Mayo, support groups from Spain, neighborhood groups, the Socialist and Communist parties, and the Association of Ex-Detained, Ex-Disappeared joined their evening marches. I was with them on one of these marches and observed that city officials had turned off the lights in the Plaza and that people closed their windows or turned away as the Mothers passed by. The only television coverage was from abroad, and the following day none of the newspapers carried stories about the march.

The Mothers also marshalled their support groups abroad to apply pressure on the Menem government. A number of new associations sprang up in Australia and Canada, and twenty-three women parliamentarians in the European Assembly created a group on behalf of the Mothers. The outrage expressed abroad had little impact on President Menem, however. He found wide sympathy for his economic policies in Europe and the United States, which muted the reaction to his pardons. The press speculated that the pardons were an attempt by Menem to mollify the *carapintadas*, their leader Mohammed Alí Seineldín, and their supporters among members of the business and landed community.[31] During Menem's election campaign Colonel Seineldín spoke favorably about him and subsequently received frequent visitors from among the president's associates. "A government which allies itself with assassins ends up resembling them," the Mothers publicly concluded.[32]

Menem's relations with the military were put to the test on December 3, 1990, when a group of several hundred *carapintadas*, led by Colonel Seineldín, occupied five national military installations—including a headquarters building two blocks from the presidential palace—a week before a visit by U.S. president George Bush. As President Menem had banked on acquiring U.S. support for his program of privatization and encouragement of foreign investments, the event was a terrible embarrassment. This time, however, there were no delays in putting down the revolt because Menem met the *carapintadas'* demands for pay increases and more modern weapons. His broad pardon of October 1989 may also have helped. He was able to receive George Bush a few days later as if nothing had happened.

Menem's next step had been anticipated by the Mothers for a long time. They kept insisting that the measures taken to placate the military and grant it a political space would result in clemency for the leaders of the junta. Shortly after the December 3 uprising, President Menem issued a pardon to former Presidents Jorge Videla and Roberto Viola of the junta; the former naval commander Emilio Massera; the top commanders of the Buenos Aires police, including Ramón Camps and Ovidio Richieri; and Carlos Suárez Mason, a former army commander who fled to the United States and was extradited to Argentina for trial. Mario Firmenich, the former head of the Montonero guerrillas, was also pardoned. Luis Moreno Ocampo, the prosecutor who helped convict the former military leaders, publicly stated that the nation had no interest in reconciling with these people and speculated that the president might have made a secret deal with the current leadership of the armed forces.[33]

The pardon completed the unraveling of the human-rights prosecutions, a process that had begun with the Easter Rebellion in 1987 and which revealed how Argentina continued to be caught in its own political history. One of the major demands of the Easter uprising and the following two revolts had been a halt to the prosecution of hundreds of military officers accused of abuses during the Dirty War. The armed forces once again gained legitimacy from a constitutional government for their unchecked use of violence, undercutting that

The Mothers march with masks representing the *disappeared*, 1988 (*photo by Gerardo Dell'Orto*)

The Mothers march with silhouettes of the *disappeared* (*photo by Gerardo Dell'Orto*)

government's authority. The pardon, its timing carefully manipulated in hopes of limiting media attention in Europe and the United States, was announced by the defense minister in the midst of a four-day weekend at the beginning of the summer, a period when many people leave for vacation. Concurrent with the pardon Menem sought to remove judges and prosecutors who had served during the trials of officers implicated in the Dirty War. Eventually, he replaced three fourths of the judiciary in an attempt to undermine its independence.

The Mothers waged a vigorous campaign against the pardons, gathering thousands of cards and letters from prominent people in politics, the arts, and the sciences as well as from workers, professionals, and students, and brought them to the Casa Rosada in huge boxes. They also embarked on a tour throughout Europe where their television appearances and press conferences unleashed a flood of letters to the president from abroad. They dedicated their tenth annual march of resistance on Human Rights Day to a condemnation of the pardon, marching under the banner REBELLION TO STRUGGLE, COURAGE TO FORGE AHEAD. They described their new slogan as a way of both condemning the military and proclaiming that ethics and politics are not mutually exclusive. "We give the example of politics with morality, morality without corruption," they said. "The way is to socialize, share, distribute, love."[34] Joining the Mothers were thousands of Argentines and human-rights groups from Canada, Europe, and Latin America. Youth groups from the Radical party and groups such as the left-wing Peronists, who generally do not march with them, also participated. Seventy percent of the Argentine people were opposed to the pardons, a recent poll had revealed.

President Menem reacted to the march by attacking the Mothers. "Where are they getting the money for all their travels abroad?" he asked, insinuating that they were being financed by outside forces. "Let's put an end to this circus and start thinking of a new world."[35] He announced that he was going to sue the Mothers, the Movement Toward Socialism (Mas), and the Communist party for painting slogans on the Plaza. "The Plaza has been left looking like a pigsty," he complained in one of the major daily newspapers.[36] The president's repeated criticism of the Mothers was proof of their continued relevance and power. That they were now on a collision course was highlighted by subsequent events.

Just before Christmas, Juana de Pargament and Hebe de Bonafini managed to slip into the Casa Rosada unobserved. They were bearing a small Christmas tree decorated with the names and photographs of the generals Menem had pardoned, while thousands of their supporters were chanting outside, "There are no loyalists, no rebels, all the military are criminals. Punishment for the guilty!" In a speech afterwards, Hebe de Bonafini told the crowds that she gave the tree to the president to remind him that those whom he freed would one day remove him from office. When the Mothers carried their battle against the pardons to Europe in February 1991, Hebe de Bonafini appeared on a television program in Spain where she was interviewed at great length. She focused all her wrath on the president, claiming that he behaved like an emperor rushing through decrees, ignoring the Congress and the country. She described the pardon as not only for the military but also for the politicians who had allowed them to function with impunity, and then referred to Menem as *basura*, or garbage.[37]

Those words cost her dearly. President Menem labeled Hebe a national traitor and began proceedings to bring her to court on charges of contempt for authority, a criminal offense in Argentina. Nevertheless, Hebe continued her criticism, claiming, "Our country is different from his. His is the military, money and the United States, power, a Ferrari. Ours is the working men and women who give their lives for it, our children, the Plaza, life, the earth."[38]

The Mothers' outspokenness provoked a concerted campaign to break up their organization. Now subjected to intimidations similar to those endured by dissident associations in former Soviet-bloc countries, they faced a three-pronged attack consisting of court proceedings against their leader, a rash of death threats, and the sacking of their office. They had not been under such pressure since the rule of the junta. On April 6 the Mothers' office on Yrigoyen Street was robbed, an occurrence that did not surprise the women and which turned out to be the first in a series of thefts. Thieves stole their awards for peace and human rights and returned to pillage in mid-May. After the Mothers complained before a judge, a police guard was posted by the door of the building that housed their office.[39] Nevertheless, when the Mothers arrived there on June 4, 1991, they discovered that the bars on the windows and the locks had been broken with professional skill, a high-voltage wire strung across the entrance. Inside, they confronted smashed furniture, empty coffers, broken windows, and the theft of all of their archives and equipment, most notably the computer containing the information they had gathered on the detention centers in operation during the junta.[40] Given the skill with which their office was robbed and the nature of the missing material, the Mothers concluded that the police were involved and publicly blamed the minister of the interior, Julio Figueroa, and the chief of the federal police, Jorge Passero. They noted that the police guard detailed to protect their office was somehow absent when the robbery occurred.

Concurrent with the robberies and the legal proceedings against Hebe de Bonafini, the Mothers began receiving death threats by phone. Because the Jewish community had been subjected to a number of anti-Semitic incidents, the Mothers had staged a demonstration in their support, stating, "For the military and the Nazis it's bad to be Jewish. For the Mothers it is a source of pride because we are friends and colleagues with Jews and have fought alongside them for years." The threatening phone calls referred to them as "shitty Jewesses." One other person who had dared to publicly criticize the president for the pardons, the noted filmmaker Fernando Solanas, was shot in the legs six times from a passing car as he left his office. That same morning Hebe de Bonafini received a phone call telling her, "You are going to get it in the head, not in the legs."[41]

By now the Mothers felt as though they were living under a state of siege. It took a great deal of aplomb and energy to carry on their organizational work in the midst of these assaults. Added to this was their lack of access to television programs and to the major newspapers, save for the Communist *El Sur* and, at times, the new paper *Pagina 12*. President Menem had shown his displeasure with frank reporting by eliminating a number of radio stations since he had come to power, one in particular that frequently had hosted the Mothers. As usual, the women responded by a round of visits abroad to denounce the efforts to destroy their organization. At home they initiated a series of marches and press conferences, raising their new slogan WE WILL NOT SURRENDER. Shortly after facing charges in court, Hebe reminded the judge in a press conference that in a free country one has the right to speak openly and that "the president showed a lack of respect and contempt for the people when he pardoned the military."[42] Characteristically, the Mothers insisted on having the last word.

The Mothers' movement was now fourteen years old, a remarkable lifespan given the fact that since 1984 the Argentine people and the government had expressed a strong desire to move forward and forget the past. The Mothers, who were middle-aged and older when their children were *disappeared*, were now in their sixties, seventies, or even their eighties, many of them struggling with poverty and ill health. It is a testament to their courage that despite years of concerted attempts to eliminate them as a political force, they were neither silenced nor cowed. They had wrested a moral space in a country that continued to ignore basic rights and had raised standards that, although we may consider them self-evident, are rare in Latin America: the value of human life, the right to economic dignity and justice, and the freedom of speech and assembly.

NOTES

1. de Cerruti, interview.

2. Madres, *Monthly Newspaper*, December 1986.

3. de Cerruti, interview.

4. Members of the Front for Human Rights, interviews by Marguerite Bouvard, November 1990.

5. de Bonafini, interview.

6. Ibid.

7. Madres, *Monthly Newspaper*, August 1987.

8. Ibid.

9. Graziano, *Divine Violence*, 56–57.

10. Madres, *Monthly Newspaper*, February 1988.

11. Ibid.

12. Ibid.

13. Gary W. Wynia, "The Peronists Triumph in Argentina," *Current History* (January 1990): 13–35.

14. *Argentina: The Attack on the Third Infantry Regiment Barracks at La Tablada: Investigations into Allegations of Torture, Disappearances, and Extrajudicial Executions* (New York: Amnesty International USA, March 1990).

15. Ibid.

16. Madres, *Monthly Newspaper*, September 1989.

17. Ibid., October 1989.

18. The year before the attack on the La Tablada barrracks, the MTP had split after members of the former People's Revolutionary Army (ERP) joined, in particular Gorriaran Merlo, who had assassinated the exiled former Nicaraguan dictator Anastasio Somoza Debayle while he was in Paraguay. Merlo's history created ample suspicion regarding his real motives. He was the only important leader of the ERP who survived the Dirty War, and he also escaped unscathed from the confrontation at La Tablada, which led many people to believe that the attack was engineered by members of the army intelligence who had infiltrated the organization and that Merlo was working with these agents. Those who support this view believe that the attack was intended to discredit President Alfonsín and force him to sign a law creating a role for the military in internal security. Other political observers regard the La Tablada incident as yet another indication of the isolation and irrelevance of the far left. Oscar Serrat (Associated Press), Buenos Aires, letter to Marguerite Bouvard, Wellesley, MA, September 16, 1991.

19. Alma Guillermoprieto, "Letter from Buenos Aires," *The New Yorker* (July 15, 1991): 63–78.

20. Madres, *Monthly Newspaper*, March 1989.

21. Ibid., February 1989.

22. Ibid., July 1989.

23. Ibid., June 1989.

24. Ibid., July 1989.

25. Ibid., December 1989.

26. Ibid., August 1989.

27. Wynia, "The Peronists Triumph," 13–35.

28. Madres, *Monthly Newspaper*, January 1990.

29. Ibid., October 1989.

30. Ibid., November 1989.

31. Guillermoprieto, "Letter from Buenos Aires," 63–78.

32. Madres, *Monthly Newspaper*, December 1990.

33. Guillermoprieto, "Letter from Buenos Aires," 63–78.

34. Madres, *Monthly Newspaper*, December 1990.

35. "Finalizó en Plaza de Mayo la marcha de la resistencia," *La Prensa* (Buenos Aires), December 7, 1990.

36. "Proceso por desacato a Hebe Bonafini," *La Prensa* (Buenos Aires), May 17, 1991.

37. Madres, *Monthly Newspaper*, April 1991.

38. "Madres de Plaza de Mayo," *La Nación* (Buenos Aires), April 10, 1991.

39. "Cuarto atentado a las Madres," *El Clarín* (Buenos Aires), June 4, 1991.

40. Madres, *Monthly Newspaper*, June 1991.

41. Ibid.

42. Madres, *Monthly Newspaper*, July 1991.

TE YERBA

The rain knocks against the windows
of the small office with its posters and chairs,
its hotplate where the water

bubbles and winks for the gourd of "maté."
The Mothers sit in a circle
after the march. The electricity has just

sputtered and died, part of the new austerity,
but they are laughing and exchanging gossip
as they pass around the gourd

with its metal straw. They are warriors
between battles, but their stories are not about
skirmishes. They have traveled the fields

of shock and numbness, the trenches
of wrath. Their heart muscles
have grown sturdy with use, their tongues

have shaped new languages. Now is the time
to cut a frosted cake, to celebrate the birth
of a grandchild in Spain. They are Mothers.

CHAPTER 9

A New Model in the Struggle for Human Rights

Because we have only a short period of life left, we feel the need to continue our way of working. There is a great need for love. There is also a great need to feel and to receive other people's love, and this is a new way.

Mothers of the Plaza de Mayo

The Mothers of the Plaza de Mayo have left an important legacy to the world, a new model for human-rights activity. Their organization is based upon equality and ties of affection among its members, the quality of these bonds as important to the Mothers as the goals they pursue. They believe they are providing a new way of life within their association, creating opportunities not only for people who live under repressive regimes but also for all those who feel alienated from political structures impervious to their needs. Under authoritarian regimes, groups based upon affection represent a powerful form of opposition; to form ties based on love is to defy systems based on force. There are also many people who live within democratic systems yet feel they lack the opportunity to define and manage their own interests. The Mothers have demonstrated that participation and sharing are not just paths to survival—they are life itself.

The Mothers came to the same conclusion as Vaclav Havel, the former leading dissident in Czechoslovakia who once ruminated from his prison cell that an improved political system could result only from a better way of life. In his essay "The Power of the Powerless," Havel suggests establishing parallel structures within an oppressive society where a different life could be lived and where the focus would be on the needs of real people.[1] Like the Mothers, he realized that Western political democracies were not the panacea for oppressive regimes because in them people could be manipulated in ways that were more subtle and refined and because mass political parties run by professionals released the population from concrete, personal responsibility. Also like the Mothers, he aimed for the moral regeneration of his society and for relationships among human beings based upon trust and solidarity rather than on the formalized, ritualized ties of official structures. The Mothers' organization, as well as the Civic Forum, which ushered in the Velvet Revolution in Czechoslovakia, defended the aims of life and humanity in the here and now rather than adopting abstract political visions of the future. Both organizations developed without an administrative structure, functioning on the basis of direct democracy and close ties among their members. They realized that creating a better life meant much more than a change of political systems; it involved living by alternative values and behaviors springing from the private sphere of free thought.

The Mothers' mutuality represents a new political form animated by the principle of self-management and shared responsibility. Unlike traditional collectivist solutions, however, the Mothers' concord is not based on self-abnegation. Rather, it is so demanding that only strong, vigorous individuals can sustain such ties. They explain: "We are not ordinary mothers or ordinary women because we are very strong and that is why we are in the organization. We wish to be together, discussing and disagreeing, not vegetating in front of a television set. Because we are strong, we will continue to be together. We have special courage."[2] This solidarity has been celebrated in a small town in Holland where five statues rise out of the central square, commemorating outstanding human-rights activists around the world. In addition to the Mothers they honor Gandhi, Martin Luther King, Jr., Steve Biko, and Jerzy Popelieszko. The statue for the Mothers of the Plaza de Mayo is of a group of women because the Mothers are interested in projecting their common effort rather than their individual personalities. While Western political thinking celebrates the autonomous, separate individual who joins with others to create a consensus, without impinging on his or her separateness, the

Mothers' social understanding reflects perceptions common to many women—that the key to morality lies in a lifetime of responsiveness to relationships.[3]

Although they did not theorize about gender differences, the Mothers of the Plaza de Mayo were determined to project their experience of attachment and affection onto their political style and goals. Like working-class women in other societies they rejected the label of feminism while developing ideas and concerns falling within the repertoire of feminism. They were keenly aware that they viewed the world and their mission differently from the other groups engaged in politics and human-rights activity and were determined to maintain not only the truth of the *disappearances* but also the truth of their perceptions and experiences.

Initially, the Mothers came together because they were bent on the same journey. They shared a common goal, a similar pain, and a phenomenal courage, given that most people were afraid to come forward and ask for information about their children. From the pursuit of their shared aim and from navigating the dangerous shoals of the dictatorship sprang an affection much deeper than comradeship. In their first bulletin, which they published clandestinely, the Mothers noted, "The fact of working together, and looking for our children, helped us feel each other's pain. In difficult moments of illness, economic distress, and loss, we helped each other."[4] When Hebe de Bonafini's husband was dying of lung cancer, she wanted to drop out of the organization's commission because she was unable to travel from La Plata to Buenos Aires. Instead, the commission decided to hold their meetings in her home for the four months until Humberto de Bonafini's death. This responsiveness is the cement that holds together a group of highly diverse individuals. "We quarrel a lot," Hebe relates, "but we are much more than a family. We help each other, and that solidarity is worth a lot."[5]

"We are like links in a chain," the Mothers explain. "Every Thursday we attach a new link, a link that is making an indestructible chain that connects us to our children. With them we create a chain of love, hope, and feeling."[6] The leap from *I* to *we* is not a problem in open societies. In those societies where repressive governments use fear to divide and alienate their populations, the ability to develop mutuality and transcend personal tragedy in the pursuit of justice is a source of strength. The security police who make repeated attempts on Hebe de Bonafini's life are so convinced of the effectiveness of physical intimidation they cannot understand that the organization will continue undiminished if Hebe is assassinated.

In preserving the strength of their group throughout the time of the repression and in the face of a more veiled but equally dangerous pressure today, the Mothers defy an age-old technique of domination. In 345 B.C., Aristotle outlined the ways in which tyrannies can be maintained, listing the very techniques used by the junta as well as some used by the present government: removing persons of spirit, forbidding common organizations, prohibiting anything likely to produce mutual confidence and an independent spirit, utilizing a secret police to infiltrate private and public meetings, and sowing mutual distrust between people.[7] Neither he nor the junta could have imagined that an organization of women would successfully defy these methods.

The Mothers' organization has been described by Sara Ruddick as an example of "women's politics of resistance," referring to the fact that its participants are women who deliberately invoke their culture's symbols of femininity to oppose governmental policies.[8] The Mothers' reasons for organizing as women did not include claiming independence from men. Instead, they wanted to establish their distinctive voices and perceptions and mistakenly believed that they would be safer than their husbands in a society that revered women even while it marginalized them. Keenly aware that the sexes had different styles of behavior, they were also concerned that men would spend all of their time establishing a formal structure and writing reports while they were anxious for immediate action. In the early days some of the fathers did attend their meetings, but they immediately began to argue about their respective political views and the structure of the group. The Mothers believed formal practices were time consuming and inefficient in opposing a military dictatorship. They also knew that their voices and actions would be diminished in any organization that included both sexes.

The fathers responded in different ways to their spouses' incursions into the public arena. Some were fearful for their wives' safety and accompanied them, watching from the sidelines. Because of the division of labor between the sexes in Argentina, most of the men had to continue working in order to support their families. However, they, too, had to face upheavals in their personal lives as they took over some of their wives' household chores. Many of them supported their wives' new roles, but others were resentful of activities that kept the Mothers away from home. The fathers' situation had its own terrible tragedy because the cultural delineation of gender in Argentina constricts men's as well as women's behavior. Hemmed in by the ideals of *machismo*, many of the fathers were unable to express their feelings openly. "My husband died afterwards because he swallowed all of the pain," Esther Schnieder recalls. "He didn't take any action or do anything. I would come to the capital and write letters, but he stayed home alone and I would return every two weeks to see him so sad. So that is how it was; he ended his life suffering from cancer because he kept all of the pain inside. The men suffered more because they didn't take to the streets."[9] Another Mother told me, "My husband, who was not as [emotionally] strong as I am, went to work one morning and had a cardiac arrest. He was taken to the hospital and three days later he died. He was only fifty-eight years old and was always very healthy. A year after my husband died, my son's father-in-law had a heart attack and died in a bus."[10] The Mothers have many such stories.

Not surprisingly, the manner in which the Mothers conduct their affairs reflects their way of thinking. They have made a clear decision that they will not sacrifice the spontaneity, affection, and freedom of the private sphere while pursuing their political goals. They have proved it is possible to carry on an effective political organization without adopting the dominant organizational model, their distinctive political style evident in the bustle and seeming chaos of their office. Thanks to the financial help of their support groups, in 1984 the Mothers moved from their small office on the second floor of Uruguay Street to a centrally located building on Yrigoyen Street. A plaque on the door informs the visitor that one is at the *Casa de las Madres*, or, the Mothers' House.

A visitor who arrives at the house and climbs up the marble stairs to the warren of rooms on the second floor might feel as if he or she were entering a large, tumultuous household where everything is happening at once. The first time I arrived, one of the Mothers was granting an interview to a group of journalists from Norway in the small reception room at the head of the stairs while another was shepherding around a visitor from Holland, showing him the paintings, awards, and trophies the women have received from groups around the world. Hebe de Bonafini was meeting with lawyers in the front office, the telephone ringing incessantly. At the same time, in the back room, some of the Mothers were having a heated discussion with the journalists over a press release. At noon one of the women picked up her shopping bag in order to gather provisions for the midday meal.

As in their former office on Uruguay Street, a large poster with photographs of their *disappeared* children dominates the main meeting room, which also serves as a dining room. The Mothers hold press conferences in that setting as well as sponsor workshops on political issues, freedom of the press, and human rights. A constant flow of visitors from universities and high schools throughout Argentina and human-rights activists from abroad trickles through the rooms. Because few of the Mothers were able to complete their education, they regularly read and discuss books on politics and human rights from their library. They also attend classes on various subjects taught by young volunteers who come to the Mothers' House once a week. Every morning they read all the newspapers, from the Centrist *La Nación* to the Peronist *El Clarín*.

The space is also a moral court, a testimony to past events as well as the seat of political work seeking to transform the future. One of the journalists who writes for the newspaper devotes a special page each month to the "Gallery of Repressors," featuring one of the torturers who operated the detention centers during the time of the Dirty War. The *Casa* is the space of memory in a society that keeps trying to exorcize the events of the past.

On May 30, 1985, one of the Mothers gave testimony in this office to a military prosecutor trying the officers responsible for torture during the Dirty War. According to Argentine law, "A woman of honest character is able to make a declaration in the location of her choice." A Mother who had been detained under the junta was cited to appear in Military Court 36, in Artilleria Group 1, where a detention center was located. Reluctant to appear where such horrible deeds had occurred and determined to give a clear signal that the Mothers repudiated the decision to try these crimes before a military tribunal, the woman insisted on giving her testimony at the Mothers' House.[11] When the military officers arrived they encountered a row of Mothers in their white scarves standing before the poster of their children. With perfect dignity the Mother recounted the details of her nightmarish imprisonment in the concentration camp, Arena, providing the names of those involved.

This is the underlying reality at the office: the Mothers deliberately have chosen to remember their suffering because to do so will serve their goal of seeking justice and transforming the political system. Beneath that reality are the many layers of activity that take place in this setting. The Mothers make their space available to people needing help, such as numerous neighborhood groups and the parents of the young people involved in the La Tablada incident.

Although there are regularly scheduled meetings of the commission, the planning and discussion of political events also occurs over lunch and tea. Various Mothers have gravitated toward certain jobs according to their inclinations, but the writing of press releases and announcements takes place on a continuous basis and is sandwiched among other activities. I have seen the Mothers return from a demonstration during which there was a fierce encounter with the police and immediately plunge into the task of writing a press release. On another occasion, I watched two of the Mothers hurriedly clear a desk in the back office and install a sewing machine to complete a banner for an evening demonstration.

The Mothers' House opens at 10:00 A.M. and frequently remains open until 1:00 A.M., when the newspaper is going to press or when the young people are helping to prepare for a march or demonstration. The Mothers are always on hand, cooking dinners for their young helpers or for the journalists, and the offices ring with the noisy exchange of work and banter.

Some of the Mothers' organization and political style reflect the principles and practices of anarchism, a movement that flourished in the nineteenth and twentieth centuries in Argentina and which was inspired by immigrants from Italy and Spain who swelled the city of Buenos Aires. The anarchists included leaders like Gori Maletestsa, who inculcated the labor unions with ideas of communal anarchism from Russia before being crushed by General José Uriburu's government in the 1930s.[12] The Mothers' spontaneity, their strong populist language, evangelical solidarity, and antimilitarism resemble that movement. Like groups practicing communal anarchism, the Mothers intend to adjust differing social interests by free and open agreement.

This was also the solution proposed by Vaclav Havel when he wrote that parallel social structures within an oppressive regime should be organized from below, forming dynamic and free communities that engage in mutual cooperation. He believed that these small communities could serve as rudimentary models, ultimately becoming the foundation of a better society after the collapse of the Communist regime.[13] While Havel was searching for a more humane organizational form, he was also describing the way of life practiced by the Mothers.

"In a certain way, we are anarchists because we don't accept the established norms," María del Rosario de Cerruti told me.

> For instance, the Mothers have just participated in an International Festival of Students and Youth in North Korea. It is a Communist country. The Mothers wanted to demonstrate as they do in Argentina, but they were sent to a place where no one would see them. The two Mothers wanted to have a march with their banner just as we do in the Plaza. They entered the room where the festival was being held with their sign held up high. Even though everybody said it couldn't be done, they did it. The Mothers say, "When you want to, you can do it." They marched in when speakers were discussing anti-imperialism. The Mothers said, "If we are talking about human rights, we cannot be in a corner." Everyone stood up and applauded. Then they invited Hebe to go to the head table. She said, "I'll go to the head table if I can talk. Otherwise, I won't go because they have to know what the Mothers are fighting for." This is the Mothers' anarchism. When we go to a place we do what we think we should do. We don't ask for permission. For us, laws don't exist, or homage, all those foolish things. We don't mean the anarchism of killing people, we don't kill anybody, but we will fight until we go to jail, until the last minutes of our lives.[14]

Although there is a broad range of anarchist thought, practices, and attitudes toward change, the unifying spirit of all types of anarchism is one of rebellion toward the established order. What characterizes the Mothers as anarchists is their rebelliousness and their aim of a complete transformation of Argentine society. "We can't have liberation without revolution, without solidarity, without participation, and without the growth of grass-roots organizations," they argue. "There is a need for mutual support and solidarity, for working both inside and outside the political parties so that they maintain dignity and morality."[15] Characteristically, anarchists evaluate society with respect to its fulfillment of human potential, freedom, and justice. When the Mothers raised their banners to include the right to work, a dignified wage, and an adequate health-care and educational system, they focused their criticism on the economic and social structures underpinning the government as well as on its failure to rout the military and prosecute its human-rights abuses.

The Mothers also opposed the inertia of rigid institutions in the country and their imperviousness to the people's needs and desires. When the General Confederation of Labor (CGT) invited the Mothers to participate in a labor rally under their slogan FOR LIFE in November 1990, the Mothers agreed to attend but insisted on marching under their own banner. The day of the rally they appeared in the square under their standard: FOR LIFE WITHOUT A TRADE UNION'S BUREAU-CRACY, ASSASSINS AT LIBERTY, AND A TRAITOROUS GOVERNMENT.

Like the nineteenth-century French anarchist Georges Sorel, who advocated a general strike as a way of toppling the French government, Hebe de Bonafini exhorted the CGT to bring the whole country to a halt in the case of government oppression. In February 1990 she incited the workers who gathered in the Plaza de Mayo not to pay their electricity, gas, or utility bills and urged the grass roots of the labor unions and the political parties to develop a rebellious consciousness. "It would be good for the people to say 'enough.' "[16]

The Mothers' experiences with the church have led them to criticize it as an oppressive institution. "The church subjugates by fear of the devil, hell, purgatory," Hebe explains. "As soon as you get to a church, you have to kneel down. The church imposes silence on you, tells you to keep your pain and pray."[17] The Mothers have noted that whenever mothers of the *disappeared* in other Latin or Central American countries have become affiliated with the church, they wind up accepting its reconciliation with the murderers of their children. In one of their newspaper editorials the Mothers complained, "They always show Christ crucified, never working. It seems as if the church is saying, 'Watch out, the same can happen to you.' If God is everywhere, why do we need to go to church? We can pray at home."[18] They have waged a war of words against the church for its complicity during the Dirty War and for turning its back on the families of the *disappeared*. After the restoration of constitutional government they condemned it for supporting both the government's reconciliation with the military and the granting of pardons to members of the armed forces. They have repeatedly criticized the church hierarchy—in particular, Cardinal Aramburu and the archbishop of La Plata, Antonio Plaza—for its complicity within the detention centers and have brought their charges to the pope himself. When the pope visited Argentina in 1987 the Mothers greeted him with an editorial in their newspaper condemning the church on the basis of the Ten Commandments. "The Pope should place himself at the service of the suffering," they wrote. "Why doesn't he speak out on behalf of life, truth, and justice? Why doesn't he give Communion to the Mothers, or in a poor neighborhood, without military and plainclothesmen in attendance?"[19]

In June 1990 at the thirteenth national meeting of their chapters the Mothers drew up an anarchist platform. "We are reconstituting the bases of organizations, helping them to overcome fear and to reject bureaucratic intrigues and directives. We are beginning to mobilize, giving birth to new forms of organization, resisting and combating in each sector, and creating important modifications in the public's consciousness."[20] In keeping with their political style, the Mothers' association with anarchism is more practical than theoretical. They maintain a dialogue with one of their most fervent supporters, the historian Osvaldo Bayer, who lives in exile in Germany and has written extensively about anarchist movements in Argentina. He has contributed a number of articles about anarchism in nineteenth-century Argentina to the Mothers' newspaper, and the women are avid readers of his books. Their anarchist stance, however, is primarily a result of their own experiences and their own perceptions of power and authority.

One of the Mothers, Mercedes Mereno, grew up in Spain during the civil war as the daughter of a member of the National Confederation of Workers (CNT), the anarchist labor federation. She witnessed a social revolution by millions of workers and peasants who were fighting not to restore a republican regime but to reconstruct Spanish society along anarchist lines. These experiences have inspired Mercedes's political activism and reinforced the Mothers' tendencies toward rebellion. The Mothers' activism is reminiscent of the university students' anarchism that swept Western Europe like a tidal wave in the late 1960s and which was directed not only against governments but also against all the institutions of power—economic, social, and educational. The students prompted people to think of power as residing not just in the economy or in governmental institutions but within all of the structures in which society lives and works. Throughout Europe young people repudiated political parties as irrelevant while the highly bureaucratized parties of the left, such as the Communist party, vacillated between criticizing them and trying to capitalize on their success.

What the Mothers have in common with historical examples of anarchism are their revolutionary methods and their anarchist vision of equality and self-determination through direct participation. In a society such as Argentina's where relations fostered by the church, the military, and powerful interest groups are based upon domination and subordination, the Mothers have forged an agenda of self-determination for the workers and the dispossessed. Their anarchism is reflected in the structure of their organization, which is flexible and democratic, avoiding the creation of committees and the writing of reports, both of which take time and hinder immediate responses to situations. Hebe de Bonafini is a powerful leader, yet she acts only with the full consent of each member; no decisions are taken unless there is agreement among the fifteen-member commission.

Commission meetings are held every Tuesday and whenever important decisions need to be made. Often assembling before the Mothers' Thursday march in the Plaza de Mayo, commission members help clarify the lines of a speech Hebe or another Mother will give, or sketch out a press release after an important event. Since most members are at the Mothers' office much of the week, a gathering can assemble at a moment's notice. The discussions usually involve a heated exchange, the Mothers expressing themselves vigorously and passionately. When there is a thorny problem to solve, the Mothers will often debate for three or four hours. Final decisions are then communicated to the forty active members of the Buenos Aires chapter.

Because decision making occurs with such frequency and spontaneity, the Mothers are able to engage in unpredictable political actions. For example, on July 6, 1990, the eve of the annual celebration of Argentine independence, a number of political parties contacted the Mothers and asked them if they needed help in any way. The Mothers responded with a polite and firm no. They understood that everyone was concerned about demonstrations by the Mothers that might mar Independence Day celebrations and that the offers of help were really a way of trying to fathom their plans for the day. As the Independence Day celebrations commenced, the Mothers caught all the government officials and political parties off guard. They appeared in the Plaza just as the president, flanked by government officials and an honor guard, strode to the cathedral for a solemn High Mass. Despite the fact that they were denied entrance, the Mothers stood at the cathedral door during the Mass, holding aloft pictures of their children. In the intervals between the homily and the hymns, the Mothers shouted, "Hypocrites, assassins, where are our children?" The fact that they were surrounded by a cordon of police did not prevent them from adding their own voices and actions to the celebrations. "They never know what we are going to do next," the Mothers comment with satisfaction.

Within the organization, the Mothers speak with many voices, but when they mobilize as a group they are like a flock of geese arriving and departing, fanning through crowds with precision and determination. Unlike geese, however, the Mothers do not scatter under attack. I have seen them in the midst of a police assault, moving swiftly in a single wave, making sure they remain together, surrounded by the linked hands of their support group. In 1987, when a group of armed policemen dragged off one of the Mothers and put her in a squad car, the women surrounded the car with a cordon made of their pañuelos while their young supporters sat down with a single movement in front of the car, forcing it to back out of the Plaza.[21]

The Mothers have been practicing direct action since their days under the junta. Today, they continue to engage in surprise political forays and keep appearing throughout the country. They also maintain a presence in the province of Buenos Aires, supporting squatters who have taken over abandoned buildings and heading marches of resistance against instances of police brutality in some of the poorer suburbs. They seem to be everywhere, making speeches, setting up tables in the streets, and handing out pamphlets explaining their position. The Mothers' political activities intend to demonstrate that although the president can pass measures by decree, circumventing the Congress, he cannot bypass the people.

Because of their many support groups, the Mothers in Buenos Aires are able to draw thousands of people together on short notice; their chapters in the interior of the country stage similar if smaller demonstrations. When the notorious priest from the Night of the Pencils, Father Christian Von Wernich, was reinstalled as pastor of a church in the suburb of Bragado in 1988, the Mothers led a community march against him. That same year they headed a march of resistance in San Francisco Solano, denouncing the assassination of two young people by the Buenos Aires police.[22]

Since 1981 every December they have staged a twenty-four-hour resistance march in the Plaza de Mayo to celebrate Human Rights' Day. These marches are the occasion for stirring speeches and have become an established drama, an opportunity to claim space for the humane values of the opposition. The week prior to the march, doctors who support the mothers fortify them with vitamins and minister to them so they can sustain such a rigorous event. The cafés that line the Plaza put out chairs for the Mothers and make their facilities available to the marchers. These demonstrations, typically drawing well-wishers from other Latin American countries, Europe, the United States, and Canada, reveal how the Mothers consistently defy the stereotypes of women and the elderly in a society that has sought to ridicule them. The processions are not only a means of entering the political dialogue, but they also demonstrate the cohesion of their participants, providing a form of popular participation for those who have no access to the channels of power.

Through their marches, the Mothers have displayed a repertoire of new techniques to manifest an alternative and higher set of values than those promoted by the political system, drawing upon a powerful symbolism. In 1985, for instance, the Mothers initiated a campaign of Linking Hands. They printed thousands of white flyers with the outline of a hand topped by the insignia of the Mothers: PEACE, LOVE, AND JUSTICE. People from around the country and abroad were invited to sign their names and to add messages of goodwill. President Sandro Pertini of Italy sent an impression of his left hand to the Mothers with the message, "This is my left hand, the hand of the heart, filled with anguish at the cruel fate of the disappeared." A nine-year-old child wrote beside his signature, "I don't know you. I know you are some-where, but wherever you are, I want you to know we will keep fighting for you." When the Mothers had gathered thousands of hands they strung them together in rows of banners in the Plaza to show that "each person is a participant, a person exercising his or her right, who decides, who helps to create democracy and to show that justice is indivisible. We link our hands so that everyone can see that we are together, that we wish to live, work, and think without fear."[23]

The Mothers' demonstrations are also a form of street theater similar to the medieval morality plays. At the time of the trials of the junta, the Mothers marched with the Association of Ex-Detained, Ex-Disappeared, carrying chains and hoods as symbols of the terror. In the late 1980s groups of artists working for the Mothers created white masks representing the *disappeared*. Thousands of young people wearing these masks paraded down the main streets in a display aimed at keeping the plight of the *disappeared* in the public consciousness. The artists have also created props of life-size white silhouettes for the Mothers' marches. Watching a parade of hundreds of ghostly silhouettes or chalk-white masks file silently through the streets is a powerful, emotionally jarring experience.

These events are also a way of publicizing the names and deeds of those who were responsible for the tortures and abductions. Whenever the army stages a parade, the Mothers are there with their banners and the photos of their children. On the anniversaries of the military coup, the Mothers stage a four-day event, Against Injustice, with stands for political parties and human-rights groups. One year a number of fine-arts students painted a twenty-foot mural that depicted political pris-oners and the torture they endured. In the background a radio station, installed by the Mothers' support group, played some of General Videla's speeches. In 1987 the Mothers launched a Behind Bars event on the streets to represent the enactment of justice. Their support group pasted huge posters, with the names of those responsible for the terror, as well as the names and locations of all the detention centers, on buildings, splashing black prison bars over them. The paintings were installed with great dispatch in a single morning while the Mothers surrounded their helpers with a cordon of white shawls to protect them from the police. When the armed forces marched by that afternoon, many of them found their names on the walls.

The Mothers demonstrate in 1988 against the granting of amnesty (*photo by Gerardo Dell'Orto*)

The police arrest a Mother in the Plaza de Mayo and search a supporter, 1987 (*photo by Gerardo Dell'Orto*)

In 1988, the year of two military uprisings, the Mothers launched a campaign to distribute posters throughout the country and to send lists of signatures abroad. ARMED FORCES, ASSASSINS, the posters proclaimed, and the leaflets with the signatures were entitled AGAINST AMNESTY, FOR LIFE, AGAINST DEATH. The Mothers appeared everywhere—in the parks, in the plazas, and in the streets—gathering signatures. They mailed their leaflets to the European Parliament, the United Nations, and the Organization of American States, and shipped huge bundles to the Argentine president, the Congress, and members of the judiciary to show them that much of the population opposed the granting of amnesty. They also printed and circulated pamphlets entitled I AC-CUSE, which listed the names of all those responsible for the terror and the *disappearances*. Each of these campaigns has been intended to catch the government off guard, to elicit the participation of as many people as possible in order to counter efforts by the government, the police, and the army to manipulate the public into states of apathy and hopelessness. "The government should know that the people think for themselves," the Mothers proclaimed, "that they rebel, that they wish to transgress, that they want change."[24]

"Wherever there are '*disappeared*,' we are there," the Mothers have said. In a society alienated by fear and memories of repression, the Mothers' goal is to bring back the value of the person to the center of national concerns. Therefore, they avoided establishing a large, bureaucratized organization and instead created a true democratic anarchism, a federation of fourteen chapters across the nation whose members cooperate both formally and informally on the basis of equality. Although the Buenos Aires chapter is now the largest and was the first to establish itself formally, serving as a model for other affiliates, it does not dominate the federation. These chapters meet every three months to hammer out the national program and to make major decisions. Since 1981 they have scheduled yearly gatherings during which the Mothers make a public statement on both the state of affairs in the country and their goals. The chapters also hold frequent regional meetings in order to help them reach wider audiences in the population. In the intervals between meetings, the Mothers travel to each other's offices in support of their respective projects.

The various chapters operate under differing political conditions, and, as a result, their activities are diverse. Some chapters are unable to schedule marches in the central plazas of their cities because of the hostility of the local governments, while some have acquired a column in local newspapers and time on local radio programs. The chapter in Luján maintains a strong presence because of a radio program it produces, "To Be a Woman," which airs for two hours every day and hosts women from all walks of life. It also produces a companion television program once a week that has helped the Mothers gain publicity. In Tucumán, where the army initiated its clandestine policy of *disappearances* even before the junta came to power, it is still dangerous to be a political dissident. The police operate a museum of subversion there that is open to the public and which exhibits body parts of captured "terrorists" in bottles of formaldehyde.[25] The Mothers in the Tucumán chapter are headed by Graciela Jaeger, a brilliant woman with a strong charisma and a gift for political analysis that she uses frequently and publicly.

Many chapters, such as the San Juan Mothers, suffer from a declining membership. From a high of thirty Mothers and a number of wives of the *disappeared*, the San Juan chapter has dwindled to two members. The wives of the *disappeared* either have remarried or are burdened with the dual task of childrearing and earning a living. Some of the Mothers stopped coming because of age and ill health, others because of their husbands' objections to both their *disappeared* children's politics and their wives' participation in the chapter. The government of San Juan opposes the Mothers and has refused to grant them permission to demonstrate. Given the political climate and trying personal circumstances, it is remarkable that two of the San Juan Mothers continue their political activity. On Sundays they keep a stall in the plaza where people sell crafts, and they are there from 6 P.M. until midnight in the summer, selling the Mothers' newspapers and answering questions. In 1990 they participated in a strike, which gave them new contacts and helped create a support group of young people. Esther Schnieder is one of the two Mothers who keep the chapter alive. Her daughter, who was studying psychology at the University of Córdoba, was living in a boardinghouse when twenty armed men came to drag her away at dawn on December 6, 1977. Through the Mothers' information network of *ex-detained-disappeared*, Esther found out that her daughter was in La Perla concentration camp but never learned her ultimate fate. She told me, "Many people have retired, the older mothers whose health is failing. So I was left trying to keep this little light burning, illuminating the fact that our sons and daughters fought for something noble and that we continue with their banners raised high."[26]

The different chapters are assisted by support groups; in Buenos Aires, the Mothers are also supported by personnel and constitute a quasi-utopian community where no money is exchanged for service. Most people who work with the Mothers have outside employment. A team of lawyers has represented the Mothers for the past eight years, and a married couple, Primi and Héctor Mohina, films every important demonstration and keeps a chronicle of events in the life of the organization. A number of doctors periodically check on the Mothers' health and prepare them for the more arduous marches and events. The reporters and photographers who work on the Mothers' newspapers donate their time, and when the paper is in production they frequently work throughout the night. A few of them are at the *Casa* every day, helping the Mothers refine their press releases and serving as a sounding board for some of their ideas.

As the Mothers were marching around the Plaza de Mayo in the early years of their organization, a woman expressing her support for their plight came to join them. They discovered that she was a psychologist, and some of them asked for her help in facing their difficulties. Thus began the support of a team of therapists who donate their services not only to the Mothers but also to the families and relatives who suffered the emotional and psychological problems of losing a sibling or parent under such horrendous circumstances. Among the Mothers are many who are rearing their grandchildren because both a son and daughter-in-law were *disappeared* or whose grandchildren are being brought up by the opposite set of grandparents and have only minor visitation privileges. The services of these psychologists have been a significant source of support to the Mothers in dealing with such pressures, and, until recently, the professionals maintained a suite of offices on the top floor of the *Casa de las Madres*. The relationship has been a dynamic one, the Mothers imparting the fruits of their increasing political sophistication to the psychologists. They have actually helped the therapists face the difficulties of practicing their profession under a repressive system. In 1988 this group scheduled a debate for mental health professionals and invited psychologists from the Foundation for Social Assistance of the Christian Churches in Santiago, Chile, which has worked with victims of torture since 1975.[27] Professionals in both countries who work with families of the *disappeared* have come to view their roles in more political terms—as helping victims of state terrorism who have experienced profound alterations in their legal, social, and political lives.[28]

The Mothers are aided as well by a group of young students and workers called the *Juventud*, or Youth, who perform most of the manual tasks needed to get ready for the marches and help prepare for important demonstrations and events. The Mothers, however, see their most important assistance and their future as coming from the Front for Human Rights. The hidden political agenda of the Front poses one of the problems endemic to an anarchist organization, the omnipresent possibility of becoming undermined not so much from outside forces, which are clearly visible, but from well-organized minorities within who conceal their purposes. Given this problem, the most accurate way of viewing the organization's future is to see the Mothers as a historical example whose influence is not limited to Argentina or to the following generation, but which will continue to inspire groups around the world, as did the work of Steve Biko in South Africa or the Velvet Revolution in Czechoslovakia. Instances of extraordinary courage and the enduring power of moral integrity are like sparks that fly throughout the globe, catching flame at different periods. Thus, while the Mothers may have no immediate heirs in the next generation, their example will certainly awaken similar efforts in other places and times. In 1989, for instance, a group of four hundred Mexican-American mothers in a district of East Los Angeles donned white shawls and started a campaign of weekly marches and letter-writing to block the construction of a state prison and an incinerator in an area near dozens of schools. This was the beginning of a long campaign against the injustices visited on their community. Like the Mothers they entered politics not as individuals channeling their grievances through traditional routes but as a group working on behalf of issues affecting their households and community, linking the public and private in a new form of political behavior.

In creating their organization the Mothers inspired similar efforts throughout Latin America: delegations of mothers of the *disappeared* from Chile, Guatemala, El Salvador, Nicaragua, and Honduras frequently visit the Mothers of the Plaza de Mayo, learning organizational and political skills and marching with them. The Mutual Support Group (GAM) of mothers of the *disappeared* in Guatemala was formed in 1984, stirred by the Mothers and by the *Co-Madres* in El Salvador.[29] All three organizations draw the bulk of their membership from the working and peasant classes. As long as military regimes continue to *disappear* young adults and perpetuate economic policies that exacerbate poverty, Mothers' groups will confront military brutality and protest the conditions of the poor.

The Mothers have also influenced the grass roots of labor unions disaffected with their leadership and have worked with the Mapucho Indians, groups of retired people, and slum dwellers. They see their work—empowering disenfranchised sectors of the population and challenging the institutions of government—as proof of the relevance of revolutionary anarchism. Although it is the nature of anarchism to be short-lived because of its spontaneity, its openness, and its refusal to establish bureaucratic structures, anarchist movements have had an influence disproportionate to their size and strength. Like the Mothers' organization, other anarchist experiments have served as mirrors in which the larger society could see its faults. Both have been scorned for their impracticality and praised for their humane ideals. Throughout history, communal anarchist movements have created new social practices that were ultimately adopted by the broader society.

Features of communal anarchism recently have appeared among people defying established institutions and seeking to create new forms of popular participation, notably the democratic movement in China that briefly flowered in Tienanmen Square in 1989. Revolutionary communal anarchism is a recurrent theme in the ongoing human struggle to create political change. Viewed in this light, the Mothers' organization is a crucial episode in the continual search for human freedom and dignity. What makes it unique is that it was founded and is governed by women. In establishing their organization the Mothers have created a model that allows both women and men to experience continuity between humane values and political behavior and that regards relatedness as an end as well as a means. It has proved a resilient model of resistance to an oppressive regime, demonstrating a flexibility that has enabled it to reflect changing political circumstances while steadfastly maintaining the values of its creators. The Mothers have proved that it is possible to work openly with democratic values in authoritarian settings, contradicting a political history in which those oppressed by the state have in turn often adopted oppressive methods.

NOTES

1. Vaclav Havel, "The Power of the Powerless," in *Vaclav Havel: Or, Living in Truth*, ed. Jan Vladislav (Boston: Faber and Faber, 1986), 36–122.

2. Sánchez, *Historias de vida*, 171.

3. Carol Gilligan et al., eds., *Mapping the Moral Domain: A Contribution of Women's Thinking to Psychological Theory and Education* (Cambridge, MA: Center for the Study of Gender Education and Human Development, 1988), 3–19.

4. Madres, *Boletín*, no. 1 (no date).

5. de Bonafini, interview.

6. Madres, *Monthly Newspaper*, January 1991.

7. "Causes of Revolution and Constitutional Change," in Bk. 5, *The Politics of Aristotle*. trans. Ernest Barker (New York: Oxford University Press, 1974), 244.

8. Ruddick, *Maternal Thinking*, 222.

9. Esther Schnieder, interview by Marguerite Bouvard, November 1990.

10. Hebe Mascia, interview by Marguerite Bouvard, November 1990.

11. Madres, *Monthly Newspaper*, June 1985.

12. Osvaldo Bayer, *Los anarquistas expropiadores* (Buenos Aires: Legasa S.A., 1984).

13. Vaclav Havel, "The Power of the Powerless," 117.

14. de Cerruti, interview.

15. Madres, *Monthly Newspaper*, January 1989.

16. Ibid., February 1990.

17. de Bonafini, interview.

18. Madres, *Monthly Newspaper*, March 1991.

19. Ibid., March 1987.

20. Ibid., June 1990.

21. Héctor and Primi Mohina, *Video History of the Mothers of the Plaza de Mayo* (Buenos Aires, August 1987).

22. Madres, *Monthly Newspaper*, June 1988.

23. Ibid.

24. Ibid.

25. Mères de la Place de Mai, *Bulletin Liaison de SOLIMA* (Paris), no. 14 (March 1992).

26. Schnieder, interview.

27. Madres, *Monthly Newspaper*, September 1988.

28. Kordon et al., *Psychological Effects of Political Repression*, 24.

29. Jennifer G. Schirmer, "Those Who Die for Life Cannot be Called Dead: Women and Human Rights Protest in Latin America," *Feminist Review* 29 (Summer 1988): 41–65.

THEY TRY TO MAKE YOU INVISIBLE

In the early years, they spray-painted your office
terrorist cell. The next day
you were on the street with tables and chairs
passing out hand-printed pamphlets.
At the height of the repression, the newspapers
were afraid to carry your ad
listing your missing children. When you found
one that was brave enough, you took up
a collection because you had no money.
You borrowed a typewriter because
you had no equipment. They abducted your leader
to try to silence you, but you placed the ad
anyway. Today the newspapers
are still afraid, so you publish your own paper.
You are always one step ahead of them,
painting the names of the torturers
on the cobblestones
the night before a military parade,
surrounding your young helpers with a cordon of pañuelos
while they paint murals of colonels behind bars
on the buildings of a main street.
You call a demonstration on behalf of justice,
but when you gather in the plaza
the evening of the march, they turn off the lights.
As you surge through the avenues, past
the hotels and theaters,
past the elegant apartments, the good citizens
move indoors. The television crews
are from abroad. But you have 10,000 followers
marching behind you. You have shown
again and again that you can fill the streets,
that nothing can make you invisible.

CHAPTER 10

Taking Space: Women and Political Power

The Mothers did not start out as political thinkers. Rather, they began their quest within what Vaclav Havel called "the hidden sphere," the private self reexamining a new reality and responding to it.[1] Remaining true to their vision of what had happened to their children was a tremendous undertaking that involved unmasking government propaganda and assurances of normality while braving physical assaults and death threats. To serve the truth they decided to use the method of truthfulness, working in the open through a free and democratic organization based upon their own views. In so doing they reunited the spheres of the private and the public. They revealed that living with dignity and honoring life in a society that denied the most basic rights was a political statement.

The story of Carmen d'Elia, a woman who has been one of the Mothers' most active supporters since the days of the junta, illustrates how living with integrity and serving the truth can constitute a powerful political position. When the junta came to power Carmen was a prime candidate for the policy of *disappearance* because of her socialist politics. She knew she had been targeted, but by continually changing residences she managed to elude the security forces. She told me that at that time it felt as if all Argentines were living in a concentration camp, one perhaps less ferocious than the detention centers but a prison nevertheless. During this period Carmen developed a tumor in her breast, which medical tests revealed as cancerous. Shortly afterward, in the fall of 1979, she saw the Mothers standing in line to talk with members of the Organization of American States' Commission on Human Rights, denouncing the junta in public. That sight changed her life. Even though security police had been looking for her and her chest ached from her recent surgery, she joined the Mothers on their march around the Plaza de Mayo. Carmen then interpreted her illness as a hidden desire to die rather than live under a political system that made her feel impotent. She told me that her decision was a matter of claiming her own moral space, of deciding to live with dignity rather than succumb to despair. In a repressive regime to choose to do so is a form of power, which is why individuals in totalitarian societies who have tried to act upon their integrity have been sent to concentration camps if they were unknown, into exile if they enjoyed a reputation.

These individual acts illuminate the chinks in the regime's armor. When they take the form of collective action they begin to defy the propaganda, the set of lies that serves as the glue holding together an unwieldy and pervasive bureaucracy of terror, for no regime can exist on terror alone. Ideology or a particular interpretation of national security, such as the junta's claim of preserving "Western, Christian values against atheistic terrorism," guarantees the internal coherence of the power structure and acts as one of the pillars of its external stability. Unlike national myths, which may achieve a semblance of reality in the lives of a people, the junta's ideals of national security existed on shaky grounds. While the junta insisted that the *disappeared* were terrorists who had gone abroad or had died, the Mothers revealed the ugly facts of the detention centers. They continually pointed out that the majority of the *disappeared* were not terrorists, as the junta claimed, but loyal members of the opposition, including people who had never engaged in politics and even some members of the establishment. Further, the Mothers proclaimed that their life within their organization was based upon true Christian values; the junta, however, failed to honor the very values it claimed it was protecting. In shattering the lies that served as a rationale for the junta's terror, the Mothers exposed the glaring weakness of the entire system. They opened a crack in the junta's armor that would widen into a yawning gap after the Falklands War.

Denied access to the institutions of power, first under the junta and then under the newly restored constitutional government, the Mothers claimed spaces in which power could be expressed in novel ways. They chose to work by direct action, out on the streets and in the Plaza. Direct action, however, is not only a decision to work outside the given structures for the expression and articulation of interests; it also represents the independent development of political consciousness. Its many facets include: interpreting a situation, defining a problem, and inventing ways of solving the problem. According to British social theorist Barry Barnes, empowerment begins when the consciousness of powerless people shifts, enabling them to assume greater control over their own lives.[2] One of its premises is that the powerful do not have absolute control over the powerless, and that cracks in such control can be identified, explored, and expanded through both individual and group resistance. When the Mothers refused to consider themselves helpless victims but rather active agents, first in searching for their children and later in demanding that those responsible for the junta's crimes be brought to justice, they were continually exceeding the limits set by the government on permissible action. Under the junta they explored every possible chink in the bureaucratic structure. The military junta, as well as the police and security forces still active today, believed that it is possible to exercise total control over sectors of the population and that power is based upon physical force. The Mothers have proved otherwise, blatantly expanding the interstices of control.

In so doing the Mothers also increased their capacity for risk taking, which allowed them to transcend the socially prescribed barriers established for women as well as the ban on political activity enforced by the junta. In Argentina women are expected to remain passive and isolated from each other. One of the Mothers, Juana de Pargament, gives a telling comment on the limits of state power:

> Sometimes we go on a big march with lots of people. They don't know what we are going to do, so they set up barricades to prevent us from going ahead. Therefore we take down the barricades and

they don't understand how we were able to do it so quickly. We don't give them any time to think. It's ridiculous to see the police with their uniforms trying to look so important and then a group of women with white scarves make them run. That ridiculous role they play makes us feel that we are strong. We look at them and see that the only things they have are their uniforms and their arms, but in the presence of dignity, they are dishonorable.[3]

As women in a traditional society imbued with the values of *machismo*, the Mothers had to overcome the psychological, social, and political barriers that kept them in the sphere of the household. "What will people think if I go out to demonstrate?" most of the Mothers wondered. Many of them feared that to act in such a manner would cause scandal in the family. Not only were women's activities circumscribed by social views of what is proper for female behavior, but those who transgressed such norms also were subject to ridicule. The government's reference to the Mothers as *Las Locas*, or the crazy ones, was intended to undermine their credibility in the public's eyes and to keep them in their places—that is, marginal and invisible. As part of their new sense of self the Mothers began to assume control over their lives, expanding their spheres of activity and moving beyond society's restraints as they marched in public, appeared at public events, and raised their banners and posters. They refused to be controlled and insisted on bringing their activities and visions into national awareness through their bulletins and, during a time when newspaper editors and publishers were being *disappeared*, by publishing poetry and books containing their children's photographs. In flaunting social custom and physical danger they took personal and emotional risks, thereby paving the way for their continual growth.

In departing from set norms and expected behavior, they enlarged their political space and the space for their perceptions, for thought and activity occur in an inextricable relationship. They brought to their newly acquired political space the consciousness of women, the concrete thinking defined by Sara Ruddick and exemplified by Hebe de Bonafini's comment to a television interviewer that she considered herself a housewife and also a political activist, defying the simplification of the male/female, private/public spheres. Ruddick contrasts maternal thinking with the abstract thinking often engaged in by

The Mothers "put the torturers behind bars" in 1987 with murals posted before a military parade (*photo by Gerardo Dell'Orto*)

Independence Day celebrations, 1990. Denied entrance to the cathedral for Mass, the Mothers demonstrate outside with photos of their *disappeared* children (*photo by Gerardo Dell'Orto*)

Susanna de Gudano, selling the Mothers' newspaper in the Plaza de Mayo

María del Rosario de Cerruti, editor of the Mothers' newspaper (*photo by Gerardo Dell'Orto*)

governments that simplifies, generalizes, and sharply defines. Mothers around the world work and think with a double vision—the near and the banal, such as supervising a child's homework; and the larger questions of purpose for the child. This vision enables them to make connections between the spheres of their lives. "In their work, the Mothers learn to ponder circumstances and consequences, to listen sympathetically to the uncertainties of another's experiences," Ruddick writes.[4] Thus, the concreteness of maternal thinking reflects the complexities of life, tolerates ambiguity, and multiplies options rather than accepts the terms of a problem.

Another unique aspect of the consciousness articulated by the Mothers is the reuniting of thought and feeling from their artificial separation into reason, on the one hand, and emotion, on the other. Psychologist Jean Baker Miller, who has written that thought and feeling reinforce each other and that connecting closely with what we are experiencing enables us to tap our inherent creativity, believes that the more opportunities we have to put our thoughts into action, the more completely we can feel, and that the more women can act in terms of their own conceptions, the more complete, authentic, and strong they feel.[5] "Feeling is what keeps us alive," the Mothers have commented. They are always rewriting themselves, demonstrating an inherent creativity and enlarging the range of their experience.

Sara Ruddick has noted that although some kinds of thinking are more separable from feeling than others (computer programming, for instance), a mother is dependent on her sensibility to name and construct the world she observes. For example, sentiments are tested in terms of protection and worry on the part of the mother, a sense of safety as experienced by the child. "In protective work, feeling, thinking, and action are conceptually linked. Feelings demand reflections, which are in turn tested by action, which is in turn tested by the feelings it provides. Thoughtful feeling, passionate thought, and protective acts together test and reveal the effectiveness of preservative love."[6] Certainly, the Mothers refer to love as a motivating force in their political work and as an approach to their actions. For them, love is not an abstraction but is instead embodied in the strength of their ties, the quality of their relations with other groups, the bonds of affection with their *disappeared* children and all the children and dispossessed of Argentina, and in their goal of creating a more just society.

The other side of love is hatred and anger, and the Mothers are equally fueled by an anger for which they are continually criticized, their fury wholly out of keeping with the passive, grieving model of motherhood held up in the tradition of *marianismo*. Carolyn Heilbrun notes in *Writing a Woman's Life* that anger, together with the open demand for power and control over one's life, is one of the key prohibitions experienced by women.[7] In order to curb their anger, she says, women have been criticized as shrill and strident, and she concludes that a woman must destroy herself in order to create her most authentic self and act in the public domain. Hebe de Bonafini, for example, contrasts herself today with Kika, the nickname she used among family and friends. Kika was naive and trusting—Hebe is politically astute and expresses outrage regardless of the consequences.

Many Argentines urged the Mothers to forgive, forget, and move on. They refused to relinquish their rage, though, because they recognized that it was their anger and their pain that fueled their political action. Hebe de Bonafini recalled that once a politician participating in a radio debate made the moderator ask why the Mothers have so much hatred in them. "So I answered, 'Yes, I loathe people who torture and rape.' And then the politician said, 'I don't feel any hate,' and I answered, 'Listen, if after knowing how they tortured and raped our sons and daughters, you don't feel any hate, you are a hypocrite.' "[8] The church has also criticized the Mothers for expressing their rancor toward those responsible for the tortures during the Dirty War. Hebe de Bonafini has continually responded on behalf of the Mothers that suppressing detestation means becoming a hypocrite and that the women have transformed their hatred into their political efforts. The Mothers shattered the limits of permissible female behavior when they demonstrated by their actions and words that anger and pain are both appropriate and useful and that feelings cannot be controlled. Writing about the Holocaust and meditating on the strains of good and evil in all human beings, Israeli psychologist Israel Charny commented, "Each of us must bear full responsibility for the choices we make whether or not to be destroyers. There can be no forgiveness; there can be no dampening of our outrage and protest against the killing of men."[9]

Psychologists have noted that the duality in human beings must be continually intertwined, that we must call on the two natural sides of ourselves to work together—the toughness and tenderness, the loving and hating. Catholic theologian Thomas Merton wrote about the interconnection between love and hate, commenting, "As long as we believe that we hate no one, that we are merciful, that we are kind by our very natures, we deceive ourselves. Our hatred is merely smoldering under the gray ashes of complacent optimism. We are apparently at peace with everyone because we believe we are worthy. That is to say, we have lost the capacity to face the question of unworthiness." [10] Drawing upon their experiences in the private sphere, the Mothers weave their duality and the full range of their emotions into their political work. They have sloughed off their old selves, who once placed trust in institutions, and assumed new and fuller identities that express rage, scorn, irony, and derision.

Their anger enabled the Mothers to move beyond fear. During the days of the junta they recognized that the pervasive fright among the population left it paralyzed, unable and unwilling to oppose the government. After the return of constitutional government the security forces, police, and military remained omnipresent threats to dissenters like the Mothers, yet the women continued their political work. I remember the transformation I underwent as a result of being with the Mothers. On my first visit I felt a deep sense of unease as they were followed and videotaped by the ubiquitous security police. If fear flares up in one's imaginings, however, it disappears the minute one decides to move beyond it and react with anger to those who wish to oppress. On my second trip I lost my fright as I marched with the Mothers when, in their linked arms, in their casual disregard of the security forces, and in their determination, I felt their courage around me. When I looked at a group of policemen striding through the Plaza de Mayo during a trade union rally, I exploded inside at the realization that my apprehension had made me overly cautious. The anger that authorities seek to repress sparks rebellion and is thus powerful, as the Mothers have proved. "Fear is a prison without bars," Hebe de Bonafini once claimed. "It is the worst jail because it doesn't let you think."

As women in a male-defined society, the Mothers broke through the barriers of ridicule and social prohibition to create new identities and a public space for themselves. They also deliberately placed themselves outside of the norms of female beauty by refusing to pay attention to their looks. "We are not stars," the Mothers say. "We are not going to care about our appearances on television or when we are photographed." They will not wear makeup when they are on television or in public because they regard their wrinkles and their lines of suffering with respect. In so doing, they refuse to be made objects or to have their plausibility defined by the culture. Hebe de Bonafini feels completely comfortable with her affectionate nickname, *La Gorda*, or the fat one. María del Rosario de Cerruti once commented, "I used to spend hours shopping for a dress, a pair of shoes." She now typically wears T-shirts to work, and one is immediately aware of her intrinsic beauty, the sharp intelligence in her dark eyes, her deft and capable movements not as she folds laundry or tucks in a bed but as she lines up the marchers before a demonstration. The Mothers defy not only the general image of women in Argentina and the world but also the particular image of aged women, who are usually regarded as ineffective and politically irrelevant. Just when women are supposed to settle down, make preserves, and care for their grandchildren, the Mothers began a rebellion against their own political system and against patriarchal values the world over.

Carolyn Heilbrun, observing women writers, stated that women are often in their middle years when they begin to create their own story. The Mothers have demonstrated that rather than turning into public images of crones or hags, they have become braver as they age, unconcerned about the opinions of others. By their actions they demonstrate that while young people have time, older people have possibilities; they know about the range of choice, the moral dimension of political issues, and the real meaning of life. Heilbrun notes that to allow oneself at fifty and beyond a fuller and freer self-expression has no male counterpart in the Western world. If men revolt they do so at a younger age, and by the time they reach their middle years they are much less likely to express hidden ideals or revolutionary hopes. "It is only in old age, certainly past fifty, that women can stop being female impersonators, can grasp the opportunity to reverse their most cherished principles of femininity," she argues.[11] For the Mothers, these cherished principles included political naïveté and the mistaken belief that they could entrust their destiny to others. Their new identities include a joyful participation in significant political work.

Their new-found freedom and selfhood is also expressed in their capacity for laughter and happiness. One of the Mothers commented, "I don't know if people can understand that despite the pain and horror I have lived through, I can be happy. I am happy that people listen to me and understand how a woman whose children have been snatched from her can become a lion, that we can all do it. I believe women have a great destiny. We have a lot to do in this world."[12] The laughter and pleasure in companionship that the Mothers experience daily in the Mothers' House on Yrigoyen Street is indicative of their changed life. They know how to enjoy themselves, whether celebrating the birth of a grandchild or laughing at a good joke. Heilbrun remarks, "Women laugh together only in freedom, in the recognition of independence and female bonding. It marks the end of fantasy and daydreaming, the substitution of work, the end of the dream of closure."[13] Out of the confidence they have gained from their new-found authenticity the Mothers have invented a political narrative where there was none and have developed a tone in which to speak with authority.

The first time Hebe de Bonafini addressed a public forum was in 1980 at the United Nations. The Center for Legal and Social Studies (CELS) and the Families of the Disappeared came well prepared with written speeches and offered to speak on behalf of the Mothers, who insisted upon speaking for themselves. They spoke simply, without notes, explaining their positions and what they were working for. After the presentations were over most of the questions were directed toward the Mothers. They were able to speak spontaneously in so many different settings because they held fast to the truth of their own situation and their political aims. Because they were not contending for power, but instead claiming space for the opposition, they were not forced to compromise their language or their goals. Voice is an important part of political dialogue; the Mothers' voice is bold, forthright, challenging, and reflects women's experience in a male-dominated world. "We say things the way we think. We don't want to be pleasant."[14] When the junta fell and constitutional government was restored, the Mothers insisted on "jail for those who committed genocide, for those who violated, tortured, robbed, and disappeared thirty thousand people. Jail for those criminals set free by corrupt judges and for politicians without scruples." On the eve of the trials of junta members, the Mothers demanded "judgment and punishment for all culprits." These slogans were both a rallying cry against the government and an effort to create a new political reality based upon justice and human dignity.

During the time of the junta the government peppered the country with posters that asked, "Do you know where your child is?" suggesting that the *disappeared* had been involved in clandestine terrorist activity. In the campaign the Mothers waged in 1990 against the pardon of the convicted members of the junta, their banners and posters queried, "Do you know where those who tortured and assassinated our children are? Do you know what positions they hold, what they are involved in?" These questions were intended to demonstrate how many of those who had participated in the Dirty War continued to hold positions of authority. The Mothers noted how the government undermined the significance of words when the president referred to his administration as democratic yet made use of decrees to bypass the Congress. "If there is anything we have gained in the years of struggle," they explain, "it is space to shout, to protest, to mobilize, to gather to our side people that really don't like this government, and to demand at last a government for and by the people. We are the 'No,' the drums, the protest, the street, and the beginning of that other revolution which will abolish privilege and establish respect for human dignity."[15]

The government and the military found themselves forced to respond. Until he was pardoned the notorious Ramón Camps, former chief of police of the province of Buenos Aires, wrote newspaper columns for *La Prensa* from his cell, unleashing a barrage of criticism against the Mothers for their "orgy of hatred, madness, and blasphemy against the army, the police, and the church, against everything that signifies order and hierarchy."[16] The attention devoted to creating negative images of the Mothers was an indication of the status they had acquired.

More important, the Mothers enlarged the terms of the political debate to include ethical values. As they had joined thought and feeling in their powerful words, they wanted to combine ethics and politics, saying, "It is a lie that politics and ethics cannot go together. We have to defend love among ourselves, a political ethics and an ethical politics."[17] When the Mothers marched against the granting of a pardon to the convicted members of the junta, they described themselves as "fighting against fear, against pragmatism, and above all against indifference and the manipulation of conscience."[18] Like the dissidents in former Communist regimes, the Mothers were drawing upon ethical values both to criticize the political system and to suggest an alternative political future. While the government sought to contain the dialogue within the established channels of partisan politics on the one hand, and their bargains with the military on the other, the Mothers expanded the frame of reference of political debates.

From the early days of their organization the Mothers have revealed that truth consists both of speaking and of modes of being. They have proved that, because it reveals the inconsistencies and weakness of the system, truth constitutes a form of power in a repressive political regime. Speaking the truth openly and at great personal risk to the world of power constitutes what Vaclav Havel referred to as the "power of the powerless." The Mothers agree: "We think that to be able to tell the truth, as difficult as it might be, to be able to face the powerful without violence, to face them as we do, gives us strength, a different kind of power, not their kind."[19] In 1992 they were rewarded for their efforts with the Sakharov Prize for Freedom of Thought from the European Parliament, an honor previously conferred upon South Africa's Nelson Mandela, Czechoslovakia's Alexander Dubcek, and Burma's Aung San Suu Kyi.

The moral stature the Mothers have gained acts as an unwelcome mirror and a measuring stick for the government and its policies. In calling out the truth of their perceptions—that behind the orderly facade of democratic institutions lie arrangements with nonofficial sources of power—the Mothers expose the real basis of the state. Vaclav Havel insists that as long as an alternative exists to the political system, it does not matter how large a space it occupies. Its effectiveness relies not upon numbers but in the light it casts on the system and its foundations.[20] The power of truth-telling is inherently destabilizing, which explains the savagery with which the government has turned on the Mothers, especially during President Saúl Menem's tenure. Havel notes that speaking the truth and standing up for human rights do not bear immediate fruit. Too frequently the immediate results are death, imprisonment, and continual harassment, all of which the Mothers have suffered.

As Gandhi and Martin Luther King, Jr., pointed out, nonviolent action reveals the inherent violence within a political system and highlights the oppressiveness and injustice of the governing forces. The sight of police turning water cannons on peaceful demonstrators for civil rights, for instance, gave the world a stark image of the U.S. political system in the 1960s. The sight of the Mothers marching peacefully in the Plaza and being attacked by police on horseback, or surrounded by plainclothesmen with their video cameras trained on them, gives the world a clear picture of that other Argentina which is so carefully masked in the media.

As the junta in its tyranny erupted into the private space of Argentines, the Mothers responded by bringing emblems of that space into public places as an act of defiance and a dramatization of a different social order that combined the two spheres. From the beginning the Mothers decided to work in prominent public arenas—the Plaza de Mayo and the streets—to denote the value of openness as well as the temporary suspension of total governmental control. During the time of the junta, which categorized all public demonstrations and gatherings as subversive, the Mothers defied physical assault and their own fear by gathering in its vast empty spaces. The Plaza became a sacred arena where they could assume their dignity, the right to think and act as human beings against a repressive government. Defying death threats, the Mothers marched straight into the seat of power, demanding government accountability. Because the junta ultimately was unable to eject them from that space, except for brief periods, the Mothers felt that it belonged to them.

The Plaza is the space they have claimed for their children from a government that sought first to eliminate them and then to deny their very existence, the place where their children receive a social and political existence. "If I miss a Thursday, I miss my child," the Mothers have told me. "The Plaza is in my skin. It's in my body. . . . It is a space that is ours. After fourteen years, it cannot belong to anyone else. Going to the Plaza is an encounter, not only with the son you are not going to find, but also with the young activists that come in our support, who will follow in our steps when we are no longer here. Our children were tortured and killed, but their ideas remain. They were planted in the Plaza. No one can destroy them. No one can torture them."[21] In December 1990 the Mothers carried out their tenth march of resistance to commemorate Human Rights Day and to condemn the recent military uprising, indicating that nothing could stop them from continuing their work. In a moving ceremony during that march the daughter of one of the deceased Mothers scattered her ashes over the flower beds around the central pyramid in deference to her mother's last wishes.

An important feature of the Mothers' newspaper, entitled "Mothers in the Streets," includes articles about affiliates in other parts of the country and important demonstrations in Buenos Aires. There is something startling about that title in a society that traditionally has relegated women to the home and to silence. The Mothers have taken to the streets to press their demands, highlighting the contrast between working in the open and working in the secret space behind the scenes where deals are made between members of the military, powerful interests, and a government bypassing the Congress. By gathering the radical opposition and the dispossessed around them, the Mothers defy the space of privilege and its resistance to change, dramatizing the true nature of the government by exposing themselves to its wrath.

Within Latin America, the Mothers receive support from the Uruguayan Mothers of the Disappeared and sometimes combine their efforts with the Latin American Federation of Families of the Disappeared. While they have met with and given advice to mothers' groups in El Salvador, Nicaragua, Honduras, and Guatemala, they have disagreed with them over the issues of their cooperation with either the church or with political parties, perceiving such ties as a loss of independence.

Like the groups seeking to overthrow colonial rule in the late 1960s, the Mothers have also learned the importance of capturing attention in the foreign media from the early years of their organization. Their travels to the United Nations, the Organization of American States, and West European countries are intended to place pressure on the Argentine government as well as garner support for their cause.

Because of the number of Argentines of Italian origin or with dual nationalities, the Mothers have had considerable success in their travels through Italy, meeting with municipal councils, organizations of judges, labor unions, prominent politicians, and student groups. Their efforts have inspired public condemnation of the terror and, later, of the passage of the due obedience and full stop laws. The Mothers are also beloved in Spain, where streets and public squares have been named after them and where they regularly appear on television, eliciting support from human-rights groups, labor unions, students, and lawyers' organizations.

Their first and most important source of support, however, came from a group of women in the Netherlands. In 1978, Amnesty International organized a meeting between the Mothers and a group of Dutch women traveling to Argentina, an assembly including journalists, writers, teachers, and members of parliament. These women were deeply moved by their visit and on their return established the Support Group for the Mothers of the Plaza de Mayo (SAAM). They began a campaign to inform the public about what was happening in Argentina and to raise funds for the Mothers' work. Among its leaders was the late Lisbeth Den Uyl, wife of a former prime minister and president of the Social Democratic party. Every Mother's Day these women place an announcement in the newspapers along with a photograph of the Mothers: "When you buy flowers, think a minute about those other mothers in Argentina, looking for their children since the military coup of 1976."[22] SAAM, a diverse group including Christian Democrats, Social Democrats, and parties on the left, has been responsible for much of the economic support the Mothers have received from abroad. They are active throughout the Netherlands, organizing conferences in various towns and university centers. As a result of their efforts the Dutch Trade Union Organization provides the Mothers with financial assistance.

Numerous support groups exist in various German cities where the Mothers have been frequent guests at peace conferences sponsored by the church. The Mothers' most fervent support in Germany comes from the Catholic and Protestant churches, an ironic contrast to their relations with the Argentine church. Given the number of Argentine exiles in France, it is not surprising that Support for the Mothers of the Plaza de Mayo (SOLIMA) was formed in 1979 to give the Mothers economic, political and moral backing. Even before SOLIMA was created, however, groups demonstrated against the junta in front of the Argentine embassy. One of the Mothers' most notable supporters has been Mme. Mitterrand, wife of the French president. In addition, a number of other groups work on behalf of the Mothers, such as the Christian Action for the Abolition of Torture, the Association of Parents and Friends of the French Disappeared in Argentina, and the Ecumenical Service of Human Rights, to name a few.

The number of support groups in Switzerland, Sweden, Norway, and Denmark, as well as throughout Western Europe, necessitated some form of coordination. Ada Alessandro, the leader of SOLIMA, began orchestrating the activities of these groups in 1989.[23] In addition to managing the Mothers' travels, fund raising, and publicity, she sees her most important task as ensuring the security of the Mothers in Argentina. Each attempt against the Mothers has unleashed a flood of letters and telegrams to the Argentine president from the various support groups. The government knows that while it can harass the Mothers, its image would be greatly damaged by a member's death.

Recently, deputies from the European Parliament of the European Economic Community have formed a group to assist the Mothers. Another special support group includes notables such as Elie Wiesel (Nobel Peace Prize, 1986), Roald Hoffmann (a 1981 Nobel Prize winner in chemistry), and members of various parliaments in European countries. The Mothers have also inspired the formation of new auxiliary groups in Canada and Australia. These women, who rarely left their own neighborhoods, have become used to meeting with political leaders and addressing the public and the press around the world, joining the hundreds of nongovernmental organizations that are active in the international arena.

The Mothers' presence abroad enhances their efforts within Argentina and demonstrates their belief that their place is wherever political decisions affecting human rights are being made. As they broke through social barriers within their own country, they broke the barriers of protocol by addressing international organizations where they had no official status and by traveling to any country that would receive them, regardless of that country's politics. They did so as easily as they tore down the police barricades intended to stop them from demonstrating.

The Mothers of the Plaza de Mayo have carried out their politics under the banner of Motherhood, which has opened them up to criticism from feminist groups. This raises the question of whether there can be a role for mothers in national politics. Instances of mothers entering the political arena at the national level have occurred regularly, such as the banding together of mothers across ethnic groups in 1991 in the former Yugoslav republic of Slovenia to protest the drafting of their sons into the military. The Women's Peace Movement, which is now active throughout the former Yugoslav republic, initially rose up as a movement to release the members' conscripted children from the army but soon expanded into efforts to protect each other's national monuments. In a country riven by ethnic hatred, they represent all the nationalities and have remained avowedly nonpartisan, despite the attempts of many political parties and groups to co-opt them. National Public Radio news commentator Sylvia Poggoli said they numbered in the several thousands, although an exact count had not been made. The official press ignored them and the traditional political forces were angered at their refusal to enter into partisan politics, but the mere existence of a peace movement in that war-torn area was an extraordinary accomplishment.

Other such examples include the former nuclear freeze movement in Britain and the United States and the formation of the Sri Lankan Mothers' Front. In Sri Lanka, a country torn by ethnic violence between majority Sinhalese and the minority community of Tamils, the Mothers' Front is the only group that has taken to the streets to promote peace and protest the excesses of the military. Eighty-four percent of the women in Sri Lanka are illiterate, and conservative tenets of Hindu society have effectively restricted the majority of the women to the home. Yet women from all classes and creeds have banded together in the Front to protest the *disappearances* of their children, husbands, and brothers.[24] They have used nonviolent methods, such as hunger strikes and demonstrations, to protest the use of military force and to demand peace with justice. They organize sit-ins, fasts, and prayer meetings. They march in processions, holding up placards to express their grievances, and have demanded audiences with the president. Like the Mothers they publish books of poetry, distribute pamphlets to educate people about their association, and promote campaigns to collect signatures aimed at stopping the violence and oppression. Their continual mobilization and defiance serve to dramatize the limits of physical intimidation and terror and provide an alternative model of political organization and action. Because such movements do not fit the conceptual framework we have developed for analyzing political phenomena, they have remained relatively unknown, and information on groups like the Mothers' Front or the Yugoslav mothers is difficult to obtain.[25] Once women have entered the political domain as resistance fighters, however, it is not unusual for them to continue their political activism under a new regime, adapting their associations to face new challenges. That the Mothers of the Plaza de Mayo have remained a presence under the constitutional government indicates an enduring role for them as political actors.

There has been little long-term research on women's accomplishments in peace movements, although scholars have documented resistance and political activism among women in the United States and in Latin and Central America.[26] Women have entered politics as groups representing neighborhoods, workplaces, and self-help efforts, reflecting a political consciousness that makes connections between the issues that affect them and their families in the differing spheres of their lives.[27] That they also may be mothers demonstrates the fact that such women, especially working-class mothers, regularly confront institutions that affect their lives on many fronts and thus may come to an understanding of the power relations that affect them as well as their ability, as a group, to influence these forces.

What the Mothers in particular, and women's resistance efforts in general, demonstrate is a politics rooted not in abstract ideas but in concrete thinking grounded in personal, everyday experience. Most important, this experience is founded upon integrity and the reality of human relationships in our lives. Although perhaps not an exclusively female experience, this new political consciousness offers the possibility of enlarging concepts of the democratic polity that has been defined by men since the time of Aristotle.

NOTES

1. Havel, "The Power of the Powerless," 58–61.
2. Barry Barnes, *The Nature of Power* (Urbana: University of Illinois Press, 1988), 65.
3. de Pargament, interview.
4. Ruddick, *Maternal Thinking*, 93.
5. Jean Baker Miller, *Toward a New Psychology of Women* (Boston: Beacon Press, 1986), 112.
6. Ruddick, *Maternal Thinking,* 70.
7. Carolyn G. Heilbrun, *Writing a Woman's Life* (New York: W. W. Norton, 1988), 12.

8. Madres, *Monthly Newspaper*, March 1991. Hebe de Bonafini's interview with Jesús Quintero.

9. Israel W. Charny, *How Can We Commit the Unthinkable? Genocide: The Human Cancer* (Boulder, CO: Westview Press, 1982), 34.

10. Thomas Merton, *A Thomas Merton Reader*, ed. Thomas P. McDonnell (New York: Harcourt, Brace and World, 1962), 349.

11. Heilbrun, *Writing a Woman's Life*, 126.

12. Madres, *Monthly Newspaper*, March 1991.

13. Heilbrun, *Writing a Woman's Life*, 129.

14. de Cerruti, interview.

15. Madres, *Monthly Newspaper*, April 1990.

16. Ibid., January 1989.

17. Ibid., October 1990.

18. Ibid., December 1990.

19. de Bonafini, interview.

20. Havel, "The Power of the Powerless," 56–57.

21. de Pargament, interview; de Berrocal, interview.

22. Madres, *Monthly Newspaper*, December 1985.

23. Ada Alessandro, interview by Marguerite Bouvard, July 1991.

24. Anita Nesiah, "*Satyagrapha* (Non-violence) as Women's Weapon in the Struggle for Peace and Justice in Sri Lanka" (paper, 1989).

25. The only reference I found to the Yugoslav mothers was a commentary by Sylvia Poggoli on WBUR in June 1991, and a talk by the human-rights lawyer Eva Brantley at Brandeis University in January 1993.

26. Shulamit Reinharz, "Women as Competent Community Builders: The Other Side of the Coin," in *Social and Psychological Problems of Women: Prevention and Crisis Intervention*, ed. Annette U. Rickel et al. (Washington, DC: Hemisphere Publishing, 1984), 19–41.

27. Ackelsberg, "Communities, Resistance, and Women's Activism," 305.

BIBLIOGRAPHY

BOOKS AND ARTICLES

Ackelsberg, Martha A. "Communities, Resistance, and Women's Activism: Some Implications for a Democratic Polity." In *Women and the Politics of Empowerment*, edited by Ann Bookman and Sandra Morgan, 297–313. Philadelphia: Temple University Press, 1988.

Ackelsberg, Martha A., and Shanley, Mary Lyndon. "Gender, Resistance, and Citizenship: Women's Struggle with/in the State." Paper delivered at meetings of the International Political Science Association, Buenos Aires, July 1991, and at the 17th annual meeting of the Social Science History Association, Chicago, November 5–8, 1992.

————. "From Resistance to Reconstruction: Madres de Plaza de Mayo, Maternalism, and the Transition to Democracy in Argentina." Paper presented to a works-in-progress seminar of the Smith College Project on Women and Social Change, and to the annual meeting of the Latin American Studies Association, Los Angeles, September 1992.

Arendt, Hannah. *The Origins of Totalitarianism.* New York: Meridian Books, 1958.

Aristotle. *The Politics of Aristotle.* Translated by Ernest Barker. New York: Oxford University Press, 1974.

Aron, Raymond. *Peace and War: A Theory of International Relations.* New York: Doubleday, 1966.

Barnes, Barry. *The Nature of Power.* Urbana: University of Illinois Press, 1988.

Bayer, Osvaldo. *Los anarquistas expropiadores.* Buenos Aires: Legasa S.A., 1984.

Calvert, Susan, and Calvert, Peter. *Argentina: Political Culture and Instability.* Pittsburgh: University of Pittsburgh Press, 1989.

Charny, Israel W. *How Can We Commit the Unthinkable? Genocide: The Human Cancer.* Boulder, CO: Westview Press, 1982.

Diago, Alejandro. *Hebe de Bonafini: Memoria y esperanza.* Buenos Aires: Ediciones Dialectica, 1988.

Dolgoff, Sam. *The Anarchist Collectives: Workers' Self-Management in the Spanish Revolution, 1936–1939.* New York: Free Life Editions, 1974.

Duhalde, Eduardo Luis. *El estado terrorista argentino.* Buenos Aires: Ediciones Caballito, 1983.

Elstain, Jean Bethke. "The Passion of the Mothers of the Disappeared in Argentina." *New Oxford Review* (January-February 1992): 4–10.

Feijoó, María del Carmen. "The Challenge of Constructing Civilian Peace: Women and Democracy in Argentina." In *The Women's Movement in Latin America: Feminism and the Transition to Democracy.* Edited by Jane S. Jaquette, 72–94. Boston: Unwin Hyman, 1989.

Fisher, Jo. *Mothers of the Disappeared.* Boston: South End Press, 1989.

Freire, Paulo. *Pedagogy of the Oppressed.* New York: Herder and Herder, 1971.

Garcia, Cristina. "En Argentine: La démocratie avance grâce aux femmes." *Alternatives Non Violentes* 78 (March 1991): 23–39.

Gilligan, Carol. *In a Different Voice: Psychological Theory and Women's Development.* Cambridge, MA: Harvard University Press, 1982.

Gilligan, Carol, et al., ed. *Mapping the Moral Domain: A Contribution of Women's Thinking to Psychological Theory and Education.* Cambridge, MA: Center for the Study of Gender, Education, and Human Development, Harvard University Graduate School of Education, 1988.

Graham-Yooll, Andrew. *A State of Fear: Memoirs of Argentina's Nightmare.* New York: Hippocrene Books, 1986.

Graziano, Frank. *Divine Violence: Spectacle, Psychosexuality, and Radical Christianity in the Argentine "Dirty War,"* Boulder, CO: Westview Press, 1992.

Guest, Iain. *Behind the Disappearances: Argentina's Dirty War against Human Rights and the United Nations.* Philadelphia: University of Pennsylvania Press, 1990.

Guillermoprieto, Alma. "Letter from Buenos Aires." *The New Yorker* (July 15, 1991): 63–78.

Havel, Vaclav. *Vaclav Havel: Or, Living in Truth.* Edited by Jan Vladislav. Boston: Faber and Faber, 1986.

Heilbrun, Carolyn G. *Writing a Woman's Life.* New York: W. W. Norton, 1988.

Kordon, Diana R., et al. *Psychological Effects of Political Repression.* Buenos Aires: Sudamericana/Planeta, 1988.

Lewis, Paul. "The Right and Military Rule, 1955–1983." In *The Argentine Right: Its History and Intellectual Origins, 1910 to the Present.* Edited by Sandra McGee Deutsch and Ronald H. Dolkart, 147–80. Wilmington, DE: Scholarly Resources, 1993.

Manor, James, ed. *Sri Lanka in Change and Crisis.* London: Croom Helm, 1984.

Martin, Alfredo. *Les mères "folles" de la Place de Mai.* Paris: Renaudot et Cie., 1988.

Merton, Thomas. *A Thomas Merton Reader.* Edited by Thomas P. McDonnell. New York: Harcourt, Brace and World, 1962.

Mignone, Emilio. *Iglesia y dictadura.* Buenos Aires: Ediciones del Pensamiento Nacional, 1986.

Miller, Jean Baker. *Toward a New Psychology of Women.* Boston: Beacon Press, 1986.

Nesiah, Anita. "*Satyagrapha* (Non-violence) as Women's Weapon in the Struggle for Peace and Justice in Sri Lanka." Paper, 1989.

Partnoy, Alicia. *The Little School: Tales of Disappearance and Survival in Argentina.* Pittsburgh: Cleis Press, 1986.

Plato. *The Republic of Plato.* Translated by Francis M. Cornford. New York: Oxford University Press, 1945.

Poneman, Daniel. *Argentina: Democracy on Trial.* New York: Paragon House, 1987.

Reinharz, Shulamit. "Women as Competent Community Builders: The Other Side of the Coin." In *Social and Psychological Problems of Women: Prevention and Crisis Intervention.* Edited by Annette U. Rickel et al., 19–41. Washington, DC: Hemisphere Publishing, 1984.

Rock, David. *Argentina 1516–1987: From Spanish Colonization to Alfonsín.* Berkeley: University of California Press, 1987.

Ruddick, Sara. *Maternal Thinking: Toward a Politics of Peace.* Boston: Beacon Press, 1989.

Sánchez, Matilde, ed. *Historias de vida Hebe de Bonafini.* Buenos Aires: Fraterna del Nuevo Extremo, 1985.

Scarry, Elaine. *The Body in Pain: The Making and Unmaking of the World.* New York: Oxford University Press, 1987.

Schirmer, Jennifer G. "Those Who Die for Life Cannot be Called Dead: Women and Human Rights Protest in Latin America." *Feminist Review* 29 (Summer 1988): 41–65.

Senkman, Leonardo. "The Right and Civilian Regimes, 1955–1976." In *The Argentine Right: Its History and Intellectual Origins, 1910 to the Present.* Edited by Sandra McGee Deutsch and Ronald H. Dolkart, 119–45. Wilmington, DE: Scholarly Resources, 1993.

Shumway, Nicolas. *The Invention of Argentina.* Berkeley: University of California Press, 1991.

Simpson, John, and Bennett, Jana. *The Disappeared and the Mothers of the Plaza.* New York: St. Martin's Press, 1985.

Stevens, Evelyn P. "Marianismo: The Other Face of Machismo in Latin America." In *Female and Male in Latin America.* Edited by Ann Pescatello, 90–101. Pittsburgh: University of Pittsburgh Press, 1973.

Tambiah, Stanley J. *Sri Lanka: Ethnic Fratricide and the Dismantling of Democracy.* Chicago: University of Chicago Press, 1986.

Thornton, Lawrence. *Imagining Argentina.* New York: Doubleday, 1987.

Timerman, Jacobo. *Prisoner Without a Name, Cell Without a Number.* New York: Alfred A. Knopf, 1981.

Westin, Alan F. *Privacy and Freedom.* New York: Atheneum, 1967.

Wynia, Gary W. "The Peronists Triumph in Argentina." *Current History* (January 1990): 13–35.

DOCUMENTS
Mothers of the Plaza de Mayo

Acta constitutiva asociación Madres de Plaza de Mayo. La Plata, August 22, 1979.
Boletín informativo, nos. 1–22 (1980–1984).
Historia de las Madres de Plaza de Mayo. Buenos Aires, 1988.
Mohina, Héctor and Primi. *Video History of the Mothers of the Plaza de Mayo.* Buenos Aires, 1985–.
Monthly Newspaper (1984–1993).
Nuestros sueños: Taller de escritura. Buenos Aires, 1991.

Amnesty International

Argentina: The Attack on the Third Infantry Regiment Barracks at La Tablada: Investigations into Allegations of Torture, Disappearances, and Extrajudicial Executions. New York: Amnesty International USA, March 1990.
Argentina: The Military Juntas and Human Rights: Report of the Trial of the Former Junta Members. London: Amnesty International, 1987.
"Disappearances," A Workbook. New York: Amnesty International USA, 1982.
Testimonio sobre campos secretos de detención en Argentina. London: Amnesty International, 1980.
Testimony of Graciela Geuna on La Perla Camp (Córdoba). London: Amnesty International, 1980.

Other

L'Honneur perdu des évêques argentines: La collaboration des évêques catholiques dans la pratique des disparitions forcées et de la torture. Geneva, Switzerland: Cahiers de l'Association Internationale contre la Torture, 1990.
Communautés européennes. Parlement européen. Documents de séance: Proposition de résolution sur les droits de l'homme en Argentine. December 3, 1990.
Delgado, Ariel. *Las luces se van Apagando.* Argentina, 1990.
Epelbaum, Renée S. Correspondence with author, January 21, 25, 1993.
Noblit, Kevin. Associated Press Document 12740. January 26, 1989.
———. Associated Press Document 13718. January 27, 1989.
———. Associated Press Document 28186. March 1, 1989.
Nunca Más: The Report of the Argentine National Commission on the Disappeared. New York: Farrar, Straus, and Giroux, 1986.
Serrat, Oscar J. Correspondence with author, September 16, 1991.
Truth and Partial Justice in Argentina. Washington, DC: America's Watch, 1987.

NEWSPAPERS

"Argentina, Shaken and a Little Stirred." *The Economist.* December 6, 1990.
"Ataque estilo mafioso anoche contra Solanas." *Ambito Financiero.* May 23, 1991.

"Bonafini pasó por Tribunales." *El Clarín.* May 24, 1991.

"Bonafini: Vivimos amenazadas." *Cronica Matutina.* May 24, 1991.

"Cenizas en la Plaza de Mayo." *Cronica Matutina.* December 7, 1990.

"Children of the Disappeared." *World Press Review.* May 1991.

"Controversia por la actitud de Bonafini." *La Razón.* March 12, 1985.

"Cuarto atentado a las Madres." *El Clarín.* June 4, 1991.

"Dejaron un chiquero." *Diario Popular.* December 7, 1990.

"Desde la Casa Rosada se vio el acto como un fracaso." *La Nación.* November 16, 1991.

"Dictaron proceso a Hebe de Bonafini." *Ambito Financiero.* May 19, 1991.

"Exhumación de cadáveres en Mar del Plata se llevara a cabo esta semana." *Diario Popular.* March 13, 1985.

"Exhumaciones: Debate las Madres ratificaron su posición tras los sucesos de Mar del Plata." *La Voz.* March 13, 1985.

"Extrañeza por la actitud de Bonafini." *Diario Popular.* March 13, 1985.

"Finalizó en Plaza de Mayo la marcha de la resistencia." *La Prensa.* December 7, 1990.

"Hebe de Bonafini, Madre de Plaza de Mayo, denuncio amenaza: 'A vos no te vamos a dar en las piernas, sino en la cabeza.' " *Cronica Vespertina.* May 23, 1991.

"Hebe de Bonafini, seremos muchos contra el indulto." *Pagina 12.* December 5, 1990.

"Impiden exhumación de NN un grupo de Madres intervino en el cementerio de Mar de Plata." *Diario Popular.* March 11, 1985.

"Incidente en Cementerio: Hebe de Bonafini impidió la exhumación de tres cadáveres." *Diario Cronica.* March 11, 1985.

"Las Madres bajo amenazas." *Cronica Matutina.* April 11, 1991.

"Madres de Plaza de Mayo." *La Nación.* April 10, 1991.

"Marcha de la resistencia." *El Clarín.* December 7, 1990.

"Menem cuestionó la marcha de las Madres porque ensucian la Plaza." *Pagina 12.* December 6, 1990.

"Mothers Hold New March." *Buenos Aires Herald.* December 7, 1990.

"Nuevo robo a las Madres de Plaza de Mayo." *La Nación.* June 4, 1991.

"Nuevo saqueo y amenazas a Madres de Plaza de Mayo." *La Prensa.* May 11, 1991.

"Organismos de derechos humanos, condenas y buena memoria." *Pagina 12.* December 4, 1990.

"Otra de los conocidos de siempre." *Pagina 12.* April 10, 1991.

"Para las Madres, no hay dos sin tres." *Pagina 12.* May 10, 1991.

"Persecución politica." *La Nación.* May 24, 1991.

"Procesan a Bonafini, 'no pediré la excarcelación.' " *Pagina 12.* May 17, 1991.

"Proceso por desacato a Hebe Bonafini." *La Prensa.* May 17, 1991.

"Rechazan une orden de exhumación." *La Razón.* March 3, 1985.

"Robaron a las Madres." *La Pampa.* April 10, 1991.

"Robo en sede de las Madres." *Diario Popular.* April 10, 1991.

"Ubaldini reclamó cambios en la primera jornada nacional de protesta, la marcha de la Bronca." *Pagina 12.* November 16, 1991.
"Un robo por mes en la sede de las Madres de Plaza de Mayo." *Cronica.* June 4, 1991.
"Videla, Massera, Viola y Firmenich en la Gaera, indulto para Navidad." *Nuevo Sur.* December 9, 1990.

INTERVIEWS WITH THE AUTHOR

Mothers of the Plaza de Mayo

Cota (Ada María Feigenmuller), August 1989, November 1990.
de Aguilera, María Estela Gomez, November 1990.
de Alvarez Rojas, Noemie, November 1990.
de Andreotti, Aurora Alonzo, November 1990.
de Berrocal, María del Carmen, August 1989, November 1990.
de Bonafini, Hebe Pastor, August 1989, November 1990.
de Cerruti, María del Rosario, August 1989, November 1990.
de Da Re, Rogelia Higuera, August 1989, November 1990.
de Gudano, Susanna, August 1989, November 1990.
de Mansotti, Elsa Fanti, August 1989, November 1990.
de Nolasco, Gloria Fernandez, November 1990.
de Palazzo, María Rosa, November 1990.
de Pargament, Juana, August 1989, November 1990.
de Pauvi, Josefa Donato, August 1989.
de Petrini, Evel Aztarbe, August 1989, November 1990.
de Senar, Ada María, August 1989.
de Triana, Elvira Díaz, August 1989, November 1990.
del Hodel, Aline Moreno, November 1990.
Gutman, María, August 1989.
Mascia, Hebe, August 1989, November 1990.
Mereno, Mercedes, August 1989, November 1990.
Schnieder, Esther, November 1990.

Siblings and Children of the *Disappeared*

de Bonafini, Alejandra, November 1990.
de Pratti, Arturo, November 1990.

Support Groups of the Mothers of the Plaza de Mayo

Alessandro, Ada (SOLIMA, Paris), July 1991.
Delgado, Ariel (radio commentator and producer), November 1990.
d'Elia, Carmen (journalist for the Mothers), November 1990.
Edelman, Lucila (psychologist), August 1989.

Front for Human Rights: Raúl, Ines, Alejandro, Andrea, Alberto, Juan Carlos, Diego, Ariel, Cecilia, Monica, Carlos, November 1990.

Mohina, Héctor and Primi (video historians for the Mothers), August 1989, November 1990.

Pampa (journalist for the Mothers), November 1990.

Schiller, Herman (journalist for the Mothers), November 1990.

Other

Former member of the Communist party, currently member of a group seeking to unify the democratic left (name withheld for safety), November 1990.

INDEX

ABOUT THE AUTHOR

Marguerite Guzmán Bouvard spent time with the Mothers in Argentina while researching this book and has also written *With the Mothers of the Plaza de Mayo*, a volume of poems about them. She is the author of several books in the fields of political science, psychology, and poetry, and she has edited *Landscape and Exile*, an anthology of literature by displaced writers.

She has been a professor of political science, a fellow at the Bunting Institute and the Wellesley College Center for Research on Women, and a writer-in-residence at the University of Maryland. Currently, she is a visiting scholar with the Women's Studies Program at Brandeis University, where she organizes lectures on human rights.

Latin American Silhouettes
Studies in History and Culture

William H. Beezley and
Judith Ewell
Editors

Volumes Published

William H. Beezley and Judith Ewell, eds., *The Human Tradition in Latin America: The Twentieth Century* (1987). Cloth ISBN 0-8420-2283-X Paper ISBN 0-8420-2284-8

Judith Ewell and William H. Beezley, eds., *The Human Tradition in Latin America: The Nineteenth Century* (1989). Cloth ISBN 0-8420-2331-3 Paper ISBN 0-8420-2332-1

David G. LaFrance, *The Mexican Revolution in Puebla, 1908–1913: The Maderista Movement and the Failure of Liberal Reform* (1989). ISBN 0-8420-2293-7

Mark A. Burkholder, *Politics of a Colonial Career: José Baquíjano and the Audiencia of Lima*, 2d ed. (1990). Cloth ISBN 0-8420-2353-4 Paper ISBN 0-8420-2352-6

Kenneth M. Coleman and George C. Herring, eds. (with Foreword by Daniel Oduber), *Understanding the Central American Crisis: Sources of Conflict, U.S. Policy, and Options for Peace* (1991). Cloth ISBN 0-8420-2382-8   Paper ISBN 0-8420-2383-6

Carlos B. Gil, ed., *Hope and Frustration: Interviews with Leaders of Mexico's Political Opposition* (1992). Cloth ISBN 0-8420-2395-X Paper ISBN 0-8420-2396-8

Charles Bergquist, Ricardo Peñaranda, and Gonzalo Sánchez, eds., *Violence in Colombia: The Contemporary Crisis in Historical Perspective* (1992). Cloth ISBN 0-8420-2369-0   Paper ISBN 0-8420-2376-3

Heidi Zogbaum, *B. Traven: A Vision of Mexico* (1992). ISBN 0-8420-2392-5

Jaime E. Rodríguez O., ed., *Patterns of Contention in Mexican History* (1992). ISBN 0-8420-2399-2

Louis A. Pérez, Jr., ed., *Slaves, Sugar, and Colonial Society: Travel Accounts of Cuba, 1801–1899* (1992). Cloth ISBN 0-8420-2354-2 Paper ISBN 0-8420-2415-8

Peter Blanchard, *Slavery and Abolition in Early Republican Peru* (1992). Cloth ISBN 0-8420-2400-X   Paper ISBN 0-8420-2429-8

Paul J. Vanderwood, *Disorder and Progress: Bandits, Police, and Mexican Development.* Revised and Enlarged Edition (1992). Cloth ISBN 0-8420-2438-7   Paper ISBN 0-8420-2439-5

Sandra McGee Deutsch and Ronald H. Dolkart, eds., *The Argentine Right: Its History and Intellectual Origins, 1910 to the Present* (1993). Cloth ISBN 0-8420-2418-2   Paper ISBN 0-8420-2419-0

Jaime E. Rodríguez O., ed., *The Evolution of the Mexican Political System* (1993). ISBN 0-8420-2448-4

Steve Ellner, *Organized Labor in Venezuela, 1958–1991: Behavior and Concerns in a Democratic Setting* (1993). ISBN 0-8420-2443-3

Paul J. Dosal, *Doing Business with the Dictators: A Political History of United Fruit in Guatemala, 1899–1944* (1993). ISBN 0-8420-2475-1

Marquis James, *Merchant Adventurer: The Story of W. R. Grace* (1993). ISBN 0-8420-2444-1

John Charles Chasteen and Joseph S. Tulchin, eds., *Problems in Modern Latin American History: A Reader* (1994). Cloth ISBN 0-8420-2327-5 Paper ISBN 0-8420-2328-3

Marguerite Guzmán Bouvard, *Revolutionizing Motherhood: The Mothers of the Plaza de Mayo* (1994). Cloth ISBN 0-8420-2486-7 Paper ISBN 0-8420-2487-5

William H. Beezley, Cheryl English Martin, and William E. French, eds., *Rituals of Rule, Rituals of Resistance: Public Celebrations and Popular Culture in Mexico* (1994). Cloth ISBN 0-8420-2416-6 Paper ISBN 0-8420-2417-4